The field of missional hermeneutics of Scripture, to our great encouragement, continues to produce abundant fruit. This collection of essays offering a diverse range of missional readings of 1 Peter is a worthy successor to the editors' earlier collaboration in *Reading Hebrews Missiologically: The Missionary Motive, Message, and Methods of Hebrews*. The book is outstanding not only in the breadth and detail of the topics covered along with extensive bibliographies for further enquiry, but significantly for the diversity of the contributors, many of whom bring illuminating insights and applications from their majority world contexts. A most welcome and enriching contribution to the task of reading the whole Bible with a missional lens.

Christopher J. H. Wright, PhD
Langham Partnership
Author, *The Great Story and the Great Commission*

Whether you are a seasoned scholar, a seminary student or a minister, *Reading 1 Peter Missiologically* invites you to step into a world where exegesis meets missiology and theology encounters culture. The essays present both traditional and fresh readings of 1 Peter informed by exegetical analysis and socio-cultural locatedness in specific and diverse settings from around the world. Written by an international team, the book presents a biblically rooted and theologically sophisticated visions of mission that draw together countless exegetical, missiological and theological threads. Readers will find this a resource for many questions that arise from the interpretation and application of 1 Peter, but even more, they will find an inspiring and enriching chorus of appreciation for the Word and mission of God.

Sofanit T. Abebe, PhD
Lecturer in New Testament and Greek, Oak Hill College, London

Reading 1 Peter Missiologically

The Missionary Motive, Message, and Methods of 1 Peter

Abeneazer G. Urga,
Jessica A. Udall,
Edward L. Smither,
Editors

visit us at missionbooks.org

Reading 1 Peter Missiologically: The Missionary Motive, Message, and Methods of 1 Peter

© 2024 by Abeneazer G. Urga, Jessica A. Udall, and Edward L. Smither.
All Rights Reserved.

No part of this book may be reproduced, stored in a retrieval system, or transmitted in any form or by any means—electronic, mechanical, photocopy, recording, or otherwise—without prior written permission from the publisher, except brief quotations used in connection with reviews. This manuscript may not be entered into AI, even for AI training. For permission, email permissions@wclbooks.com. For corrections, email editor@wclbooks.com.

William Carey Publishing (WCP) publishes resources to shape and advance the missiological conversation in the world. We publish a broad range of thought-provoking books and do not necessarily endorse all opinions set forth here or in works referenced within this book. WCP can't verify the accuracy of website URLs beyond the date of print publication.

Chapters 1, 4, 12, 15: All Scripture quotations, unless otherwise indicated, are taken from the ESV® Bible (The Holy Bible, English Standard Version®), Copyright © 2001 by Crossway, a publishing ministry of Good News Publishers. Used by permission. All rights reserved.

Chapters 2, 10, 11: All Scripture quotations, unless otherwise indicated, are taken from the Holy Bible, New International Version®, NIV®. Copyright ©1973, 1978, 1984, 2011 by Biblica, Inc.™ Used by permission of Zondervan. All rights reserved worldwide. www.zondervan.com. The "NIV" and "New International Version" are trademarks registered in the United States Patent and Trademark Office by Biblica, Inc.™

Chapter 3: All Scripture quotations, unless otherwise indicated, are taken from the New Revised Standard Version Bible, copyright © 1989 National Council of the Churches of Christ in the United States of America. Used by permission. All rights reserved worldwide.

Chapters 6, 7: All Scripture quotations, unless otherwise indicated, are taken from the NET Bible® https://netbible.com copyright ©1996, 2019 used with permission from Biblical Studies Press, L.L.C. All rights reserved.

Chapter 8: All Scripture quotations, unless otherwise indicated, are taken from the Christian Standard Bible®, Copyright © 2017 by Holman Bible Publishers. Used by permission. Christian Standard Bible® and CSB® are federally registered trademarks of Holman Bible Publishers.

Chapter 9: All Scripture quotations, unless otherwise indicated, are taken from the Akan version (New Revised Asante Twi).

Published by William Carey Publishing | 10 W. Dry Creek Cir
Littleton, CO 80120 | www.missionbooks.org

William Carey Publishing is a ministry of Frontier Ventures
Pasadena, CA | www.frontierventures.org

Cover and Interior Designer: Mike Riester

ISBN: 978-0-87808-585-0 (paperback)
      978-0-87808-587-4 (epub)

Printed Worldwide

28 27 26 25 24   1 2 3 4 5   IN

Library of Congress Control Number: 2024938761

Contents

Preface vii

PART 1: THE MISSIONARY MOTIVE OF 1 PETER

Chapter 1 3
Salvation of the Nations: The Vision of God's Mission in 1 Peter 1:10–12
By Joshua Bowman

Chapter 2 19
Like Father Like Son: Holiness and *Missio Dei* in 1 Peter
By Gift Mtukwa

Chapter 3 35
Mission by God's Living Stones:
Watchman Nee's Missional Exegesis of 1 Peter 2:5–11
By Jacob Chengwei Feng

Chapter 4 51
Embodying God's Mission in an Unfriendly World:
The Identity and Missionary Mandate of the Church in 1 Peter
By Boubakar Sanou

Chapter 5 65
The Role of the Spirit in Mission in 1 Peter
By Yimenu Adimass Belay

Chapter 6 79
Eschatology and Mission in 1 Peter
By Grant LeMarquand

PART 2: THE MISSIONARY MESSAGE OF 1 PETER

Chapter 7 99
Salvation and Judgment as Missionary Message in 1 Peter
By Markus T. Klausli

Chapter 8 115
The Missiological Message of Hope in 1 Peter
By Sarah Lunsford

Chapter 9 129
Mission to the Dead and the Resurrection of Jesus:
1 Peter 3:18–22 and Ancestor Christology in Africa
By Rudolf K. Gaisie

PART 3: THE MISSIONARY METHODS OF 1 PETER

Chapter 10   145
   Missional Hospitality: Responding to Physical and Spiritual Alienation
   By Tricia Stephens

Chapter 11   163
   Suffering in God's Mission: Reflections from 1 Peter
   By Edward L. Smither

Chapter 12   181
   Ethical Living as Proto-Evangelion:
   Holiness, Honor, and Hope in 1 Peter
   By Jessica A. Udall

Chapter 13   193
   Evangelism in 1 Peter:
   The Verbal Proclamation of a People Awaiting the Return of Their King
   By Will Brooks

Chapter 14   209
   Missional Implications of Christ's Proclamation to the Spirits
   By Sigurd Grindheim

Chapter 15   225
   The Pilgrimage Motif in 1 Peter and Its Implications for Evangelism
   By Sofia Papaspyrou

About the Contributors   241

Scripture Index   245

Preface

There are numerous books on the New Testament theology of mission, but most of these volumes pay scant attention to the contribution of the General Epistles. Our book seeks to fill this gap in missiological scholarship. Written by a diverse array of biblical scholars and missiologists hailing from and living in countries all over the world, *Reading 1 Peter Missiologically* seeks to demonstrate that the Bible as a whole is a missional document and that the book of 1 Peter—while not often cited by those discussing mission-related themes—has much to contribute to our understanding of the mission of God and our participation in it. This book will consider 1 Peter's missionary theology in three parts: the missionary motive, the missionary message, and the missionary methods of 1 Peter. The motive is the reason behind missionary efforts (the why), the message refers to the content of what missionaries communicate (the what), and the methods are prescribed or described strategies for mission (the how). Instead of putting forth a single definition of "mission" at the outset of the book, we have allowed each contributor to flesh out this complex concept in their own way as relates to their topic. Thus, we believe this book as a whole makes the idea of mission shine, highlighting multi-faceted aspects in unique and edifying ways.

Part 1 opens the discussion of the missionary vision of 1 Peter with Joshua Bowman's chapter, "Salvation of the Nations." He focuses on 1 Peter 1:10–12, drawing from the Old Testament to flesh out Peter's statement that believers are benefitting from and seeing the fulfillment of what the prophets spoke long ago about Jesus, the foundation of our faith and the one we proclaim in mission. Using African Biblical Hermeneutics, particularly focusing on the comparative aspects of the Shona proverbs that speak about imitation or resemblance, Gift Mtukwa demonstrates the crucial connection in 1 Peter between living holy lives—following the example of Christ—and the mission of the people of God.

Jacob Chengwei Feng explores Watchman Nee's missional exegesis of 1 Peter 2:5–11, shedding light on the idea that God's means of mission is corporate in nature. Boubakar Sanou focuses on Peter's exhortation and consolation for the scattered Christians across Asia Minor, arguing that God's people's identity is inseparably linked to their responsibility of carrying out God's mission on earth. Yimenu Adimass Belay emphasizes the role of the Holy Spirit in mission in 1 Peter with insights from the Ethiopian contemporary context. Placing the mission of the church in broad perspective,

Grant LeMarquand concludes the section by showing 1 Peter's emphasis on living in the reality of the eschaton inaugurated by the incarnation, death, and resurrection of Jesus the Messiah.

Part 2 examines the missionary message of 1 Peter, opening with Markus T. Klausli's examination of Peter's focus on the missional expression of God's saving work before a hostile culture while believers sojourn in the world and bear witness to the power of God and his gospel. Sarah Lunsford argues that the living hope that Peter tells believers that they have is intrinsically missiological in its evangelistic testimony as well as its discipleship implications. Employing an Akan reading of 1 Peter 3:18–22, Rudolf K. Gaisie closes this section by considering some aspects of a functional Ancestor Christology for the modern Christian mission in Africa and beyond.

Part 3 explores the missionary methods of 1 Peter. Tricia Stephens begins the section by discussing missionary hospitality as a response to the physical and spiritual alienation of believers both in Peter's day and in our own. Tracing the story of Peter's own ministry and martyrdom, Edward L. Smither focuses on how suffering relates to the mission of God in 1 Peter. Jessica A. Udall explores 1 Peter's emphasis on the essential nature of a truly Christian lifestyle of proto-evangelion that removes barriers—such as preconceived ideas and prejudices—for sharing the gospel.

Will Brooks demonstrates that Peter's missiological and eschatological vision compels believers to engage the world around them through verbal proclamation of Christ and his work. Sigurd Grindheim exegetes 1 Peter 3:18–22 in an attempt to remedy the Western tendency to overlook the idea that Jesus preached to imprisoned spirits, suggesting that this passage is meant to undergird Peter's call toward evangelism and is an encouragement to all who experience spiritual warfare in mission. Sophia Papaspyrou employs a case study to explore the connection between pilgrimage and mission and its evangelistic implications in 1 Peter and in the modern day.

We hope that the contents of this book will encourage readers with the missiological purposes of God in 1 Peter and inspire believers toward missional engagement with the world, "proclaim[ing] the excellencies of him who called [us] out of darkness into his marvelous light" (1 Pet 2:9).

Abeneazer G. Urga, Addis Ababa, Ethiopia
Jessica A. Udall, Addis Ababa, Ethiopia
Edward L. Smither, Columbia, South Carolina

May 2024

Part 1
The Missionary Motive of 1 Peter

Chapter 1

Salvation of the Nations

The Vision of God's Mission in 1 Peter 1:10-12

Joshua Bowman

Concerning this salvation, the prophets who prophesied about the grace that was to be yours searched and inquired carefully, inquiring what person or time the Spirit of Christ in them was indicating when he predicted the sufferings of Christ and the subsequent glories. It was revealed to them that they were serving not themselves but you, in the things that have now been announced to you through those who preached the good news to you by the Holy Spirit sent from heaven, things into which angels long to look. (1 Pet 1:10–12)[1]

Introduction

In 1 Peter 1, Peter encouraged Christians to rejoice in suffering because they have a precious salvation that will result in glory to Christ. The focus text of this chapter is 1 Peter 1:10–12, where Peter emphasizes that his readers are the beneficiaries of the Old Testament prophets' inquiry, anticipation, and service. Peter wrote about how believers could have confidence in their identity in Christ and endurance despite ongoing trials. Although their present circumstances were troubling, Peter's hearers were privileged to see fully what Old Testament saints only saw partially.

This passage opens doors to exploring key themes related to the Messiah and salvation about which the Old Testament prophets inquired. The longing and desire of the prophets, which are now fulfilled, provide confidence for those waiting for their final redemption and escape from persecution. The Holy Spirit revealed the message that believers have, and angels long to investigate it. Finally, this revealed salvation prompts faithful Christians to endure suffering, preach the word, walk in obedience, and engage in God's mission to the nations. Instead of shrinking back in fear, the great salvation of 1 Peter 1 provides a solid biblical and theological basis for engagement in missions.

---

[1] Unless otherwise noted, all Scripture quotations in this chapter are from the English Standard Version.

Reading 1 Peter 1 missiologically forces us to consider some of the following questions: How do verses 10–12 motivate suffering Christians to engage in the mission of God?[2] What is the great salvation that prophets inquired about and that angels long to understand? How did the prophets serve us?

The primary goal of this chapter is to evaluate how 1 Peter 1:10–12 provides motivation and mandate for Christians to endure suffering and engage in missions. This passage teaches that suffering believers can proceed in joy, hope, and confidence because God has revealed what the prophets longed to know about salvation in Christ, which is the foundation of our faith and motivation for missions.

Suffering, Salvation, and Motivation in 1 Peter 1

Peter addressed his letter to Christians scattered across Asia and living as aliens (1 Pet 1:1). He wrote to people living in culturally inhospitable contexts. They were "distressed by various trials" (1:6), treated harshly just as Christ was (2:21), and exhorted not to "be surprised at the fiery ordeal" that tested them "as though some strange thing were happening to you" (4:12).

Suffering was not only a future possibility but an ever-present reality to those Peter addressed (4:16, 19; 5:1, 8–10).[3] Peter placed the hardships of these brothers and sisters in the context of Jesus's suffering. The prophets predicted Jesus's suffering (1:12); he was the rejected stone (2:7); his suffering is an example to Christians in their distress (2:21); his suffering was on behalf of sinners (3:18); and our suffering causes rejoicing as we share in Christ's suffering (4:13). Finally, our suffering is merely for a "little while," and it unites us with the experience of other Christians suffering around the world (5:9–10).

---

[2] Seland expounded on Peter's suffering theme by saying, "We thus find in 1 Peter that the author envisages Christians who have to stand up for their faith; we do not always get a clear picture of what kind of problems they have to cope with, but the author's emphatic use of 'sufferings' and his exhortations fully demonstrate the need for both theological and practical comfort." Seland, "Resident Aliens in Mission," 588.

[3] Flemming said, "Words for suffering appear more in this letter than any other New Testament book. Peter sews this thread into the whole fabric of the letter (see 1:6–7; 2:12, 18–25; 3:13–18; 4:1–6, 12–19; 5:8–10). But what does suffering have to do with mission? In the first place, Peter sees the experience of undeserved suffering as something quite normal when God's people engage their world. Christians should not be surprised when they find themselves coming under fire, 'as though something strange were happening' (3:12)." Flemming, "Won Over without a Word," 60.

In the context of distressing trials, Peter wrote about grace, peace, and hope (1:2–3). He described an inheritance reserved in heaven. Imperishable, undefiled, and reserved—these are the Spirit-inspired adjectives that describe this heavenly inheritance (1:4). Peter's main point is to assure suffering believers that God protects their salvation. Martin Williams argued that salvation is the central theme of 1:3–12, pervading the opening section and the entire book.[4] Salvation here is key as Peter stresses its timing, surety, and revelation.

Therefore, based on the reality and assurance of their coming salvation, the primary response of God's people should be rejoicing (1:6). Considering the hardship and stress of persecution that scattered believers across Asia, fear and anxiety would have been a normal, fleshly response. Instead, Peter elicited the opposite. Confidence, peace, and even joy come from faith in the promised salvation of the Lord. A careful reader can already ascertain deep theological truths that motivate believers to engage in God's mission, regardless of circumstance or convenience.

Though salvation is a motivating factor, according to Peter, the primary joy comes from the glory and honor that will be received (1:7–8). After God reveals salvation (1:5), next comes the response of faith leading to "the salvation of your souls" (1:9). It seems oxymoronic to acknowledge distress yet frame it in the context of joy. Yet, scattered people living under religious persecution have peace to the fullest (1:2).

The focus text of this chapter, 1 Peter 1:10–12, begins by referring to "this salvation," which is best understood in the context of the two preceding references to salvation listed above (1:5, 9). In these three verses (1:10–12), salvation is desired by and revealed to the prophets, which motivates believers to engage in missions and obey the ethical instructions in the remainder of Peter's letter.[5]

Salvation Desired

In verses 10–12, Peter made a theological argument that served as a basis for confidence in suffering, obedience to ethical instructions, and participation in God's redemptive mission. Peter encouraged and exhorted

---

4 Williams, *Doctrine of Salvation*, 149–50.

5 Muriithi points to how 1 Peter is a book looked to by Africans to "find answers to questions about how the truths concerning salvation and faith apply in such circumstances. How can they live as Christians in the midst of persecution, poverty, and sickness?" Muriithi, "1 Peter," 1544. Furthermore, "This message speaks to African Christians who are suffering the ravages of war, famine, and disease, and who want to know where God is when they suffer like this." Muriithi, 1543.

faithfulness among scattered believers based on the glorious salvation that is sure to come. The challenge for readers of the epistle was that their recent experiences of suffering tempted them to doubt the timing and surety of salvation. Therefore, suffering in 1 Peter is a catalyst that intensifies the search for understanding Old Testament prophecy.[6]

Summarizing the structure of 1 Peter, D. Edmond Hiebert asserted that 1 Peter 1:1–12 provides the doctrinal foundation for three cycles of practical exhortations. He explained,

> The opening paragraph (1:3–12), setting forth the glories of our salvation in Christ, provided a solid foundation for Peter's series of exhortations that were intended to strengthen and stimulate the suffering readers. The first cycle of exhortations is grounded in the readers' personal experience of salvation (1:13–2:10); the second appealed to them on the basis of their position in the world (2:11–3:12). The remainder of the epistle is devoted to exhortations dealing with the crucial theme of Christian suffering (3:13–5:11).[7]

Joy and glory were promised to these disciples, but the recent trials tested their strength. Paul Achtemeier described how Peter's appeal to prophetic searching compels confidence in this struggling Christian community: "The reference to the OT prophets searching out the grace in which the NT community stands points to the continuity of God's purpose and thus the unity of divine revelation, which in its turn underlines the certainty of the announced salvation in Christ in the midst of circumstances that contradict rather than confirm it (cf. v. 6)."[8]

Peter attempted to bolster the faith of sufferers by attaching current hope to past predictions of Old Testament prophets. Thomas Schreiner explained Peter's reference to the past by saying, "The link between vv. 9–10 is the term 'salvation' (*sōteria*). The salvation believers experience now, which will be consummated in the future, was also prophesied in the past. Believers in Christ represent the fulfillment of prophecy."[9] Peter was not merely offering empty promises or platitudes to those living in hostile environments whose lives were in danger. Instead, he reminded them to look back. He asked them to consider how the prophets foretold Christ's coming, suffering, and glorification.

---

6   Davids, *First Epistle of Peter*, 62.
7   Hiebert, *First Peter*, 20.
8   Achtemeier, *1 Peter*, 108–9.
9   Schreiner, *1, 2 Peter, Jude*, 71.

The consistent, accurate, and bold predictions comforted and emboldened Peter's audience to stand confidently, knowing that their faith rested on trustworthy evidence. Those engaged as disciples of the Lord will face hardship due to gospel proclamation. Therefore, Peter connected past revelation with current realities to show how both were expected and will be overcome.

Verse 10 ends with Peter describing the "careful searches and inquiries" made by the prophets about their own prophecies and the "grace that would come to you." In order to understand Peter's argument, an overview of several Old and New Testament passages that describe this prophetic quest is in order.

Prophetic Inquiry

Peter's reference to Old Testament prophets emphasizes the unity of all Scripture and assures his audience that appeals to joy and glory are not illusions meant to spark false hope. Douglas Harink connected Petrine themes of suffering, glory, and prophetic expectation by saying,

> It becomes clear that the Messiah did not come lately upon the scene—unprecedented, unanticipated, unheralded—as if only those who live after the birth and death of Jesus share in the grace of the Messiah. The Spirit of the Messiah (*pneuma Christou*) was already at work long ago, inciting in the prophets of Israel an intense inquiry into the *kairos* of the Messiah and bearing advance witness (*promartyromenon*) through them to the sufferings and the subsequent glorification.[10]

Jesus's identity, suffering, deity, and glorification were not fabricated by a band of followers after his death on a Roman cross. The prophets saw in part, trying to discern things that did not come into focus during their lifetimes. The mystery was partially revealed, and they had enough information to search and ask questions. Since the inquiry started in antiquity, Robert Leighton succinctly reminds us that "the prejudice of novelty is removed."[11]

Daniel 9 provides an example of one prophet who carefully studied the prophecies of those who came before, seeking to discern the times of desolation, judgment, and the coming Messiah. Verse 2 says, "I, Daniel, perceived in the books the number of years that, according to the word of the Lord to Jeremiah the prophet, must pass before the desolations of Jerusalem." Daniel continued in prayer to confess that Israel "has not listened to our servants the prophets" (v. 6). Israel had been punished because they refused

---

10 Harink, *1 & 2 Peter*, 50.
11 Leighton, *Commentary on First Peter*, 62.

to obey the law of Moses (v. 11). As Daniel prayed, Gabriel spoke of a coming "anointed one, and prince" who would atone for iniquity and provide everlasting righteousness (vv. 24–25). Daniel looked to Moses, Jeremiah, and the direct revelation he received to discern the times and workings of the Lord.

The book of Daniel concludes with Daniel asking questions as he tries to understand the visions of the end. He asked questions like, "How long shall it be till the end of these wonders?" and "What shall be the end of these things?" (12:6, 8). His inquiries were not satisfied as he remained without understanding (v. 8). He was told that others would be blessed at the end of the allotted time, but he would need to rest (vv. 12–13). The search is on, but this prophet's questions remain unanswered. He writes what he is told, but the message is "shut up and sealed until the time of the end" (v. 9).

Old Testament prophecies about the coming Savior abound. However, most prophets did not state their inquiry as explicitly as Daniel. Instead, they simply recorded the Spirit-inspired revelation about the descendant who would bruise the serpent's head (Gen 3:15), the coming ruler holding the scepter of Judah (Gen 49:10), and the prophet to whom the nation should listen (Deut 18:15–18). Several New Testament passages provide the interpretive lens and clarification about what the Old Testament prophets saw partially but tried to understand more fully.

Peter was the disciple who preached the message on the day of Pentecost when three thousand souls were added to the church (Acts 2:14–47). In Acts 2:30–31, Peter quoted the words of David recorded in Psalm 16:8–11. David spoke of the Lord being at his right hand and how his Holy One would not see corruption. Peter explained that David "foresaw and spoke about the resurrection of Christ, that he was not abandoned to Hades, nor did his flesh see corruption" (Acts 2:31). In this sermon, Peter used the evidence of King David to prove that Jesus is both the expected Messiah and the one rejected and crucified by the house of Israel (2:36). God used this gospel message, which was largely reliant on David's prophecy, to convict the crowds, leading to widespread repentance and the birth of a church.

As the disciples multiplied and the word of God increased (Acts 6:7), the crowds and religious leaders did not always respond like Peter's audience at Pentecost. In fact, they seized Stephen and brought him before the council, where he addressed the high priest by summarizing the history of Israel, including Abraham, Moses, and the prophets (7:1–53). Stephen argued that the history of Israel and the progressive revelation of the prophets led to Jesus as the fulfillment of God's promises. Stephen confronted them with the fact that they had rejected God's prophet and now killed God's righteous Son. The nation should have known, but they only added to the heap of their mounting guilt. The crowds could no longer bear the indictment, so they bludgeoned him with stones as he commended his spirit to the Lord Jesus (7:54–60).

In Matthew 13, Jesus used parables to teach about the kingdom of God. This confused the disciples since the meaning of these stories was hidden from the crowds and often from Jesus's own disciples. In Matthew 6:14–15, Jesus quoted Isaiah 6:9–10, which refers to the people's dull hearts that do not hear or understand. Jesus then said, "But blessed are your eyes, for they see, and your ears, for they hear. For truly, I say to you, many prophets and righteous people longed to see what you see, and did not see it, and to hear what you hear, and did not hear it." Some people had no understanding, and others longed to understand but could not. Like Peter's audience in 1 Peter, believers today are blessed because they have the explanation and insight into what others sought but failed to experience.

Throughout the New Testament, the nation, religious leaders, and even Jesus's disciples failed to see all Scripture reveals about the Messiah. God revealed his plan to the prophets, who communicated faithfully and frequently. They searched the Scriptures, and warned God's chosen people, but all too often, the message fell on deaf ears.

On the road to Damascus, after the resurrection, Jesus pointed to Moses and the prophets to interpret "things concerning himself" (Luke 24:25–27). Similarly, the apostle John affirmed that the Scriptures point to Christ, but many still refused to see and believe. According to Jesus, Moses himself will accuse them before the Father, because he prophesied about this day (John 5:39–40, 45–47).

Jesus's and Peter's words affirmed the prophets' search and its outcome, which resulted in a message that was meant to be understood and obeyed. The examples show that Jesus was disappointed that the religious leaders did not discern what the prophets said because, if they had understood, they would have followed him. Furthermore, these examples show the outcomes of the prophets' inquiries described in 1 Peter 1:10. Their prophecies both expect and confirm that Jesus is the Messiah, sent by the Father to bring salvation to the nations.[12] The New Testament teachings affirm these facts based on the Old Testament prophets.

---

12 Chou, "They Were Not Serving Themselves," 220.

Salvation Revealed

Remember, as this chapter focuses on 1 Peter 1:10–12, the broader themes of Peter's epistle are suffering, future glory, and sure salvation. Current sufferings should not surprise Christ's disciples because they are called to share Christ's suffering now and his glory in the future (1 Pet 4:12–16). Therefore, the historic, prophetic testimony of the faith is vital to current confidence and future hope.

The assurance of things foretold and now fulfilled provided the necessary theological foundation for Peter's audience to endure hardship and participate in God's mission. According to John Lillie, "The story of salvation provides them with a hermeneutic for their suffering, as well as for the epistle's ethical instructions. Their persecutions and trials are reinterpreted, in the context of God's eschatological salvation, as the arena of salvation."[13] Therefore, the prophets' quests and revelations provide missiological motivation and confidence.

The content of the prophets' inquiry in 1 Peter 1:10–11 can be broken into four parts. First, they were concerned with "salvation," which Peter referenced twice in the preceding verses (1:5, 9). Second, Peter referred to "what person or time the Spirit of Christ in them was indicating." Third, in alignment with Peter's overall theme, the prophets were interested in the sufferings of Christ. Finally, they inquired about the glories of Christ after his suffering. In order to understand Peter's argument and the missiological motivation it provides, the following section will provide examples of each part of the prophetic inquiry. Some examples will touch on several or all four categories, while others will reference a single category.

Salvation in General

Peter's reference to the prophets certainly included all those in the Old Testament canon, but he does seem to have a particular affinity to Isaiah. John Elliott observed that Isaiah is likely to be foremost in Peter's mind because of "the frequent appeal to Isaiah in this letter (approximately 18 citations or allusions …), the similarity of the language in 1:12 and 1:24–25 (citing Isa 40:6–8), and especially by the use of Isaiah 53 in 2:21–25 in speaking of the innocent and vicarious suffering of Christ."[14] Peter's emphasis in 1:10–12 focuses on the salvation foretold in the past but now fulfilled.[15]

---

13   Lillie, *Lectures*, 89.
14   Elliott, *1 Peter*, 348–49. Elliott lists the following references or allusions to Isaiah in 1 Peter: Isaiah 8:12–14; 53:4–13; 52:7, 13; 40:9; 42:12; 50:9.
15   Elliott, 345.

In Isaiah 52, the prophet spoke of God's past faithfulness to save the nation from Egyptian slavery and, later, Assyrian oppression (v. 4). God desires to be known among the nations, and this will surely come to pass as faithful messengers publish salvation (v. 7). Isaiah proclaimed, "All the ends of the earth shall see the salvation of our God" (v. 10). Isaiah moves from the proclamation of salvation to the person—called a servant—who will be lifted up (vv. 13–14). In chapter 42, Isaiah prophesied about a coming salvation and predicted the suffering of the Messiah, which is precisely what Peter explained to suffering Christians in his New Testament epistle (1 Pet 1:10–11).

The inclusion of the nations in God's redemptive plan is another example of how the Old Testament prophecies were clarified by the New Testament apostles. The prophets consistently revealed a coming day when the nations will come to the holy mountain, learn about the one God, and enjoy salvation with Israel (Isa 2:2–3).

In Genesis 12:3, God promised to bless all nations through a descendant of Abraham. Despite Israel's ethnocentric tendencies, God had a plan from the beginning for his salvation to reach the ends of the earth. An example of this mystery is how Egypt will come to the LORD "in that day" (Isa 19:16–22). Amazingly, the former enslavers of God's chosen people "will know the LORD in that day and worship with sacrifice and offering," and "he will listen to their pleas for mercy and heal them" (vv. 21–22).

Paul explained the revelation he received from God and the responsibility given to preach the riches of salvation to the gentiles. In Ephesians 3:4–6, he clarified any confusion surrounding the inclusion of the nations in God's mission by proclaiming gentiles as "fellow heirs." Paul did not preach a new doctrine of salvation. Instead, he built upon previous revelation though he acknowledged Old Testament saints did not see as New Testament apostles did. Paul's closing doxology in Romans 16:25–27 summarizes these truths:

> Now to him who is able to strengthen you according to my gospel and the preaching of Jesus Christ, according to the revelation of the mystery that was kept secret for long ages but has now been disclosed and through the prophetic writings has been made known to all nations, according to the command of the eternal God, to bring about the obedience of faith—to the only wise God be glory forevermore through Jesus Christ! Amen.

Paul, in the passage above, and Peter, in 1 Peter 1:10–12, both recognized that God's people awaited a Savior. God promised that salvation was coming, and faithful prophets looked to the blurry horizon with hope and conviction that redemption was near. They prayed, searched, and waited for the fulfillment of covenant promises made by a faithful God.

Time and Person

Peter said the prophets looked for specifics about the Messiah (1 Pet 1:11). The Gospel writers, Mary, Zechariah, and Jesus all confirm that Jesus is the person and that now is the time foretold by those prophets. The New Testament begins with three names—Jesus, David, and Abraham—before detailing the genealogy of the promised Messiah (Matt 1:1–17). Mary understood the angel Gabriel's message as a confirmation and remembrance of God's previous covenant with Abraham (Luke 1:46–55). John the Baptist's father, Zechariah, prophesied after his son's birth. He quoted Old Testament prophets and linked the birth of this child to the covenant promises of salvation through the Messiah (Luke 1:67–79). Jesus's identity is ultimately confirmed by the voice of God the Father, who expressed his good pleasure as Jesus ascended from his baptism (Matt 3:16–17).

Old Testament saints fixated on the time and person of the Messiah, and some of these same concerns carried over to his disciples. After Christ's resurrection, his followers had assumptions about Christ's rule and reign. They naively assumed he was going to set up his kingdom and asked him, "Lord, will you at this time restore the kingdom to Israel?" (Acts 1:6) The questions of both the prophets and apostles validate the prior expectations of both groups based on earlier revelation.

In John 8, Jews listening to Jesus's self-assessment of his identity and relationship to Abraham showed their disapproval by picking up stones to punish him for blasphemy (v. 59). Jesus had just told them, "Your father Abraham rejoiced that he would see my day. He saw it and was glad… . Truly, truly, I say to you, before Abraham was, I am" (vv. 56, 58). In short, Jesus confirmed that Abraham, like many other Old Testament saints, knew the Messiah was coming.

These examples from the Gospels and Acts summarize the vast prophetic inquiries and revelations described in 1 Peter 1:11. Faithful Israelites who worshiped the God of Abraham, Isaac, and Jacob were waiting, looking, and trying to discern his identity and arrival. Peter advances the New Testament conviction that Jesus is the Messiah, and Jesus's fulfillment of specific prophecies related to the timing of his arrival, ministry, and suffering confirm his identity and message.

Sufferings of Christ

One clear example of the prophetic inquiries regarding the suffering Messiah described by Peter (1 Pet 1:11) is found in Psalm 22. As Jesus hung on the cross, some of his final words were a quote of Psalm 22:1. He said, "My God, my God, why have you forsaken me?" (Matt 27:46). Jesus was pierced, mocked, and beaten in accordance with this Old Testament prophecy. His clothes were divided (Ps 22:18; Matt 27:35). Ultimately, his suffering will end in the worship of the Messiah by all families of the earth (Ps 22:27–28). The suffering servant of the Old Testament will thereafter be the one who rules the world.

Isaiah 53 portrays the man of sorrows who will suffer for the sins of the people. God will crush him as a substitute and satisfaction for our sins so that we can be accepted and redeemed. In this chapter, we see the Messiah who is despised, rejected, pierced, and crushed. Because of this sacrifice, he will "make many to be accounted righteous, and he shall bear their iniquities" (v. 11).

Paul's evangelistic method was to point out these truths from the prophets in order to persuade Jews and gentiles to confess Christ as Lord. The fact that the prophets foretold Jesus's suffering was a significant apologetic. In Acts 17:2–4, we learn of Paul's method at Thessalonica, which was to preach on the suffering and resurrection of Christ. The Holy Spirit worked through Paul's exposition of prophetic texts that expected the Messiah to suffer. In the end, many were convinced and followed Paul's teaching.

Peter comforted his audience of suffering believers by reminding them that Christ suffered and that his suffering was foretold long before he was born. Christ's sufferings were followed by subsequent glories (1 Pet 1:11), setting a pattern for disciples of Christ who suffer while awaiting the second coming.

Subsequent Glories

As previously noted in this chapter, suffering precedes subsequent glories. Williams explained this by saying, "Peter's choice of the word 'sufferings' to speak of Christ's death enables him, as at 3:18, to link the experience of Christ in suffering and glory (1:11) with that of believers in order to encourage them that, like Christ, their present experience of suffering will one day give way to glory (1:6–7)."[16] Suffering was present with the Messiah, a significant point of 1 Peter 1:10–12. Furthermore, this pattern of

---

16 Williams, *Doctrine of Salvation*, 183.

suffering first and glory later provides a bridge to Peter's readers who need encouragement to stand firm amidst persecution in their own lives.

The covenant promises of God to the patriarchs and their descendants point to eschatological fulfillment and enjoyment of blessings. This was undoubtedly clear to Abraham, who was childless in Genesis 12:3, and therefore, the promises of land, descendants, and blessings to all the nations through him were still unseen. Something glorious is coming. This inspires hope and demands faith because the things promised are not yet seen.

God's covenant with King David promised a future ruler whose kingdom and throne would be established forever (2 Sam 7:12–16). David was overwhelmed as he began to understand the magnificence and future glory associated with this promise. He turned to God and asked, "Who am I, O LORD God, and what is my house, that you have brought me thus far?" (v. 18). He declared the exclusive deity and worth of God and prayed that his name would be magnified (vv. 22–26).

Space does not allow for a full assessment of the Psalms, but Psalms 57, 67, 86, and 117 are examples of nations bringing praise, thanks, and honor to the one God who created the heavens and earth. A common theme of these psalms is evident in the following praise: "Be exalted, O God, above the heavens! Let your glory be over all the earth!" (Ps 57:11).

In the New Testament, Hebrews 11 names men and women of faith who hoped in the promises of God. Relevant to our discussion is the fact that the people listed endured incredible hardship because they were looking to the subsequent glories described in 1 Peter 1. Despite torture and mistreatment, God's people have continued because suffering is not the end. With their eyes on salvation and trust in God's promises, these saints continued since something better was coming (Heb 11:35–40). Readers of Peter's letter are benefactors of these promises and see that the suffering of Old Testament saints and Jesus himself is worth it because of the promised fulfillment of redemption through the Messiah.

Salvation as Motivation

After Peter acknowledged the prophets' desire and reception of divine revelation about salvation, he alerted his present audience to their privileged status. 1 Peter 1:12 says, "It was revealed to them that they were not serving themselves, but you, in these things which have now been announced to you through those who preached the gospel to you by the Holy Spirit sent from heaven—things into which angels long to look." Peter showed how many Old Testament saints wanted what those in Peter's audience now had.

Even angels are amazed and want to know more. But Peter's audience—who happened to be suffering—had heard and understood the gospel message. John Lillie accentuated this privilege by saying, "Here in 1 Peter the thought heightens the exclusive privilege granted the addressees: not the ancient prophets, not even angels in heaven—despite their efforts or desires—have seen or heard the things proclaimed only to you!"[17] The gospel is the treasure, and Peter's audience had it.[18]

The next word of Peter's argument in verse 13 is "therefore," which transitions the letter from theological groundings to outcomes and implications. Based on the desire, revelation, and reception of the gospel message, suffering saints can persevere and press on in obedience. Ultimately, the victory and glory attained by the resurrection will be realized. But first, Peter commanded his audience to prepare, hope, and conform based on the theological foundations of the Old Testament prophets.

Peter looked back and said that his audience had something which even the prophets and patriarchs did not fully receive. Furthermore, of all the things angels could give their attention to in the universe, this is of particular interest and amazement to them. Whether or not Peter's audience saw, believed, or felt the privilege and blessing of being "insiders" to these promises, he exhorted them that it is true.[19] Svetlana Khobnya drew the following two implications from Peter's affirmation of these Christians' identity. She said, "First, their standing is with the God of Israel. Second, God's actions not only had a positive effect for Israel in the past but they also have direct consequences for the present audience. The author evaluates these consequences in the light of Christ's suffering and the new or renewed status of his readers in Christ."[20] Therefore, they should have courage, faith, and endurance in what Peter acknowledged is a challenging race.

God has not abandoned these dear believers to suffer alone. Edmund Clowney helpfully summarized Peter's juxtaposition of suffering and glory. He said,

---

17 Lillie, *Lectures*, 350.

18 "Of all the times to be alive in human history, it is a supreme privilege to be alive in the period of history following the coming of Christ, when the gospel is clearly preached. Through the witness of those who saw and heard Jesus, subsequent generations also see and hear. Peter, however, does not press the privileged status of his readers. Rather, he builds on the unity of the OT prophetic message with the Christian gospel as an apology for the cross and a foundation for his exhortations that follow." Jobes, *1 Peter*, 103.

19 Michaels, *1 Peter*, 50.

20 Khobnya, "So That They May," 10.

Sufferings now, glories to follow. Peter wants to encourage Christians who face the first to look for the second. He has pointed our hope to the glory of Christ, and to his return. Now he would have us remember that the Christ of glory is the Christ of the cross. The sequence of our lives follows the sequence of Christ's life. He suffered first, then entered into his glory. So must we. Jesus understood that order well. It was the pattern predicted for the Messiah in the Old Testament.[21]

In 1 Peter, believers are not discouraged by suffering but recognize a long-expected pattern of hardship that assures them of their future salvation. Williams explained it this way:

> Peter's main point was that believers are greatly privileged to be living in the time when the prophecies of salvation are being fulfilled. Moreover, in the activity of the prophets the Spirit of Christ bore witness to the fact that saving grace would, as in the experience of Christ, involve a pattern of present suffering followed by future glory. Far from calling into question the reality of their salvation, the believers' present experience of suffering confirms their Christian experience. It provides a firm basis for their future hope and glorification (salvation).[22]

Suffering is normal for those who want to follow the Lord. Suffering is expected because the prophets of old experienced and predicted the same. Their suffering is blessed because they are unified with Christ in his suffering. Finally, their suffering is neither pointless nor endless since future glory is promised when the Messiah returns a second time.

1 Peter 1 is not a direct summons to preach, plant a church, or cross an ocean, so should we read this book missiologically?[23] Mark Boyley asked the same question and answered, "Decisively, yes. Peter is concerned with encouraging his readers to mission. Suffering is not present in such a way as to prevent such activity."[24] This admission does not diminish these verses or the whole book to missiological irrelevance. Instead, these connections to salvation and messianic fulfillment provide a theological and biblical basis for bold engagement in God's redemptive mission.

---

21 Clowney, *Message of 1 Peter*, 55.
22 Williams, *Doctrine of Salvation*, 187.
23 Akin says, "Peter's emphasis throughout the letter on missional identity, the missionary lifestyle, the urgency of evangelism, and the hope of heaven emphasizes a missiological motivation behind the writing of this letter." Akin, "Missiological Motivation," 19.
24 Boyley, "1 Peter: A Mission Document?," 86.

Bibliography

Achtemeier, Paul J. *1 Peter: A Commentary on First Peter*. Hermeneia. Minneapolis: Fortress Press, 1996.

Akin, Paul. "The Missiological Motivation of 1 Peter." *Southern Baptist Journal of Theology* 23, no. 3 (2019): 7–21.

Boyley, Mark. "1 Peter: A Mission Document?" *Reformed Theological Review* 63, no. 2 (2004): 72–86.

Chou, Abner T. "'They Were Not Serving Themselves, but You': Reclaiming the Prophets' Messianic Intention." *The Master's Seminary Journal* 33, no. 2 (2022): 211–37.

Clowney, Edmund P. *The Message of 1 Peter: The Way of the Cross*. Bible Speaks Today. Downers Grove, IL: InterVarsity Press, 1988.

Davids, Peter H. *The First Epistle of Peter*. New International Commentary on the New Testament. Grand Rapids: Eerdmans, 1990.

Elliott, John H. *1 Peter: A New Translation with Introduction and Commentary*. Anchor Bible 37B. New York: Doubleday, 2000.

Flemming, Dean E. "'Won Over without a Word': Holiness and the Church's Missional Identity in 1 Peter." *Wesleyan Theological Journal* 49, no. 1 (2014): 50–66.

Harink, Douglas. *1 & 2 Peter*. Brazos Theological Commentary on the Bible. Grand Rapids: Brazos Press, 2009.

Hiebert, D. Edmond. *First Peter: An Expositional Commentary*. Chicago: Moody Press, 1984.

Jobes, Karen H. *1 Peter*. Baker Exegetical Commentary on the New Testament. Grand Rapids: Baker Academic, 2005.

Khobnya, Svetlana. "So That They May Be Won Over without a Word: Reading 1 Peter through a Missional Lens." *European Journal of Theology* 29, no. 1 (2019): 7–16.

Leighton, Robert. *Commentary on First Peter*. Grand Rapids: Kregel, 1972.

Lillie, John. *Lectures on the First and Second Epistles of Peter*. Minneapolis: Klock & Klock, 1978.

Michaels, J. Ramsey. *1 Peter*. Word Biblical Commentary 49. Grand Rapids: Zondervan, 2015.

Muriithi, Sicily Mbura. "1 Peter." In *African Bible Commentary: A One-Volume Commentary Written by 70 African Scholars*, edited by Tokunboh Adeyemo, 1543–50. Nairobi: WordAlive, 2006.

Schreiner, Thomas R. *1, 2 Peter, Jude*. New American Commentary 37. Nashville: Broadman & Holman, 2003.

Seland, Torrey. "Resident Aliens in Mission: Missional Practices in the Emerging Church of 1 Peter." *Bulletin for Biblical Research* 19, no. 4 (2009): 565–89.

Williams, Martin. *The Doctrine of Salvation in the First Letter of Peter*. Society for New Testament Studies Monograph Series 149. Cambridge: Cambridge University Press, 2011.

Chapter 2

Like Father, Like Son

Holiness and *Missio Dei* in 1 Peter

Gift Mtukwa

Introduction

This chapter argues that the author of 1 Peter connected his exhortations on living holy lives to the mission of the people of God. The call to live as resident aliens, to be holy in all they do, and their identity as chosen people are all connected to living properly "among the pagans," who would see the good deeds of the believers and as a result "glorify God" (1 Pet 2:12).[1] Joel B. Green rightly noted that Peter wanted his readers to "embrace the missional vocation to be 'holy'—that is, 'different,' or 'distinctive'—in the midst of Gentiles."[2] For Peter, the people of God are to be known for doing good rather than evil, and if they should suffer, they should do so because of doing good. All this is predicated on the example of Christ (2:21). In the words of Christopher J. H. Wright, the people of God are to be "recognizably, visibly, and substantively different, as the people belonging uniquely to Yahweh and therefore representing his character and ways."[3] This chapter makes use of African Biblical Hermeneutics, particularly focusing on the comparative aspects of the Shona proverbs that speak about imitation or resemblance. These proverbs will be used to read 1 Peter heuristically. The study will conclude that holiness for Peter is at the core of the mission of God. There cannot be *missio Dei* without holiness.

Even though the essential theme of 1 Peter is eschatology, it is indeed true that the goal of the epistle is holiness.[4] The holy life as envisioned by the epistle is not an end in itself. Dan O'Connor noted, "No part of the New Testament speaks out more eloquently on [the] theme of holiness of life as a way of Christian witness [than does 1 Peter]."[5] Peter's primary concern is to shape the identity of his churches; as such he "writes a missional letter to

---

1 Unless otherwise indicated, all Scripture quotations are from the NIV.
2 Green, "Living as Exiles," 316.
3 Wright, "Old Testament Ethics," 6.
4 Davids, *First Epistle of Peter*, 17.
5 O'Connor, "Holiness of Life," 17.

a missional people."[6] Holiness has two sides to it, one side has to do with setting oneself apart from what is evil and the other side has to do with becoming like God who demands holiness.

African Context: Resemblance/Imitation among the Shona People

In her book *African Hermeneutics*, Elizabeth Mburu argued that we need an African hermeneutic in which we use hermeneutical models that are developed in Africa rather than in the West so as to "derive practical applications" from an African perspective.[7] Such a hermeneutic for Mburu takes what Africa has to offer seriously, and she suggested a four-legged stool that consists of the parallels from the African context, historical and cultural context, literary context, and theological context, which are the four critical issues that must be looked at as we interpret Scripture.[8] I will use this methodology to interpret 1 Peter and explicate its relationship between holiness and mission.

The Shona people of Zimbabwe, just like other Bantu groups, have a lot of wisdom conveyed by their proverbs, particularly the proverbial lore.[9] In Shona, proverbs (*tsumo*) are not the same as *madimikira* (allusive idioms) or even *zvirevo* (picturesque sayings), even though the three are related.[10] Proverbs are "characterized by terseness of expression, an economy of words with much left to implication, and by traditional popular acceptance."[11] They are an effective way of teaching wisdom among the Shona people. One proverb that is pertinent to the idea of looking alike is *Mbudzi kudya mufenje kufana nyina*, which means "If a goat eats cabbage-tree leaves, it imitates its mother."[12] Other variants include *Gavi rakabva kumasvuuriro* ("A fiber came from its bark") and *Chitiyo kupinda muzai kuona mai* ("When the chicken enters an egg, it sees its mother").[13] The basic meaning of these proverbs is equivalent to the English saying "Like father, like son."[14] Through these

---

6 Flemming, *Recovering the Full Mission*, 209.
7 Mburu, *African Hermeneutics*, 5.
8 Mburu, 66.
9 Hamutyinei and Plangger, *Tsumo-Shumo: Shona Proverbial Lore*, xiii.
10 Hamutyinei and Plangger, xiii.
11 Hamutyinei and Plangger, xiv.
12 Hamutyinei and Plangger, 226.
13 Hamutyinei and Plangger, 226.
14 Hamutyinei and Plangger, 226.

proverbs, the Shona understand that children must follow the behavior of their parents. A son or daughter who contradicts the way his or her parents act is considered deviant, and such a person is to be despised. It is my contention that these proverbs can help us convey the idea of looking like God or being holy as God is holy. Just like children represent their parents even when the parents are absent, the people of God are to represent God to others since they resemble him. I will use these lenses of imitation and resemblance in reading 1 Peter.

Be Like Your Father

The letter of 1 Peter begins by establishing the identity of the people to whom Peter wrote. They are identified in 1:1 as "God's elect, strangers in the world," yet the elect are situated in a particular location: "Pontus, Galatia, Cappadocia, Asia and Bithynia." The election has happened "through the sanctifying work of the Spirit," resulting in the holiness of the people of God, which is the idea of resemblance or imitation that we saw in Shona proverbs. This theme is picked up in 1 Peter 1:14–16, which elucidates the nature of holiness. Peter used the participial phrase μὴ συσχηματιζόμενοι ("do not conform") to speak about what they must not become. This is a negative resemblance to what the Shona would refer to as imitating the wrong example—instead of imitating his or her parents, the child imitates the neighbors. The participle συσχηματιζόμενοι comes from the word συσχηματίζω, which means "to form according to a pattern or mold, *form/model after* something."[15] The form they are to avoid being patterned on is the ἐπιθυμία (evil desires), which have to do with "lust." Lust has as its object various desires like sex, treasure, power, or pleasure.[16] Peter is cognizant of the fact that the life of a Christian is not one of passivity since the evil desires still influence the believers. They are to actively deny such and opt for the right thing.[17]

Holiness in verse 15 must be seen against the backdrop of "the desires" that marked their former lives.[18] Peter's call that they be "obedient children" (v. 14) and be faithful (v. 21) forms the context in which the call to be holy is made.[19] Among the Shona people, children who imitate their parents are

---

15 Danker, Bauer, Arndt, and Gingrich, *Greek-English Lexicon*, 979, emphasis original.
16 Michaels, *1 Peter*, 57.
17 Schreiner, *1, 2 Peter, Jude*, 79.
18 Green, *1 Peter*, 44.
19 Green, 44.

obedient, and those who do not obey are disobedient. For Peter the basis of that holiness was that the people of God have been "born anew" (v. 3).[20] As Green observed, "The importance of these observations is to remind us that holiness is [a] gift, grounded in relationship with God, before it is [a] command."[21] Peter had Leviticus 19:2 in mind, where holiness is related to various areas of life for the people of Israel. It makes sense then that holiness should be practiced "in every aspect of life."[22] Grant R. Osborne noted that this phrase has to do with an "aspect of our conduct [that] must reflect the holiness of God."[23] The holy life is to be seen in the believers daily conduct in all places where they have been scattered.[24] Michaels rightly noted, "The function of the modifier καλέσαντα is to indicate why the holiness of the God of Israel must be a model for the behavior of these Gentile Christians. Their identity rests in the fact that they have been 'called' (2:21; 3:9) by a holy God."[25] Yet holiness is not an end in itself; the language of calling evokes Old Testament language that always refers to the function for which one is called. For instance, when God called Abraham in Genesis 12, he was to be a blessing to others in addition to being a great nation. Given that holiness has to do with being "distinct" from the people, "the gentiles," of the locale in which they have been scattered, it is imperative for them to show them a different kind of life.[26]

Holiness is a quality that intrinsically belongs to God alone. It follows then that persons, activities, places, and objects are only holy in association with the Holy One.[27] By using Old Testament language, Peter said that what was true of Israel is now true for the scattered Christian groups. However, Peter was not concerned about ritual purity as the Old Testament was (Exod 28:2; 40:9; Lev 22:3ff.; Ezra 9:2); his primary concern is moral integrity and communion with God.[28] The command to be holy is based on the fact that God has called them; as Schreiner has stated, "Grace precedes demand."[29]

---

20 Green, 44.
21 Green, 44.
22 Green, 44.
23 Osborne, "1 Peter," 162.
24 Michaels, *1 Peter*, 59.
25 Michaels, 59.
26 Flemming, *Recovering the Full Mission*, 213.
27 Kelly, *Epistles of Peter*, 70.
28 Kelly, 70; and Marshall, *1 Peter*, 52–53.
29 Schreiner, *1, 2 Peter, Jude*, 80.

The aorist imperative γενήθητε does not convey the sense of "become holy" since they already are the holy people of God. Rather, they are to "make holiness [their] trademark once and for all."[30]

If the church now assumes the same privileges as Israel, it follows that they must also assume the same responsibilities.[31] In as much as their calling is "a command" it is also a "promise."[32] It should also be noted that the holiness of the church is patterned after the Holy God, who calls them to be holy. I. Howard Marshall rightly noted, "The holiness of God himself is both the pattern for holiness and the reason for holiness."[33] The Shona proverbs inform us here that what is required of people is to resemble the one who has called them—they are to imitate him. The difference, however, is that among the Shona people the children have to imitate their parents on their own, but here the children of God have his help in doing so. If we take the similarity seriously, it follows then that the holy people of God are to be missional in the same way in which the Holy God is missional. The people are to be holy as "the starting point" of their calling to bless the nations,[34] and they are on a mission commissioned by the Holy God.

The way Christians conduct themselves should provide the primary witness to their faith in God. In other words, it ought to reveal the character of the Holy God and act as an enticement for other people to believe.[35]

Chosen, Holy, and Sent People of God

This section will look at Peter's portrayal of the identity of the people of God (1 Pet 2:9–10); the fact that they need to "sanctify Christ in their hearts" (3:15); and the household code (2:13–3:7). The link between holiness and mission is even more explicit in 1 Peter 2:9–10. In this text, Peter established the identity of the people of God. This he did again using Old Testament language, which echoes Exodus 19:6 and Isaiah 43:20–22. As Dean Flemming observed, "Peter reads the Christian community into Israel's mission as a 'holy' and 'royal priesthood' (1 Pet 2:5, 9) and a 'holy nation' (1 Pet 2:9)."[36] These titles applied to the church are all corporate in

---

30   Michaels, *1 Peter*, 59.
31   Michaels, 59.
32   Clowney, *Message of 1 Peter*, 89.
33   Marshall, *1 Peter*, 52.
34   Pryor, "First Peter and the New Covenant," 50.
35   Marshall, *1 Peter*, 53.
36   Flemming, *Recovering the Full Mission*, 213.

nature "denoting the Church as a body rather than individual Christians."[37] This captures the African (Shona) communal worldview in that individuals are exhorted in the context of community.

Peter begins his description of the people with the fact that they are chosen. His audience are γένος ἐκλεκτόν (1 Pet 2:9), which is an echo of Isaiah 43:20 (LXX), τὸ γένος μου τὸ ἐκλεκτόν.[38] Israel as a people were the chosen ones—God had chosen them from among the nations. They were chosen as a race, which is a point of departure with the γένος ἐκλεκτόν of 1 Peter. For Peter, the chosen ones were from different races and included gentiles. Christians are chosen ones who have acquired membership among the "chosen ones," who descend from Christ through faith in him.[39] From the Shona perspective, resemblance follows the family bloodline, and here we have a point of departure in that resemblance follows the blood of one man—Jesus Christ—to whom they are not related by blood.

Even though the chosen ones receive privileges for being chosen, they also receive responsibilities. As such, "to be a chosen nation is not only an indication of privilege but also a summons to service."[40] Even in Isaiah, τὸ γένος μου τὸ ἐκλεκτόν (my chosen people) is followed by the responsibility "that they might declare my praise" (43:21). In Isaiah 2:3–4, it is the people YHWH has formed "by calling on the nations to join Israel" who "will tell [his] praise."[41] In Isaiah 2:3–4 the nations are passive, but in Isaiah 43:21 they are "active participants in the temple's worship."[42]

The second title Peter gave his audience was βασίλειον ἱεράτευμα ("royal priesthood"). They were portrayed as a "priesthood belonging to God the King"[43] or "a priesthood in the service of the king."[44] In Israel, priests were a select group of people whose work was primarily centered around the temple. Their work entailed facilitating Israel's worship in the temple. The irony here is that this work has now been universalized. Instead of a few select people, it is now for all the people of God. The people of God

---

37 Kelly, *Epistles of Peter*, 96; and Beare, *First Epistle of Peter*, 102.
38 Michaels, *1 Peter*, 108.
39 Grudem, *First Epistle of Peter*, 117.
40 Marshall, *1 Peter*, 74.
41 Watts, *Isaiah 34–66*, 677.
42 Watts, 677.
43 Michaels, *1 Peter*, 109.
44 Selwyn, *First Epistle of St. Peter*, 166.

belong to the Lord and thus experience his presence.[45] Their access to God is unmediated—they have direct access to God.[46]

The implication is that the church of Jesus Christ does not have a priest caste; rather, "every believer has both a royal function derived from Christ's kingship and a priestly one derived from His priesthood."[47] The Protestant doctrine of the "priesthood of all believers" has its roots in this text. It entails that "every Christian has in Christ the right of direct access to God without the need for any other mediator."[48] Even though the priests of the Old Testament had these privileges, they also had responsibilities. They were "to mediate God's blessings to the nations, as it [the church] proclaims the gospel."[49] The connection between what they are—a royal priesthood—and the proclamation of the gospel is implicit in verse 9. Their vocation as the royal priesthood is a "communal vocation." No one is to do it individually, and because of it they embody God's holy character.[50] The priestly role of believers is not only within the life of the church but outside the life of the church to the world at large.[51]

It is the same group of people that Peter says are ἔθνος ἅγιον ("a holy nation") and λαὸς εἰς περιποίησιν ("a people for his possession"). The two titles are related; it is because they are God's possession that they are ἔθνος ἅγιον. The purpose of these honorific titles is ὅπως τὰς ἀρετὰς ἐξαγγείλητε ("to sound the praises").

The verb ἐξαγγείλητε means "to tell out or tell forth." This suggests that "we should give a high priority to verbal declarations."[52] Some scholars have argued that ἐξαγγέλλειν has to do with worship as opposed to the missionary enterprise.[53] However, this narrowing of ἐξαγγέλλειν is not intended by the text. Is not the church by its very nature a proclaiming community? Praise in 1 Peter goes beyond worship; it also includes proclamation.[54] Indeed, the context in Isaiah 43:21 is the activity of worship. However, even this

---

45 Schreiner, *1, 2 Peter, Jude*, 115.
46 Lenski, *Interpretation of the Epistles*, 100.
47 Kelly, *Epistles of Peter*, 98.
48 Marshall, *1 Peter*, 75.
49 Schreiner, *1, 2 Peter, Jude*, 114–15.
50 Green, *1 Peter*, 62.
51 Green, 61.
52 Walls and Anders, *I & II Peter*, 31.
53 Michaels, *1 Peter*, 110.
54 Green, *1 Peter*, 62.

is not an exclusively "vertical" activity. Green states, "In Peter, however, 'praise' is expanded to include not only vertical language (worship) but also horizontal (proclamation), and has been given a particular content."[55] In both the Old Testament and 1 Peter, "such declarative praise is not a private affair between God and the worshipers, but it spills out into the public arena as one of the means by which God draws the nations to himself."[56]

Since Israel was to be a worshiping community, the church in the same manner is to be a worshiping community. God's desire is that what he does should lead his creation to praise him (Isa 43:7). Schreiner noted,

> The declaration of God's praises includes both worship and evangelism, spreading the good news of God's saving wonders to all peoples. They proclaim God's praises for calling them "out of darkness into his wonderful light." This is a description of their conversion and employs the language of Genesis 1, where God utters the word and light becomes a reality (Gen 1:3–5), pushing back the darkness.[57]

The people of God have an obligation to "declare the wonderful deeds of God to the world around [them]."[58] We have evidence in 1 Peter of what we would call mission; for instance, Peter encourages wives to make an effort to win their husbands to the faith (3:1). It should be noted that the witness by the wives is through their holy lifestyle.[59]

The content of the proclamation is also important—the word translated as "praises" in Isaiah 43:21 (LXX) is ἀρετὰς, which in 1 Peter is translated as "wonderful deeds" (2:12).[60] Various translations have different translations for "praises" (AV), "excellences" (RV), and "mighty acts" (NRSV). Mighty deeds or acts are the best translation since ἀρετὰς "when applied to a god, does not denote his virtues or intrinsic qualities but the manifestations of his power."[61] The fact that they speak of God's mighty deeds is a testament to the fact that their salvation has its origin in God. Even though they have a part to play, ultimately salvation comes from God himself.[62]

God is further identified as the one "who called you out of darkness

---

55 Green, 62.
56 Wright quoted in Flemming, *Recovering the Full Mission*, 223–24.
57 Schreiner, *1, 2 Peter, Jude*, 115–16.
58 Marshall, *1 Peter*, 77.
59 Flemming, *Recovering the Full Mission*, 218.
60 Grudem, *First Epistle of Peter*, 117–18.
61 Kelly, *Epistles of Peter*, 99.
62 Grudem, *First Epistle of Peter*, 119.

into his marvelous light" (2:9 NRSV). This phrase is significant because conversion language in Scripture is often regarded as crossing over from darkness to light (e.g., Acts 26:18; 2 Cor 4:6; Col 1:12–13).[63] Here we have a reminder of what has taken place in the lives of the people to whom Peter is writing. If the church has come from darkness to light, it follows that those who do not know God are still in darkness. Those in darkness are to be led to the light by experiencing salvation in Jesus Christ. It is indeed true that "the elect community lives between the darkness of its pagan past and the light of its eschatological future."[64]

It is self-evident that, for Peter, holiness results in outward, visible actions, which Peter called "doing good."[65] Such good acts done by the people of God are a "form of witness," and the context of such good behavior is "among the Gentiles," whom Peter assumes see these acts of kindness.[66] These gentiles are the same people who persecuted and opposed the people of God.[67] Believers' good deeds function like magnetism, which invites those who have not yet known God. As the unbelievers see these good deeds, they will change their ways of maligning the faith as they become part of it and, together with believers, will bring glory to God.[68] The Shona proverbs focus on inculcating good behavior in children. Good behavior is shown by their deeds, and it is in resembling their parents that these good behaviors come out.

Scholars have examined Peter's household code in 1 Peter 2:13–3:7 and have demonstrated that it fits into the schema of "doing good."[69] Here the believers are to "do good" within their social, political, and economic engagements in the Greco-Roman world.[70] When compared with the other household codes (*Haustafeln*), Peter's codes do not focus on interrelationships among Christians but rather on how Christians should engage with unbelievers.[71] Here both their holy lives and missions come together in a unique way. It is their conduct that enables them to missionally

---

63   Michaels, *1 Peter*, 111.
64   Michaels, 112.
65   Flemming, *Recovering the Full Mission*, 215.
66   Flemming, 215.
67   Flemming, 215.
68   Flemming, 218.
69   Flemming, 218–19.
70   Flemming, 218–19.
71   Flemming, 218–19.

engage unbelievers. Flemming believes since unbelievers can recognize what "doing good" entails, the implication is that "Christian conduct is not completely countercultural."[72] Yet since their conduct follows the example of Jesus (2:21) as Flemming recognizes, it is then completely countercultural.[73] Peter's audience are seen from the viewpoint of the life and ministry of Jesus as seen in the Scriptures, especially the exoneration of the one who suffered and yet was righteous.[74] The things that Jesus did—including not retaliating, doing good to one's enemies, or even submitting one to another—do not come naturally to humans. Just because unbelievers can recognize good does not necessarily mean that they do what is good because they lack the power that comes from God.

Given that the environment of Peter's audience was hostile toward the believers, Peter sees suffering as an occasion to respond the same way as Christ.[75] In the words of Christopher Wright, theirs is "the suffering mission of the suffering God."[76] Their response comes out of their identity as the holy people of God. The purpose of such a response is to win over the hostile world with the gospel of Christ. The witness of the believers is accomplished by means of their good deeds, which is not similar to their surrounding environment but diametrically opposed to it.[77] Green perceptively noted,

> We are not against the world; the holiness of God's people is not found in reciprocal animosity with their opponents. We do not work out our identity and sense of mission simply by negating the beliefs and behaviors of others. If we are different from the world, it is not because we set out to be so, but rather because our lives rest ultimately in a God who is different and we follow in the footsteps of Jesus Christ.[78]

In 1 Peter, it is envisioned that the people of God are to tell the world (unsaved) of the works of God (3:13–16).[79] In addition, Peter speaks of the kind of life believers should lead among the gentiles, which is intended to draw them to God (2:11–12).[80] Even though the Shona proverbs can help

---

72 Flemming, 217.
73 Flemming, 217.
74 Green, *1 Peter*, 55.
75 Flemming, *Recovering the Full Mission*, 220–21.
76 Wright, *Mission of God's People*, 240–41.
77 Flemming, *Recovering the Full Mission*, 221.
78 Green, "Living as Exiles," 324.
79 Flemming, *Recovering the Full Mission*, 224.
80 Flemming, 224.

us read the text, we need to realize that the aspect of being missional is not present among the Shonas. Children's representation of their parents has an inward rather than outward focus. As such we need to bring this aspect clearly from the text and ensure that the people understand the missional perspective of these texts. Peter writes, "But in your hearts sanctify Christ as Lord. Always be ready to make your defense to anyone who demands from you an accounting for the hope that is in you" (3:15 NRSV). Clearly, this verse envisions that the outsiders will ask the believers about their peculiar kind of life, and for Peter, this becomes an opportunity to speak about their Lord Jesus Christ. They will be asked about themselves, and they shift attention from themselves to Jesus Christ, their Savior.[81] The way that Peter structures 1 Peter 3:15 signifies the union between "word and life." Their hope stems from the command "sanctify Christ as Lord" in their hearts (3:15). The way in which they sanctify Christ as Lord is through their holy lifestyles, a way of living that manifests God's holiness.[82] In this passage we see that the people are to give a reason (proclaim their faith-mission) and sanctify Christ as Lord (be holy). Clearly, mission and holiness are intricately connected.

The people of God understand that they have a mission that is sanctioned by God himself. This mission is conducted through their mouth and lifestyle as they function as the royal priesthood.[83] For R. C. H. Lenksi, "This is the confessional and the missionary spirit and activity of God's people."[84] For them to participate in this mission, they have gone through a transformation from οὐ λαός, to λαὸς θεοῦ as they do what Israel was called to do.[85] In summary, 1 Peter 2:9–11; 3:15 and 2:13–3:7 all intimately link holiness and mission.

Synthesis and Implications for the Church

First Peter intricately weaves together holiness and mission in a way that it is impossible to have one and not the other. Being, doing, and telling come together in a unique way as valid methods for engaging in the mission of

---

81 "Believers should live as aliens in this world so that unbelievers will observe their godly lives and glorify God by coming to faith in Christ." Schreiner, *1, 2 Peter, Jude*, 118.
82 Flemming, *Recovering the Full Mission*, 226.
83 Lenski, *Interpretation of the Epistles*, 103.
84 Lenski, 103.
85 Michaels, *1 Peter*, 112.

God.[86] The believers in 1 Peter are "holy exiles, radically different" yet "fully engaged in [their] social world."[87] They are to tell others about their hope so that they may join the people of God in this living hope.[88] The holiness to which they are called is God's own holiness to the extent that "God's holiness becomes [their] holiness."[89] Holiness is patterned after the holiness of God: "He who called you is holy, so be holy in all you do" (1:15),[90] signifying that "no sphere of life is outside God's dominion."[91] Truly they must resemble God if they are to claim to be his children. Furthermore, the crucified Christ provides an example for the holy life in that "it takes the shape of the self-giving love of Jesus."[92] On the negative side, holiness also has the aspect of being separate from the world and evil desires.[93]

Peter focused on forming their identity so that they may truly be the holy people of God.[94] He used various honorific titles to identify them—chosen people, royal priesthood, a holy nation, a people belonging to God (2:9). The purpose for such titles is that "they may declare the praises of him who called you out of darkness into his wonderful light" (2:9). We discovered that "declaring the praise" is not just about worship but the proclamation of the works of God to the unbelieving world. In these texts we see holiness (identity) and mission intricately connected. They are holy so as to be on a mission which God has given them.

The ethical exhortations that follow in 1 Peter are based on this identity.[95] This is a classic case of the imperatives having a basis in indicatives. The people of God are not supposed to withdraw; it is within normal society in the midst of social, political, and economic realities that they are supposed to be holy. Even though society may be hostile to them, they are to maintain their witness in such a society. Their witness is that of word and deed—their lifestyle should be patterned after Jesus Christ. Yet they must also be able to give reasons for their hope (1 Pet 3:15) to verbalize their witness. The

---

86 Flemming, *Recovering the Full Mission*, 229.
87 Flemming, 229.
88 Flemming, 229.
89 Osborne, "1 Peter," 162.
90 Grudem, *First Epistle of Peter*, 84.
91 Schreiner, *1, 2 Peter, Jude*, 80.
92 Flemming, *Recovering the Full Mission*, 213.
93 Marshall, *1 Peter*, 53.
94 Arichea and Nida, *Translator's Handbook*, 66.
95 Arichea and Nida, 66.

mission does not start there but, for example, right in their homes as they witness to their husbands or spouses; this can be done "without a word" (3:1).

The church of Jesus Christ, particularly in Africa and elsewhere, has much to learn from this picture painted by Peter. First, we need to be holy, and second, we need to be on God's mission. This mission begins in our homes and proceeds to our immediate neighbors in the villages, towns, and cities across Africa or wherever we may live. There remain many people groups who are not yet reached with the gospel of Christ. For Africans who are scattered across the world—their mission takes place in those cities where they have been scattered. From this perspective, 1 Peter provides the impetus for reverse mission by Africans in the cities that once sent missionaries to Africa. Such a mission should not be sectarian, that is, one that only reaches out to fellow Africans. The mission field is much bigger than those who come from the missionaries' homeland.

Conclusion

We set out to investigate ways in which holiness and mission are connected in 1 Peter. We did this using Shona proverbs that deal with the issue of resemblance or imitation. Even though the missional aspect is absent within the Shona culture, these proverbs helped us to read 1 Peter from the perspective of resemblance or imitation. The call of God entails drawing nearer to him so as to mimic him since God cannot fellowship with those whose lives are anything other than holy.[96] Mission cannot be done unless the people doing it are holy. First Peter focuses on the identity of the believers and uses this as the prerequisite for engaging in God's mission.

Bibliography

Arichea, Daniel C., and Eugene A. Nida. *A Translator's Handbook on the First Letter from Peter*. UBS Handbook Series. Stuttgart: United Bible Societies, 1980.

Beare, Francis Wright. *The First Epistle of Peter: The Greek Text with Introduction and Notes*. 2nd ed. Oxford: Blackwell, 1958.

Clowney, Edmund P. *The Message of 1 Peter: The Way of the Cross*. Rev. ed. Bible Speaks Today. Downers Grove, IL: InterVarsity Press, 2021.

Danker, Frederick W., Walter Bauer, William F. Arndt, and F. Wilbur Gingrich. *Greek-English Lexicon of the New Testament and Other Early Christian Literature*. 3rd ed. Chicago: University of Chicago Press, 2000.

---

96 Davids, *Letters of 2 Peter*, 69.

Davids, Peter H. *The First Epistle of Peter*. New International Commentary on the New Testament. Grand Rapids: Eerdmans, 1990.

Davids, Peter H. *The Letters of 2 Peter and Jude*. Pillar New Testament Commentary. Grand Rapids: Eerdmans, 2006.

Flemming, Dean E. *Recovering the Full Mission of God: A Biblical Perspective on Being, Doing, and Telling*. Downers Grove, IL: IVP Academic, 2013.

Green, Joel B. *1 Peter*. Two Horizons New Testament Commentary. Grand Rapids: Eerdmans, 2007.

Green, Joel B. "Living as Exiles: The Holy Church in the Diaspora in 1 Peter." In *Holiness and Ecclesiology in the New Testament*, edited by Andy Johnson and Kent E. Brower, 311–25. Grand Rapids: Eerdmans, 2007.

Grudem, Wayne A. *1 Peter*. Tyndale New Testament Commentaries 17. Grand Rapids: Eerdmans, 1988.

Hamutyinei, M. A., and Albert B. Plangger. *Tsumo-Shumo: Shona Proverbial Lore and Wisdom*. Second edition. Shona Heritage Series 2. Gweru, Zimbabwe: Mambo Press, 1987.

Kelly, J. N. D. *A Commentary on the Epistles of Peter and of Jude*. Black's New Testament Commentary. London: Continuum, 1969.

Lenski, R. C. H. *The Interpretation of the Epistles of St. Peter, St. John, and St. Jude*. Augsburg: Fortress Press, 1966.

Marshall, I. Howard. *1 Peter*. IVP New Testament Commentary Series. Downers Grove, IL: InterVarsity Press, 1991.

Mburu, Elizabeth W. *African Hermeneutics*. Carlisle, UK: HippoBooks, 2019.

Michaels, J. Ramsey. *1 Peter*. Word Biblical Commentary 49. Grand Rapids: Zondervan, 2015.

O'Connor, Dan. "Holiness of Life as a Way of Christian Witness." *International Review of Mission* 80, no. 1 (1991): 17–26.

Osborne, Grant R. "1 Peter." *James, 1–2 Peter, Jude, Revelation*. Edited by Philip W. Comfort. Cornerstone Biblical Commentary 18. Carol Stream, IL: Tyndale House, 2011.

Pryor, John W. "First Peter and the New Covenant (II)." *Reformed Theological Review* 45, no. 2 (1986): 44–51.

Schreiner, Thomas R. *1, 2 Peter, Jude*. New American Commentary 37. Nashville: Broadman & Holman, 2003.

Selwyn, Edward Gordon. *The First Epistle of St. Peter: The Greek Text with Introduction, Notes and Essays*. Thornapple Commentaries. Grand Rapids: Baker Books, 1981.

Walls, David, and Max Anders. *I & II Peter, I, II, & III John, Jude*. Holman New Testament Commentary 11. Nashville: Holman Reference, 1999.

Watts, John D. W. *Isaiah 34–66.* Word Biblical Commentary 25. Waco, TX: Word, 1987.

Wright, Christopher J. H. *The Mission of God's People: A Biblical Theology of the Church's Mission.* Biblical Theology for Life. Grand Rapids: Zondervan, 2010.

Wright, Christopher J. H. "Old Testament Ethics: A Missiological Perspective." *Catalyst* 26, no. 2 (2000): 5–8.

Chapter 3

Mission by God's Living Stones
Watchman Nee's Missional Exegesis of 1 Peter 2:5-11

Jacob Chengwei Feng

According to church historian Richard Cook, the founding of the People's Republic of China in 1949 changed China into "a land without missionaries."[1] This statement is both true and false. It is true in the sense that Western missionaries were expelled due to the change in China's political regime. It is false because a missional spirit and activities persisted in the land, especially among the Local Churches (or the Christian Assembly, the Little Flock).[2] As an indigenous church, the Local Churches maintained no organizational and financial connection with any foreign missionary societies or enterprises,[3] despite the fact that Watchman Nee (Ni Tuosheng, 1903–72) maintained close spiritual ties with the foreign missionaries.[4] Since the inception of the Local Churches in 1922, Nee infused the movement he led with missionary dynamics, which contributed to the Local Churches' global presence and the constitution of the Local Churches in every continent by people of local origin rather than Chinese immigrants.[5]

This chapter studies Nee's exegesis of 1 Peter 2:5–11 shortly before and after China's regime change in 1949. It argues that Nee's missional exegesis of 1 Peter not only enriched his *missional* interpretation of Scripture but also provided the church and academia with a unique understanding and practice of mission as a "coordinated spiritual house," which is accomplished by all believers as living stones and priests of God and by their migration. The significance of this chapter is two-fold. First, Nee's missional exegesis

---
1 Cook, *Darkest before the Dawn*, 256.
2 For a historical account of the Local Churches by Witness Lee, one of Watchman Nee's most important and closest coworkers, see Lee, *History and Revelation*. For a historical and contemporary account of the Local Churches, see Liu, "Globalization of Chinese Christianity," 96–114.
3 It is well known that Nee's theology was influenced greatly by the British Brethren movement. However, Nee resisted the Brethren control that was attempted out of a colonial mindset. See Feng, "Against the Tide," 239–59.
4 For instance, Nee's spiritual mentor, Margaret E. Barber (1866–1929), was first sent to China by the Church Missionary Society to Fuzhou, Fujian. Later, she resigned from the mission and went to China again. This time, she returned without financial support from any mission. See Reetzke, *M. E. Barber*, 73; and Kinnear, *Against the Tide*.
5 Liu, "Globalization of Chinese Christianity," 110.

provides a fresh perspective to the worldwide Christian community in that the exegesis of Scripture does not have to be merely an academic enterprise. Instead, exegesis can be dynamically and missionally oriented. Second, Nee's missional strategy remains viable for God's mission in the third millennium.

The chapter is organized into the following structure. First, as background, I will briefly study the missionary activities in China from Nee's perspective. Second, Nee's missional exegesis of 1 Peter 2:5–11 will be presented. Third, the chapter will analyze the implications of Nee's missional exegesis for the global Christian mission in the third millennium.

Background: The Missionary Activities in China in the First Half of the Twentieth Century from Nee's Perspective

The rising and flourishing of the Local Churches in China took place in the first half of the twentieth century, an era in which a number of indigenous Chinese churches[6] began to emerge among innumerable, swirling, sociopolitical currents, both globally and in China. Cook identifies four currents that simultaneously worked together in influencing the churches in China, namely nationalism, fundamentalism, global Christianity, and imperialism.[7] One factor that Cook places under the category of nationalism is "dependency," which refers to the Western missionaries' practice of hiring local Chinese as church workers. This factor, unfortunately, produced one of the major obstacles to Nee's conversion to Christianity. Nee recounted his salvation experience in 1936:

> As a boy I did not understand the nature of preaching. When I was older, I considered it the most trifling and base of occupations. In those days most preachers were employed by European or American missionaries. They were servile subordinates to the missionaries and earned merely eight or nine dollars per month. I had no intention of becoming a preacher nor even a Christian. I could never have imagined that I would choose the profession of a preacher, a profession which I despised and considered trifling and base.[8]

---

6 For a most recent account of the indigenous Chinese churches, see Duan, *Indigenization of Christianity*.
7 See Cook, *Darkest before the Dawn*, chs. 11–12.
8 Nee, *Collected Works*, 26:453.

Nee's conversion is intimately associated with God's calling as for him, "being saved from sin and [his] life career were linked together."[9] Nee's struggle corresponds with the critics of Christianity who complained about the greed, selfishness, and sinfulness of the false Chinese church "pastors"[10] hired by the Western missionaries.

Even after his conversion, Nee continued to be bothered by the status quo of Christianity:

> I was saved in the spring of 1920. During the first year following my conversion, I was unclear regarding the truths of the church, except that the sister who led me to the Lord had told me that unfortunately there were too many nominal Christians in the church today. Also, I felt the character of the pastors I knew was too poor, for one did not ordinarily see them except when they came to ask for donations. Before my family was revived we frequently had several *mahjong* games going on at home. When the pastor would come for donations, we conveniently handed him money from the *mahjong* table. Although he knew quite well where the money came from, he still accepted it. From this observation, I felt the character of the pastors was very poor, for as long as they had money all was well. Besides this, it seemed that so many members of the church were merely nominal.[11]

In other words, both clergy and laypeople, the two major constituting elements of the Christian church, were conceived to be defiled. Nee was also concerned with the church's divisiveness and sectarianism as a consequence of the missionaries' different denominational backgrounds and goals:

> The danger which confronts the missionary is to form those he has led to the Lord into a branch of the society he represents. Since workers represent different societies, they naturally form different branches of their respective societies, and the consequence is great confusion in the work and churches of God. The immediate aim of the various workers is no doubt the same—what preacher does not hope that many souls will be won to the Lord?—but there is a lack of clarity and definiteness regarding the ultimate issue. Some workers, praise God, are out to establish local churches; others, alas! are out to extend their own denomination or to form mission churches.[12]

---

9 Nee, 26:451.

10 Cook, *Darkest before the Dawn*, 207.

11 Nee, *Collected Works*, 18:304. *Mahjong* is a tile-based game that was developed in nineteenth-century China and has spread throughout the world since the early twentieth century. In Nee's case, the game was gambling in nature, involving monetary gains or losses.

12 Nee, 30:134.

Because of his reading of Scripture, Nee chose a path based on his realization that "God's wish is to establish local churches in every city."[13] Therefore, he considered establishing and building up the local churches as one of the significant aspects of the work that God entrusted to him.[14] Moreover, the Brethren schism in 1840 and their further divisions shocked Nee, causing him to resort to the New Testament and reconsider the proper outworking of unity among the local churches.[15] As a result, Nee developed a unity-centered and mission-focused ecclesiology to meet the needs of his context.[16]

In sum, even though the Western missionaries contributed to God's missionary enterprise in the first half of the twentieth century by bringing the gospel and the word of God to China, they unfortunately—and perhaps unintentionally—caused irreconcilable damages to China's Christianity in terms of unqualified local leadership, corrupted membership, and division in the body of Christ.

Nee's Missional Exegesis of 1 Peter 2:5-11

Elsewhere, I have argued for Nee's missional ecclesiology. Namely, the church does not simply carry out mission as if mission is something dispensable to it. On the contrary, the church is missional in nature.[17] In this section, I present Nee's missional exegesis, driven by his vision of God's mission in China. On September 1, 1948, Nee gave a talk concerning the future of God's work in China. He divided God's work in the past 140 years into three periods: the gospel period (1807–1900), the revival period (1900–37), and the period of life (1937–present).[18] He discerned a "kind of hunger and thirst among the seeking saints everywhere," which is "a sign that God's work in China has gone on. Presently, however, this is the beginning of the period of life. From this point onward, God's children must have a deeper pursuit, knowledge, and experience of His life."[19] He then advised the local churches that, in order to keep up with God's work, they must attend to three matters, namely, preaching

---

13 Nee, 26:468.

14 The other three aspects are literary work, conducting overcomers' meetings, and training young people. See Nee, 26:478–79.

15 Buntain, "Exclusive Brethren, Watchman Nee," 43.

16 Feng, "Against the Tide," 241.

17 Feng, 253–54.

18 Nee, *Collected Works*, 55:43–45.

19 Nee, 55:45.

the gospel, bringing in revival, and pursuing the knowledge of life.[20] Between these lines, one can sense Nee's burning spirit for God's mission: "We are not afraid that the brothers and sisters would become too much in the matter of preaching the gospel. We only fear that they would not do enough!"[21] He presented an ambitious goal of "evangeliz[ing] China in twenty years," which believers were to carry out through their migration by following five routes from eastern to western China.[22]

Unfortunately, the regime changes in 1949 abruptly ended Nee's ambitious plan. However, driven by the continuous missionary fire, he took every opportunity to lead the church's missionary endeavor, just two years before his imprisonment by the Communist government. His missional exegesis can be analyzed from a few perspectives. First, he spoke of God's mission in 1950 by expounding on 1 Peter 2:5:

> When we were saved, we were saved individually and one by one. When we spread out as God's means, however, we spread out as the Body. When we were saved we became living stones. When we spread out, we are coordinated as a spiritual house (1 Pet 2:5). In other words, God's means is the corporate Christian—the church, not the individual Christians. Let me say a direct word to you tonight.... Our sole purpose of living on this earth is for the gospel. We do not save a few souls here and there when we feel like it. God joins all the believers together into a harmonious whole, like a body, and uses it to preach the gospel and to save others.[23]

In other words, what Nee envisions is God's mission carried out not by individual missionaries or separate missionary groups or enterprises but as a spiritual house built up and coordinated together. Nee's sense of "being built up" and "being coordinated" is echoed by Daniel Keating, who argued, "The image of a 'house' predominates here, both as a noun (*oikos*), but also as embedded in the verb 'to be built into' (*oikodomeō*)."[24] For Joel Green, the spiritual house and temple (v. 5) refer to "the community of the faithful (and not individual believers), [which] is itself the temple, [and] marks the community as sharing in the glory of God, as consecrated to God, as the

---

20 Nee, 55:45–47.
21 Nee, 55:46.
22 Lee, *Collected Works*, 2:173–74.
23 Nee, 61:122–23.
24 Keating, *First and Second Peter*, 52.

residence of the Spirit ... and as a symbol of God's power and presence."[25] Moreover, those who participate in God's mission should not be limited to a small number of Christian "elites," or only the clergy, but by all the members of the body of Christ who have been baptized into one Spirit (1 Cor 12:13) and fitly joined together (Eph 2:21).

Nee's vision of mission as a coordinated spiritual house aligns with his emphasis on "coordination" among all the believers: "Today the Lord's way is for the whole church to coordinate together to preach the gospel. God does not want to take the way of individuals; He wants the corporate service of the whole church."[26] The major hurdles to the implementation of this vision are individualism and independence:

> In our service and work, our individual element should be reduced to nothing, and our personal work should disappear in the face of corporate church service. Our work and service must be done in coordination, and our coordination must be carried out in the church. No matter how great or small we are, we are all members. No matter how small we are, we cannot be less than a member. We should have a deep feeling that we cannot be independent in any way. We must feel that we need the coordination of the other members.[27]

However, this does not mean that Nee adopted the conventional way of organizing believers into specific missionary societies. He firmly believed that, according to the scriptural mandate, there are no "headquarters" among the local churches. Each church is directly responsible to Christ as the head. No local church is joined to another church or regards another bigger church as the central church.[28]

Nee's missional exegesis led to his vision of mission as a coordinated spiritual house, which was practically implemented in his ambitious twenty-year plan to evangelize China. According to Lee's account, Nee designed five main routes, through which new Local Churches would be established through believers' migration. Each of these routes began from a coastal city (e.g., Hong Kong, Shanghai, and Yanai) in the east, where the churches were stronger, and reached the western and interior lands of China with no or weak churches.[29]

---

25 Green, *1 Peter*, 61.
26 Nee, *Collected Works*, 61:129–30.
27 Nee, 55:48–50.
28 Nee, 22:109.
29 Lee, *Collected Works*, 2:173–74.

In March 1949, right before Shanghai's takeover by the Communist army, Nee sent Lee to Taiwan to strengthen God's work there. Lee continued to implement Nee's missional strategy of a coordinated spiritual house in Taipei, which led to a thirty-fold increase within the first year of his migration. Such a rapid increase was the result of believers' highly coordinated efforts as "living stones." Namely, all the believers in Taipei were mobilized to distribute gospel tracts to every house. They formed gospel teams to parade on the streets while singing hymns, beating big drums, and beckoning people to be saved. They held weekly evangelism meetings to baptize unbelievers.[30]

Second, Nee made an interesting correlation between the "living stones" (λίθοι ζῶντες, 1 Pet 2:5) and Peter himself by drawing the believers' attention to Matthew 16:18, where Jesus says, "And I also say to you that you are Peter [*Petros*], and upon this rock [*petra*] I will build My church."[31] For Nee, Peter as *petra* represents all of Christ's believers, upon whom Christ builds his church. Each believer should follow Peter's pattern as a servant of God and participate in Christ's church. Such building work is not carried out by different believers with different agendas. Instead, all "living stones" coordinate together as a singular "rock" by following the same strategy and aiming for the same goal.

Furthermore, the word πέτρα also appears in Matthew 7:25, where Jesus gave a parable of building a house on different foundations. Nee likened the church to the house built on the rock,[32] which refers to Christ and his revelation.[33] Nee further commented:

> God's children are little stones (*lithos*) upon the unique rock. In writing the second chapter of his first Epistle, Peter said that we are God's living stones, and that we are being built into a spiritual house (v. 5). Every brother and sister is a living stone that is built upon the rock. The superstructure of the church is of the same substance as the foundation. The material for the superstructure is the same as the material for the foundation.[34]

In other words, Nee saw believers as living stones forming the superstructure of the church, whose substance and material fully match the

---

30 Lee, 2:180–81.
31 Nee, *Collected Works*, 52:92–93.
32 Nee, 52:92–93.
33 Nee, 34:109–11; 36:117.
34 Nee, 52:92–93.

church's foundation, Christ and his revelation. Green similarly detected Peter's motif "to develop the identity of his Christian audience in terms of imitation of Christ. Crucially, he does so not in terms of what his audience must become but in terms of what they already are." For Peter, Jesus is "a living stone." Those who "come to him" become "living stones" who share in his fate, both among humans and before God.[35]

Third, while exegeting ἱεράτευμα ἅγιον in 1 Peter 2:5, Nee affirmed the universal priesthood of all believers.[36] For Nee, it is the accomplishment of Christ that has unconditionally made every believer a priest (Rev 1:6; 1 Pet 2:5).[37] Services in the church should not be carried out by a small number of so-called servants of God. Instead, all believers should serve together as priests.[38] It is certainly questionable if one can exegetically connect the Protestant doctrine of the priesthood of all believers to 1 Peter 2:5.[39] However, Nee's exposition of 1 Peter 2:5 and believers' priestly roles are theologically and missionally oriented: "The gospel should not be preached just by the so-called workers. It should be furthered by all the saints striving together in one accord and in one soul for its advancement (Phil 1:5, 27)."[40] Nee's admonition is made more necessary if we heed Walter Shurden's stark criticism: "Sad to say, [the doctrine of universal priesthood] remained throughout much of Protestantism more rhetoric than reality."[41]

Fourth, Nee commented on 1 Peter 2:11 by linking it to Abraham (Gen 23:4): "We are the true descendants of Abraham (Gal 3:7). We should be pilgrims on the earth, moving and pitching our tents as he did (Heb 11:9, 13; 1 Pet 2:11)."[42] Many (if not most) biblical exegetes interpret Peter's designation of Christians as "aliens and exiles" *statically*. For instance, Green interpreted it from the perspective of Christian discipleship, in that

---

35 Green, *1 Peter*, 60.
36 Feng, "Lun shengpin jieji zhidu yu pubian jisi tixi 论圣品阶级制度与普遍祭司体系," 91–102.
37 Nee, *Collected Works*, 18:322.
38 Nee, 55:48.
39 Green affirmed that neither in 1 Peter 2:5 nor in verse 9 can we find a basis for such a doctrine, not because the doctrine lacks warrant (see e.g., 4:10–11) but because Peter's emphasis is not on the priestly role of each believer but on the priestly identity of God's people. See Green, *1 Peter*, 61. See also the excurses in Schweizer, *Church Order*, 46–47, 166–69; and Elliott, *Elect and the Holy*.
40 Nee, *Collected Works*, 55:48–49.
41 Shurden, *Doctrine of the Priesthood*, 18–19.
42 Nee, *Collected Works*, 55:51.

"the cost of discipleship for Peter's Christian audience is that they were rendered 'aliens and strangers' in their own home communities."[43] Keating noticed the verse's connection to the fate of Abraham, which is "to wander as a resident alien, never at home or settled in the land." However, when referring to God's people today, he emphasized the static Christian identity of resident aliens among the people surrounding us.[44] As a sharp contrast, Nee's exegesis is *dynamic* and *mission-oriented*. For Nee, our Christian status as "aliens and exiles" not only refers to our non-worldly identity and heavenly citizenship[45] but also has a practical implication, namely, believers' migration. Nee was saddened by the fact that "although many Christians from the coastal regions have migrated to the interior in the past ten years because of Japan's attack on China, most of them went with the motive of escaping the war, finding a job, finding a school, or finding their families; very few went for the gospel."[46] For Nee, the meaning of migration is God's command to Abraham: "Go from your country and your kindred and your father's house to the land that I will show you" (Gen 12:1).[47] The goal of migration is "to preach the gospel to all the nations and to be the Lord's witnesses to the uttermost parts of the earth (Matt 28:19; Acts 1:8)."[48] The requirements for migration are to "have an inward burden for the gospel and a will to suffer. We must be willing to absolutely obey and to give our all for the gospel."[49]

Reflecting on the missionary advancement of China, however, Nee lamented, "The gospel came to China from the West one hundred years ago. However, up to the present time, the footsteps of the gospel have only reached the coastal provinces. The interior of China and the remote areas have seen little of the gospel."[50] Nee pointed out one of the primary reasons for the lack of missionary activities in the interior part of China:

---

43 Green, *1 Peter*, 67.
44 Keating, *First and Second Peter*, 59.
45 For instance, for Watson and Callan, the coupling of "strangers and resident foreigners" in the New Testament "refers to Abel, Enoch, Noah, Abraham, and Sarah as people of God seeking their heavenly homeland (Heb 11:13–16)." Watson and Callan, *First and Second Peter*, 58. Similarly, Keener read Peter's motif statically in the sense that "life in this world is merely transitory." Keener, *1 Peter*, 149.
46 Nee, *Collected Works*, 55:52–53.
47 Unless otherwise noted, all Scripture quotations are from the NRSV.
48 Nee, *Collected Works*, 55:186.
49 Nee, 55:186.
50 Nee, 55:50–51.

In the past almost no Christians from the coastal regions migrated to the remote provinces, so it has been difficult for the gospel to move from the coast to the interior. The preaching of the gospel is like a relay race in a stadium. The [missionaries] from the West brought the gospel to the coastal regions of China and passed it on to us. We … in the coastal regions should receive the gospel and carry it to the interior and remote regions. We should not expect the [missionaries] from the West to pass us up and go there before us. If we would migrate with the gospel to all these places, the gospel would spread very quickly over the whole country.[51]

Guided by his missional exegesis of 1 Peter 5:11, Nee encouraged the churches along the coast to help the believers "in every occupation prepare themselves for the Lord's leading to take up their occupation, families, and even more, the gospel, to migrate to the remote provinces. In this way the gospel will not stop with us."[52]

Throughout their history, the Local Churches have continued Nee's missional strategy. They have encouraged the faithful to plant new churches by migrating not only from city to city in the same country but also from country to country and continent to continent. Because of the church revival in 1935, Nee and his coworkers decided to spread the churches to large cities in China through migration from Shanghai to Nanjing and from Yantai to Tianjin.[53] In the 1960s, believers from Taiwan migrated to Japan, South Korea, and the United States, and in the 1970s, to South America.[54] In the 1990s, hundreds of new churches were established in the Russian-speaking world through a joint migration by believers from America and Taiwan.[55] In the past several decades, the Local Churches in America have established new churches in strategically chosen cities through the migration of believers through an initiative called Gospelize, Truthize, and Churchize America (GTCA).[56] In the past several years, many believers migrated to Germany from Asia and the United States to participate in the Lord's Move to Europe (LME).[57]

---

51 The other reason identified by Nee is the Chinese Christians' spiritual immaturity. The gospel does not spread through excitement, ideas, or even organization. See Nee, 55:52–53.
52 Nee, 55:52–53.
53 Lee, *History and Revelation*, 1:91.
54 Lee, 2:371–81, 475–91, 505–12, 513–22.
55 Lee, *Crystallization-Study of the Epistle*, 97.
56 GTCA, *GTCA: Gospelize, Truthize*, 2023.
57 LME, *Lord's Move to Europe*, 2023.

In this section, I have presented Nee's missional exegesis of 1 Peter 2:5–11 in terms of participation in God's mission as a coordinated spiritual house, each believer as a living stone and priest of God, and mission through believers' migration. For Nee, exegesis is not merely an academic endeavor but is dynamically oriented toward mission.

Implications of Nee's Missional Exegesis toward Mission in the Third Millennium

Nee's missional exegesis has significant implications for both exegesis and mission. First, in terms of biblical exegesis, the past three to four decades have seen a steady stream of scholarly writing on the Theological Interpretation of Scripture (TIS).[58] According to Green, the scholarly interest in TIS is a reaction to the "rise of various forms of scientific exegesis from the eighteenth century forward," which not only segregates professional biblical studies from the church's everyday interpretive practices but also disconnects biblical scholarship and the Bible itself from the theological enterprise.[59] Todd Billings defined TIS as a multifaceted practice of a community of faith by reading the Bible as God's instrument of self-revelation and saving fellowship.[60] As seen in Nee's example, Craig Bartholomew and Heath Thomas are undoubtedly correct in their observation that the church has always practiced theological interpretation in some form and that such a practice is commonly reflected in the church's preaching, sacraments, and acts of charity.[61] However, Nee's exegesis prompts the following questions: If TIS is indeed a practice of a community of faith (according to Billings's definition), and if the church is genuinely missional in nature,[62] then should not the interpretation of Scripture be *missional*? Likewise, if Christopher Spinks is correct that TIS represents a "scholarly" conversation language—a *theological* language *of* the church, *for* the church—that fits well in the church,[63] then does it not imply that TIS is at the

---

58 For a succinct survey of the stream, see Spinks, "Catching Up on a Conversation," 770–73.
59 Green, *Practicing Theological Interpretation*, 4.
60 Billings, *Word of God for the People*, xii.
61 Bartholomew and Thomas, *Manifesto for Theological Interpretation*, 1.
62 Famously expressed in Vatican II's missionary document Ad Gentes: "The pilgrim Church is missionary by her very nature." See "Ad Gentes: Decree on the Mission Activity of the Church," Vatican II, accessed February 21, 2024, https://www.vatican.va/archive/hist_councils/ii_vatican_council/documents/vat-ii_decree_19651207_ad-gentes_en.html. Two standard works are Bosch, *Transforming Mission*, and Bevans and Schroeder, *Constants in Context*, 336.
63 Spinks, "Catching Up on a Conversation," 772, italics original.

same time *missional* language? Greg McKinzie rightly argued that missional hermeneutics is a radical reorientation of theological interpretation.[64] Based on McKinzie's observation that TIS remains too missionally deficient and missional hermeneutics remains too inattentive to the theological dynamics of readerly formation, McKinzie endeavored to integrate TIS and missional hermeneutics,[65] which is highly commendable and aligns with the insights offered in this chapter.

Second, in terms of mission, David J. Bosch famously enumerated thirteen thematic elements of an emerging ecumenical missionary paradigm, ranging from mission as the Church-With-Others to mission as Action in Hope.[66] Restricted by his time and context (such as the Second Sino-Japanese War from 1937–45 and the Civil War from 1927–49) and by the consequent internal and external challenges faced by the churches, Nee's vision of mission is in no way as comprehensive as Bosch's, even though a few similar insights can be detected. There are similarities, for instance, between Nee's missional ecclesiology[67] and Bosch's mission as the church-with-others,[68] between Nee's mission as universal priesthood and Bosch's mission as ministry by the whole people of God,[69] and between Nee's emphasis to gain local people (instead of Chinese immigrants)[70] and Bosch's mission as inculturation, just to name a few.[71] However, the distinct contributions of Nee and the Local Churches to the global mission can hardly be overestimated. First, I have argued elsewhere that, guided by Nee's mission-oriented, unity-centered, and locality-based ecclesiology, the Local Churches already carried out "northbound" mission at least six decades earlier than "[Philip] Jenkins' prediction that a new 'missionary century' is dawning in which the missionaries" from the Global South would travel to the Global North.[72] Second, some criticize Bosch for giving a minimal amount of attention to the Old Testament in *Transforming Mission*.[73] On the

---

64 McKinzie, "Missional Hermeneutics," 157–79.
65 McKinzie, "Hermeneutics of Participation."
66 Bosch, *Transforming Mission*, 377–522.
67 Feng, "Against the Tide."
68 Bosch, *Transforming Mission*, 377–97.
69 Bosch, 478–84.
70 Liu, "Globalization of Chinese Christianity," 110.
71 Bosch, *Transforming Mission*, 458–67.
72 Feng, "Against the Tide," 258; cf. Jenkins, *The Next Christendom*, 135.
73 Bekele, "Biblical Narrative of the *Missio Dei*," 155.

contrary, Nee provided extensive missional exegesis of the Old Testament, including Genesis, Exodus, and Song of Solomon.[74] Third, Kirsteen Kim critiqued and advanced the purported consensus of Bosch's "emerging ecumenical missionary paradigm":

> Although he propounds the theology of *missio Dei*, in which the church participates in the mission of God by the Spirit, Bosch binds the mission of the Spirit very closely to the missionary activity of the church. Thus, when he seeks to broaden mission to take account of the "comprehensive" nature of salvation, he can do so only by increasing the scope of the church's missionary activity. In this way mission still appears to be in the mold of the Enlightenment project as a *work* to be achieved by organization and strategy, rather than as a participation in the Spirit.[75]

In this aspect, Nee would wholeheartedly agree with Kim in that he opposed mission as an organization[76] and insisted on giving primacy to the Spirit in mission.[77]

Conclusion

This chapter first presented the Western missionaries' activities from the perspective of Watchman Nee. On the one hand, Nee highly regarded the missionaries who brought the Bible and the gospel to China. On the other hand, from his own experience, Nee unreservedly pointed out the problematic aspects of missionary enterprise as practiced by these Western missionaries, which led to defamed local leadership hired by the missionaries, corrupted membership, and the divisive condition among the churches caused by various missionary societies. Then, I presented Nee's missional exegesis of 1 Peter 2:5–11, in which one sees Nee's mission-oriented interpretation of Scripture. In particular, Nee stressed mission by believers as living stones of God's spiritual house and priests of God, mission as a coordinated spiritual house, and a missional strategy of believers' migration. Finally, the chapter highlighted the implications of Nee's missional exegesis for God's mission in the third millennium. With respect to exegesis, Nee's missional exegesis contributed to TIS in terms of highlighting the church's missional orientation. With respect to mission, Nee's missional ecclesiology has been

---

74 See e.g., Nee, *Collected Works*, 23:105–14, 35:15–28.
75 Kim, *Holy Spirit in the World*, 173–74.
76 Nee, *Collected Works*, 30:119–20.
77 Nee, 62:402–5.

thoroughly implemented by the Local Churches, which has led to its global presence and "northbound" mission. With Bosch's *Transforming Mission* as a missiological framework, the chapter identified Nee's missional exegesis of the Old Testament and his Spirit-focused vision of mission as particularly useful in filling up certain deficiencies of the framework, which will prove beneficial to God's global mission in the third millennium.

Bibliography

Bartholomew, Craig G., and Heath A. Thomas. *A Manifesto for Theological Interpretation.* Grand Rapids: Baker Academic, 2016.

Bekele, Girma. "The Biblical Narrative of the *Missio Dei*: Analysis of the Interpretive Framework of David Bosch's Missional Hermeneutic." *International Bulletin of Missionary Research* 35, no. 3 (2011): 153–58.

Bevans, Stephen B., and Roger P. Schroeder. *Constants in Context: A Theology of Mission for Today.* American Society of Missiology 30. Maryknoll, NY: Orbis Books, 2004.

Billings, J. Todd. *The Word of God for the People of God: An Entryway to the Theological Interpretation of Scripture.* Grand Rapids: Eerdmans, 2010.

Bosch, David J. *Transforming Mission: Paradigm Shifts in Theology of Mission.* American Society of Missiology 16. Twentieth anniversary ed. Maryknoll, NY: Orbis Books, 2011.

Buntain, William E. "The Exclusive Brethren, Watchman Nee, and the Local Churches in China." *Brethren Historical Review* 15, no. 1 (2019): 40–72.

Cook, Richard R. *Darkest before the Dawn: A Brief History of the Rise of Christianity in China.* Eugene, OR: Pickwick, 2021.

Duan, Qi. *The Indigenization of Christianity in China.* 3 vols. China Perspectives. London: Routledge, 2022.

Elliott, John Hall. *The Elect and the Holy: An Exegetical Examination of 1 Peter 2:4–10 and the Phrase βασίλειον ἱεράτευμα.* Supplements to Novum Testamentum 12. Leiden: Brill, 1966.

Feng, Jacob Chengwei 冯成伟. "Against the Tide: The Ecclesiology of the Local Churches Movement in the Colonial Context and Its Contribution to a Glocal Church." *Journal of the Evangelical Theological Society* 65, no. 2 (2022): 239–59.

Feng, Jacob Chengwei 冯成伟. "Lun shengpin jieji zhidu yu pubian jisi tixi" 论圣品阶级制度与普遍祭司体系 [On the clergy-laity system and universal priesthood]. *Kending yu fouding* 肯定与否定 [*Affirmation and Critique*] 7, no. 1 (2021): 91–102.

Feng, Jacob Chengwei 冯成伟. "Theological Method of Chinese Theology in the Republican Era (1911–1949): A Case Study of Wang Mingdao and Watchman Nee." *Journal of Chinese Theology* 9 (2023): 1–28. https://doi.org/10.1163/27726606-20230018.

Green, Joel B. *1 Peter.* Two Horizons New Testament Commentary. Grand Rapids: Eerdmans, 2007.

Green, Joel B. *Practicing Theological Interpretation: Engaging Biblical Texts for Faith and Formation.* Theological Explorations for the Church Catholic. Grand Rapids: Baker Academic, 2011.

GTCA. *GTCA: Gospelize, Truthize, Churchize America.* http://gtca.us.

Jenkins, Philip. *The Next Christendom: The Coming of Global Christianity.* 3rd ed. Oxford: Oxford University Press, 2011.

Kärkkäinen, Veli-Matti. *Hope and Community.* A Constructive Christian Theology for the Pluralistic World 5. Grand Rapids: Eerdmans, 2017.

Keating, Daniel. *First and Second Peter, Jude.* Catholic Commentary on Sacred Scripture. Grand Rapids: Baker Academic, 2011.

Keener, Craig S. *1 Peter: A Commentary.* Grand Rapids: Baker Academic, 2021.

Kim, Kirsteen. *The Holy Spirit in the World: A Global Conversation.* Maryknoll, NY: Orbis Books, 2007.

Kinnear, Angus I. *Against the Tide: The Story of Watchman Nee.* Fort Washington, PA: Christian Literature Crusade, 1973.

Lee, Joseph Tse-Hei. "Watchman Nee and the Little Flock Movement in Maoist China." *Church History* 74, no. 1 (2005): 68–96.

Lee, Witness. *The Collected Works of Witness Lee (1981).* 2 vols. Anaheim: Living Stream Ministry, 2021.

Lee, Witness. *Crystallization-Study of the Epistle to the Romans.* Anaheim: Living Stream Ministry, 2003.

Lee, Witness. *The History and Revelation of the Lord's Recovery.* 2 vols. Anaheim: Living Stream Ministry, 2020.

Liu, Yi. "Globalization of Chinese Christianity: A Study of Watchman Nee and Witness Lee's Ministry." *Asia Journal of Theology* 30, no. 1 (2016): 96–114.

LME. *Lord's Move to Europe (LME).* http://lordsmove.org.

McKinzie, Greg. "The Hermeneutics of Participation: Missional Interpretation of Scripture and Readerly Formation." PhD diss., Fuller Theological Seminary, 2021.

McKinzie, Greg. "Missional Hermeneutics as Theological Interpretation." *Journal of Theological Interpretation* 11, no. 2 (2017): 157–79.

Nee, Watchman. *The Collected Works of Watchman Nee.* 62 vols. Anaheim: Living Stream Ministry, 1992–94.

Reetzke, James. *M. E. Barber: A Seed Sown in China.* Chicago: Chicago Bibles and Books, 2007.

Schweizer, Eduard. *Church Order in the New Testament.* Translated by Frank Clarke. Studies in Biblical Theology 32. London: SCM, 1961.

Shurden, Walter B. *The Doctrine of the Priesthood of Believers.* Nashville: Convention Press, 1987.

Spinks, D. Christopher. "Catching Up on a Conversation: Recent Voices on Theological Interpretation of Scripture." *Anglican Theological Review* 99, no. 4 (2017): 769–86.

Watson, Duane F., and Terrance Callan. *First and Second Peter.* Paideia. Grand Rapids: Baker Academic, 2012.

Chapter 4

Embodying God's Mission in an Unfriendly World

The Identity and Missionary Mandate of the Church in 1 Peter

Boubakar Sanou

Introduction

The First Epistle of Peter was written during a critical time in the early church's history. The majority of Petrine scholars hold the view that much internal evidence supports the suggestion that the addressees of 1 Peter, though racially mixed, were from a predominantly gentile background.[1] As the church experienced rapid growth, the opposition faced by believers expanded beyond zealous Jews who perceived the nascent faith as a threat.

The growing number of gentiles converting to Christianity also raised concerns throughout the Roman Empire for several reasons. First, upon embracing their newfound faith, gentile converts refrained from participating in pagan temple rituals and gatherings (1 Pet 4:3–4).[2] In a context where "those who abstained from worshipping local gods were suspected of wishing trouble upon their city or regions,"[3] this shift in behavior of gentile converts greatly worried their contemporaries. The fear was that the abandonment of ancestral practices by converts to Christianity would anger the gods and lead to retributive consequences for their communities. As a result, Christians were treated with reproach and contempt (3:9; 4:4, 14–15). Second, the practice of social equality among Christians, regardless of differences in ethnicity, social status, and gender, posed a direct challenge to the established social order of the Roman Empire. Their choice to live out an alternative to Roman norms set them apart and led to exclusion and contempt.[4]

---

1 See Flemming, *Why Mission?*, 91; Schnabel, *Paul and the Early Church*, 1521; Achtemeier, *1 Peter*, 305; Papaioannou, "1 Peter," 1875–76; and Schreiner, *1, 2 Peter, Jude*, 38, 50, 116. Passages such as these serve the purpose of this argument: 1 Pet 1:14, 18, 22; 2:9–10, 15; 4:3–4, 12.

2 Unless otherwise stated, all Scripture quotations are from the ESV.

3 Wright and Bird, *New Testament in Its World*, 762.

4 Carson, "1 Peter," 1032–33; Papaioannou, "1 Peter," 1875–76; and Flemming, *Why Mission?*, 97.

Peter exhorted his socially marginalized audience scattered across Asia Minor to live steadfast and faithful lives to God in spite of the social scorn, calumny, humiliation, and persecution to which such a lifestyle may lead (5:12). To help his readers stay the course and fulfill their calling in the face of adversity and social hostility, Peter sought to firmly establish them in the awareness that they were God's special people, recipients of remarkable grace (1:2; 5:12). Or as Scot McKnight put it, "Peter intends his readers to understand who they are before God so that they can be who they are in society."[5] Peter assured them that their true identity is determined by God's verdict rather than by their social location. Even though they are disparaged by their communities because of their faith, in God's eyes they are a precious, royal, and holy people (2:5, 9–10), called to live missionally with anticipation for the realization of their promised hope—salvation with an imperishable, undefiled, and unfading inheritance (1:4–5, 7–12, 18–19, 22–23).

This chapter explores mission in 1 Peter by focusing on the two main arguments Peter used to cast his vision of the church and its mission: (1) believers' new identity as the people of God and (2) their new task as witnesses to the gospel. For Peter, there was an inherent connection between believers' special status as God's chosen people and their special responsibilities to actively participate in God's mission. New privilege and new responsibility go hand-in-hand.

1 Peter: A Missionary Document *par Excellence*

One of the purposes of 1 Peter is manifestly to strengthen its recipients who were experiencing precarious social conditions (1:6; 2:12, 18; 3:14; 4:4, 12–14). In line with Torrey Seland's argument that "the NT letters served hardly only one purpose,"[6] much internal evidence suggests that 1 Peter is more than just a pastoral epistle intended to admonish believers not to grow faint in heart when they encounter grief in various kinds of trials and opposition to their faith.

Although it does not outline an explicit systematic praxis of mission, 1 Peter is a missionary document *par excellence*. First, it deals with the issues directly related to the spread of the gospel and the outcomes of embracing Christianity. Second, significant missional themes are embedded within the overall theme of undeserved suffering for the sake of Christ. Third, it provides guidance on living out the Christian identity as a witness within

---

5 McKnight, *1 Peter*, 36.
6 Seland, "Resident Aliens in Mission," 567.

the larger unbelieving society. Fourth, it uses metaphors for the church with significant missional ramifications—its audience is addressed as a holy nation, royal priesthood, God's chosen people for the sake of proclaiming his excellencies (2:9–10), elect "exiles," and "sojourners" in this world (2:11). All these missional themes are essential components for the overall mission of the church. As such, 1 Peter cannot be faithfully read apart from the background of early Christian mission.[7] Succinctly put, the First Epistle of Peter "is not only *open* to a missional reading. It *clamors* for it."[8] In a methodical way, Peter continuously related his theology to the missionary mandate of the church.

A New Identity to Embrace

Peter began his epistle with a distinct emphasis on identity to cast his vision of the church and its mission. He addressed his readers as a chosen race, a royal priesthood, a holy nation, and God's own people and special possession (2:9–10) in his desire for his readers to conceive of themselves as the Israel of God. He conveyed the privilege gentile converts have to belong to God's people by using the language of election to ascribe to them key Old Testament allusions to Israel as a nation. That Peter used these honorifics to incorporate gentile converts into the narrative of Israel is noteworthy.[9] Peter was eager for his readers to understand that, as the primary human custodians of God's mission in their contexts, their mission was first and foremost centered on their identity, not on what they did.[10] Because their mission is anchored in who they are, understanding and fully embracing their new status in Christ constitutes a key component of their pursuit of God and witness for him.

Peter drew from the Old Testament concept of Israel as a mediatorial body and beacon of light to the nations as depicted in Exodus 19:6 (cf. Isa 43:20–21; 49:6) to convey to his audience their distinctive new identity, purpose, and significance within the framework of God's redemptive plan. In Exodus 19, Israel as a whole was commissioned as a kingdom of priests and a holy nation when God enacted his covenant with them at Sinai. Israel's priesthood consisted of mirroring the unrivaled glory of Yahweh to the nations. Like Israel in the past, the church is now called to mediate God's

---

7   Stenschke, "Reading First Peter in the Context," 108; Schnabel, *Paul and the Early Church*, 1522; Seland, "Resident Aliens in Mission," 566; Jobes, *1 Peter*, 1; and Flemming, *Why Mission?*, 89.

8   Flemming, 89. Emphasis in the original.

9   Akin, "Missiological Motivation," 8; and Papaioannou, "1 Peter," 1875–76.

10 Flemming, *Why Mission?*, 89.

blessings to the world through its proclamation of the gospel.[11] That is why Peter identified the church as a "holy, royal priesthood," "holy nation," and "a people belonging to God" (1 Pet 2:5, 9).

Peter gave an evangelistic outcome to his call of believers to holiness. The exclusive reason for the transferal of Old Testament covenant categories to the entire racially mixed church—a chosen race, a royal priesthood, a holy nation, and God's own possession—is to offer "spiritual sacrifices acceptable to God through Christ" (2:5) and to proclaim God's excellencies (2:9).

A Missional Presence to Embody

Believers' new identity as a chosen race, a royal priesthood, a holy nation, and God's own people and special possession carried significant implications for how they were to live and witness in the world. Each of the honorifics Peter used to illustrate the new identity of converts is a metaphor of the church in mission, a picture of it living out its witness in the world.[12] Although they are alienated in their own social world, they are called to actively engage it with the gospel. By identifying the church as a "holy, royal priesthood," "holy nation," and "a people belonging to God" (2:5, 9), Peter invited his audience to participate faithfully in the mission of God by both verbal proclamation and an ethical lifestyle given their current circumstances (1:13–16; 2:11–12). The believers' ethical lives were of utmost importance to Peter. For him, this was an eloquent way of witnessing to the transformative power of the gospel. Six of the thirteen New Testament references to ἀναστροφή (*anastrophē*)—conduct, behavior, way of life—are found in 1 Peter alone (1:15, 18; 2:12; 3:1, 2, 16).[13] Peter wanted their conduct to be honorable (2:12), chaste (3:2), and good (3:16). He connected correct ethical behavior to "doing good" (2:15, 20; 3:6, 13, 17; 4:19). He grounded his call for ethical living (holiness) on the fact that God who called them is holy (1:13–16) and on its potential missional effect on the onlooking gentiles (e.g., 2:12–15; 3:2, 16; 4:4). Mission and ethics are so powerfully linked in 1 Peter 2:9–10 that it becomes impossible to detach one from the other. As such, rather than withdrawing from the world into a state of secluded piety that holds little relevance to outsiders or undermining the social structure, Peter called the church to be radically different from the world but fully missionally engaged in it.[14] For him,

---

11 Schreiner, *1, 2 Peter, Jude*, 114.
12 Van Engen, "Church," 193.
13 The seven other references of ἀναστροφή (*anastrophē*) are 2 Peter 2:7; 3:11; Galatians 1:13; Ephesians 4:22; 1 Timothy 4:12; Hebrews 13:7; James 3:13.
14 Flemming, *Why Mission?*, 99.

> The church is not against the world in that it does not express holiness by reciprocating the world's animosity toward it, and neither does the church demonstrate holiness by condemning the ways of the world with self-righteous living and rhetoric. Instead the church is to be different because it is in relationship with a God who is different, and it is simply trying to stay in step with his ways in the world.[15]

In 1 Peter, ethical living includes believers being self-controlled (1:13), staying away from all forms of malice, deceit, hypocrisy, envy, and slander (2:1), abstaining "from the passions of the flesh," and keeping their "conduct among the Gentiles honorable" (2:11–12). Correct ethical behavior is also demonstrated in the way believers submit to civil leaders (2:13–17), in the way servants submit to their masters (2:18), in the way believing wives submit even to husbands who are hostile to their faith (3:1–6), in the way believers extend sincere love and hospitality to each other in the Christian community (1:22; 3:8; 4:9), and in the way Christians "honor all people" (2:17). Two readings of Peter's repeated calls to submission are possible. First, it is imaginable that Peter's counsel aimed to refute the accusations of outsiders by demonstrating that Christians lead disciplined lives, adhering to what is deemed as virtuous and acceptable conduct in Roman society.[16] Second, considering his exhortation to emulate Jesus's submissiveness in his endurance of unjust suffering (2:21–23), Peter's reiterated calls for submission are best understood as a "Christological basis for missional living"—a call for believers to engage their world with a Christlike distinction.[17]

Clearly, Peter's view of holiness and the ethical lifestyle that is linked to it is not the type of holiness that would lead believers to withdraw from society but one that is an integral part of the end imagined by God for them.[18] He was of the view that Christian witness is strengthened by the ethical conduct exhibited by the Christian community. He suggested that living ethically and honorably in the midst of hardship has the potential to lead others to inquire about the hope that Christians have (2:12; 3:15).

---

15 Beach, *Church in Exile*, 130.
16 Edwards, *1 Peter*, 106; McKnight, *1 Peter*, 166; and Jobes, *1 Peter*, 182.
17 Flemming, *Why Mission?*, 102.
18 McDonald, "Exile, Suffering, and Holiness," 69; Seland, "Resident Aliens in Mission," 570–71; Flemming noted that "this is not the type of holiness that hangs a sign on the office door that says, 'Please do not disturb. I'm being *holy*!' instead Peter envisions a church whose distinctive, self-giving, God-reflecting life, lived out 'among the unbelievers' becomes an attractive witness to the surrounding world." Flemming, *Why Mission?*, 98.

Contemporary Implications

First Peter has a universal appeal. Because of the themes it addresses (e.g., suffering, hope, promise, and divine care), the message of the epistle remains highly relevant to the circumstances of numerous contemporary Christians who encounter adverse reactions to their faith, live in constant danger of social alienation, or simply live in peril because of their faith.[19]

1 Peter: A Call to Discipleship

Peter's repeated appeals to the example of Jesus for his readers to embody a godly presence among the nations through a holy and Christlike existence is essentially a call to discipleship (2:21–25). As such, 1 Peter has something important to say about today's Christians' pursuit of God and their engagement with their cultures. This is all the more important as scholars of Christian discipleship lament the lack of depth of transformative discipleship in contemporary Christianity by pointing to the weak impact Christians have on the moral and spiritual climate of their contexts, even in countries where the vast majority of the population identifies as Christian.[20]

Peter's perspective on discipleship echoes Jesus's own teaching on the subject. In his teachings on discipleship, Jesus emphasized the need to carefully consider the cost of following him. Luke 14:25–33 serves as a key passage that outlines Jesus's terms of discipleship (see also Matt 16:24–26; Mark 8:34–37; Luke 9:23–25). Jesus used strong language to underscore the non-negotiable commitment required, calling for a love for him that surpasses all other relationships and a devotion that prioritizes him over one's own life. Taking up one's cross symbolizes total surrender and submission to Jesus, renouncing all possessions and aligning with God's agenda. Discipleship involves daily dying to self-interest and willingly enduring potential hardships for Christ's sake.

Like Jesus, Peter intimately connected suffering to discipleship (3:13–4:19). It is important to reiterate that the suffering Peter referred to is not of a generic nature, such as the death of a loved one, a chronic illness, or loss due to natural disasters. Rather, it pertains to rejection and persecution for being a Christian. As followers of Christ and participants in his suffering, Christians should anticipate receiving similar treatment to their Master. Like him, they

---

19 Charles, *1 Peter*, 292; and Jobes, *1 Peter*, 1–2.
20 Ogden, *Transforming Discipleship: Making Disciples*, 23. See also Lear, "Making Disciples Obstacles and Opportunities," 5–14; Barna and The Navigators, *State of Discipleship*; Willard, *Great Omission*; and Putman, *Real-Life Discipleship: Building Churches*.

are still called to act righteously in such circumstances. When enduring suffering for doing what is right, they can find solace in looking to Jesus, who suffered for their sins and, through that suffering, came out victorious. Peter pointed out that because of Jesus's victory, undeserved suffering for his sake provides a glimpse of his forthcoming glory. Therefore, if Christians honor Christ as Lord and follow in his footsteps, they can be confident that through suffering, they will partake in his victory. As they live in this eschatological tension, they must faithfully bear witness to their hope through both words and actions, remembering their baptismal commitment to live with a good conscience before God.[21] Although the social, cultural, and religious context of Peter's original readers is different from that of many contemporary contexts, the principles embedded in his epistle are relevant and applicable to all Christians. In the midst of prevailing cultural attitudes that promote moral relativism, 1 Peter continues to encourage "a transformed understanding of Christian self-identity that redefines how one is to live as a Christian in a world that is hostile to the basic principles of the gospel."[22]

1 Peter: A Call to Contextualized Christian Witness[23]

By transferring to the church the same perspectives that have long defined the nation of Israel, such as being a holy nation and a holy priesthood, Peter is perceived as simply contextualizing Old Testament Scriptures to suit new circumstances.[24] He did so with the intention that the biblical revelations, which were intended to reform or transform the beliefs, values, and practices of the peoples to whom they were first addressed, also serve the same purpose for his audience.

On the rationale for contextualizing the gospel in contemporary missional contexts, Dean Flemming posited,

> If modern Gospel studies have taught us anything, it is that the four Evangelists have narrated the story of Jesus according to their own theological and literary concerns and in light of how they perceived the needs of their readers. We might even say that the four Gospels are "four contextualizations" of the one story. The Gospels, then, form an important piece of the total picture of how the Christian message is reexpressed for new audiences in the New Testament.[25]

---

21 Motyer, "1 Peter," 1546; and Carson, "1 Peter," 1033.
22 Jobes, *1 Peter*, 3.
23 For a full discussion, see Sanou, "Exegeting the Bible," 371–79.
24 Flemming, *Why Mission?*, 91, 102; Beach, *Church in Exile*, 117.
25 Flemming, *Contextualization in the New Testament*, 234.

The New Testament authors' audiences provided them with the contexts within which the content of the gospel was reformulated. Doing the same in contemporary missional contexts is not an option. The social context in which every individual exists deeply influences their perspective on the world and their understanding of Scripture,[26] ultimately shaping their faith and relationship with Jesus.[27] Regardless of personal preferences, each Christian's social background significantly impacts how they interpret the Bible. Consequently, in the context of missions, where communication takes place within social and cultural frameworks, it becomes imperative to consider the social location of the recipients of the gospel. Effective communication involves not just conveying a message but ensuring it is accurately received and understood by the audience, considering their unique social realities. Missiologists and mission practitioners must be mindful of this dynamic, recognizing that mission is a ministry of the Word to the world, and to effectively minister, they must understand the world to which they are addressing.[28] To effectively contribute to the transformation of people's worldviews and promote holistic discipleship in any context, a mission approach must adhere to hermeneutically sound principles. However, it should also be culturally relevant and receiver-oriented, seeking to minimize rejection and alienation among its audience.[29] In essence, for the gospel to meaningfully engage recipients, leading to a transformation of their worldviews and a deepened relationship with Christ, communicators must creatively present the biblical message. They must ensure its content remains faithful to biblical principles while resonating with the recipients in terms of its relevance. By doing so, the message can effectively challenge individuals within their specific social context. The rationale behind this lies in the understanding that people cannot positively respond to concepts that lie beyond their frame of reference. Therefore, a balanced approach that embraces cultural sensitivity while staying faithful to the gospel is essential for fruitful missional engagement and transformation.

To faithfully present the gospel and transform the worldviews of its recipients, missionaries must diligently strive to attain cultural literacy. This proficiency aids in comprehending the diverse factors influencing how their intended audiences read and interpret the Bible, along with the

---

26 See Bauer, "Social Location and Its Impact," 75; and Vanhoozer, *Hearers and Doers*, xii–xiii.
27 Bartholomew, *Introducing Biblical Hermeneutics*, 216.
28 Vanhoozer, Anderson, and Sleasman "A Reader's Guide," 8.
29 Sanou, "Motivating and Training the Laity," 42.

underlying reasons for such perspectives. By understanding the context, missionaries can respond in ways that are biblically faithful and culturally relevant, enabling their audiences to make intelligent, life-changing decisions in favor of the gospel. Kevin Vanhoozer emphasized that culture profoundly shapes spiritual formation. Therefore, he suggested that the discipleship process should encompass both deprogramming (critiquing and correcting prevailing narratives) and reprogramming (embracing the scriptural and gospel-generated social imaginary).[30] Mission practitioners can therefore not settle down after merely articulating biblical truth; they must also propose practical and culturally relevant ways for growth in Christ, as ultimate truth resides in Jesus himself. By understanding the impact of contemporary culture on the gospel recipients and by bridging the gap between academic mission and everyday life, mission practitioners enable their audiences to see how the Bible relates to their daily experiences, empower them to navigate through diverse cultural contexts while following the path of Christ, and equip them to engage actively with culture, leaving a positive impact rather than passively succumbing to its influence.[31] By caring for both biblical faithfulness and cultural relevance, missionaries can facilitate a meaningful encounter with the gospel that brings about transformative change in the lives of their audiences.

Faithful mission extends beyond merely presenting essential truths, although acknowledging the significance of such truths is crucial. While recognizing the necessity for people to grasp scriptural truths and the demands of being Christ's disciples before surrendering their lives to him (Luke 14:25–34), I firmly believe that mere cognitive knowledge cannot fully transform a person's worldview. Throughout his ministry, Jesus devoted considerable time to teaching profound truths (e.g., the Sermon on the Mount in Matt 5–7 and parables like those in Luke 15; 18:1–14; 19:11–26; Matt 11:1; John 15:1–17). His purpose was to deepen his hearers' understanding of God's nature and will, fostering a well-informed and richer relationship with him. However, Jesus imparted truth not as mere information but as knowledge rooted in an experiential relationship with God (John 8:32; 15:1–10). He consistently challenged his listeners, particularly his disciples, to apply their intellectual understanding to their daily lives (Matt 7:24–27). In essence, faithful mission involves more than just transferring knowledge; it

---

30 Vanhoozer, *Hearers and Doers*, xiii, 15.
31 Vanhoozer, Anderson, and Sleasman, "A Reader's Guide," 7; and Vanhoozer, *Hearers and Doers*, xii.

encourages individuals to experience the truths they encounter in Scripture. Such experiential understanding enables a profound and transformative shift in one's worldview, leading to a deeper connection with God. Jesus's approach demonstrates the importance of an interactive relationship with the truth, where biblical knowledge is integrated into life experiences, allowing for genuine transformation and growth as Christ-followers.

Merely hearing and accepting the truth presented in the Bible does not conclude the Christian journey. Once believers have embraced the teachings of the Bible, they must consistently be challenged to focus on their experiential growth in Christ (2 Pet 3:18). Being loyal followers of Jesus is a defining characteristic of discipleship (Luke 16:13). One potential pitfall in biblical interpretation and mission is reducing truth to a mere topic of discussion rather than something that significantly relates to believers' daily lives, leading them to pledge allegiance to Christ. The truth that can genuinely transform worldviews and grant freedom in Christ is not solely an intellectual concept but an experienced reality (see John 8:32). Since "biblical truth is meant not just to be studied but more to be applied in life-changing ways,"[32] providing contextually relevant but biblically faithful applications of biblical truths to life's situations should be an important goal of a faithful, transformative approach to mission and discipleship. Therefore, faithful and transformative mission should aim to assist readers in understanding not only the content and meaning of specific biblical texts but, more importantly, how these texts impact their lives and their relationships with Christ. The ultimate aim of faithful mission is to firmly anchor the never-changing word of God within the ever-changing contexts of our world. To have a transformative impact on the deep-seated worldview assumptions of its audience, the understanding of biblical truth must encompass cognitive, affective, and evaluative dimensions.[33] Giving a practical application of each biblical passage is also crucial as this fosters an intimate, personal relationship with God.[34]

1 Peter: A Call to Engage in Missional Living

Reflecting on the contemporary approach to Christian ministry, church health scholar Greg Ogden compared it to "a football game with twenty-

---

32 Osborne, "Hermeneutics," 432.
33 Osborne, 432.
34 Davidson, "Interpreting Scripture: An Hermeneutical 'Decalogue,'" 109.

two people on the field in desperate need of rest, and fifty thousand people in the stands in desperate need of exercise."[35] This is a departure from the New Testament's strong emphasis on ministry as the function of the total church membership. The priestly ministry of the church advocated in 1 Peter has important implications for its missionary enterprise (2:5, 9). Offering sacrifices acceptable to God as a priest involves serving both God and others by faithfully and responsibly fulfilling one's vocation in society in accordance with the gifts of the Spirit (4:10). As such, whatever work to which God has called a believer—even the simplest, everyday tasks—should be seen as an opportunity to live out his or her priestly calling in the world.[36] From that perspective, Christ's commission to make disciples in Matthew 28:19–20 could be paraphrased, "As you go about your daily lives, make disciples of the people you interact with." Therefore, the church's holy priestly calling is an invitation to let one's faith in Christ permeate all dealings—family, school, business, and so on. By virtue of this commission and the enabling gifts of the Spirit bestowed on each believer (1 Pet 4:10), all Christians are called and commissioned, whatever their walk of life, to share their faith. God has intentionally placed each believer in their neighborhood, job, school, or other location for the strategic purpose of being outposts for his kingdom. They are the only missionaries some may ever meet or meaningfully interact with. Therefore, Christians should regard their work as a calling rather than just an occupation. When believers view their jobs as part of God's calling on their lives, they add new meaning to Christian witness. Thus, it is important for each believer to strive to connect their deeply held professional dreams with their faith in Christ and their missionary mandate. By embracing their profession as a vocation, every believer becomes a full-time minister in whatever walk of life God has intentionally placed them for the strategic purpose of being an outpost of his kingdom.

Conclusion

The First Epistle of Peter is a noteworthy missionary document. Through a skillful appropriation of Old Testament categories of a chosen race, a royal priesthood, a holy nation, and God's own people and special possession, Peter creatively communicated the essence of discipleship to his predominantly gentile audience. These categories resonated deeply with Peter's audience,

---

35 Ogden, *Transforming Discipleship: Making Disciples*, 25.
36 Allison, "Priesthood of Believers," 786–87.

reminding them of their spiritual status. They also solidified their sense of purpose and mission. By embracing their new identity, Peter's audience recognized that their ultimate allegiance lies with the heavenly kingdom, not the earthly world they temporarily inhabited. This understanding became a driving force for their mission, as they courageously navigated the challenges of living amidst a society at odds with their faith. As chosen vessels of God, they understood that they were set apart for his divine plan. As a holy and royal priesthood, they realized their calling to intercede for the world and serve as bridges between humanity and God. As a holy nation, they embodied a distinct community, living out the gospel in a way that captured the attention and hearts of those around them.

By appropriating these Old Testament categories, Peter adroitly empowered his readers to embrace their missional identity with conviction and confidence. Their faith in Jesus Christ, coupled with their chosen status and priestly calling, propelled them forward in their mission to proclaim the excellencies of God. The missional thrust of 1 Peter is further underscored as the believers were urged to display exemplary conduct in the face of suffering and persecution. Peter's missional intent came to its peak as he invited them to participate in the sufferings of Christ. He highlighted the redemptive significance of their trials, drawing a parallel between their suffering and Christ's ultimate sacrifice. This transformative perspective on suffering solidified their commitment to their mission, recognizing that their perseverance through hardship becomes a powerful testimony to the hope they have in Christ. Their mission was not simply to verbally convey a message but to embody the gospel as living testimonies of God's grace, transformative power, and salvation.

First Peter stands as a timeless testament to the inseparable connection between mission and ethical living. The epistle's themes of identity, purpose, and suffering merge into a powerful call to action, inviting believers to live out their faith with unwavering dedication and missional zeal. As modern-day readers, we are challenged to embrace the same identity as Peter's first audience, embodying the transformative power of the gospel in our lives and proclaiming the excellencies of God to a world in need of his grace and love.

Bibliography

Achtemeier, Paul J. *1 Peter: A Commentary on First Peter*. Hermeneia: Minneapolis: Fortress Press, 1996.

Akin, Paul. "The Missiological Motivation of 1 Peter." *Southern Baptist Journal of Theology* 23, no. 3 (2019): 7–21.

Allison, Gregg R. "Priesthood of Believers." In *Evangelical Dictionary of World Missions*, edited by A. Scott Moreau, 786–87. Grand Rapids: Baker Books, 2000.

Barna and The Navigators. *The State of Discipleship*. Colorado Springs: NavPress, 2015.

Bartholomew, Craig G. *Introducing Biblical Hermeneutics: A Comprehensive Framework for Hearing God in Scripture*. Grand Rapids: Baker Academic, 2015.

Bauer, Bruce L. "Social Location and Its Impact on Hermeneutics." *Journal of Adventist Mission Studies* 12, no. 1 (2016): 74–83.

Carson, D. A. "1 Peter." In *Commentary on the New Testament Use of the Old Testament*. Edited by G. K. Beale and D. A. Carson, 1015–45. Grand Rapids: Baker Academic, 2007.

Davidson, Richard M. "Interpreting Scripture: An Hermeneutical 'Decalogue.'" *Journal of the Adventist Theological Society* 4, no. 2 (1993): 95–114.

Edwards, Dennis R. *1 Peter*, edited by Tremper Longman III and Scot McKnight. The Story of God Bible Commentary. Grand Rapids: Zondervan, 2017.

Erland, Waltner, and J. Daryl Charles. *1 and 2 Peter, Jude*. Believers Church Bible Commentary. Scottdale, PA: Herald Press, 1999.

Flemming, Dean. *Contextualization in the New Testament: Patterns for Theology and Mission*. Downers Grove, IL: InterVarsity Press, 2005.

Flemming, Dean. *Why Mission?* Reframing New Testament Theology. Nashville: Abingdon, 2015.

Jobes, Karen H. *1 Peter*. Baker Exegetical Commentary on the New Testament. Grand Rapids: Baker Academic, 2005.

Lear, Heather Heinzman. "Making Disciples: Obstacles and Opportunities in Urban Congregations." *International Review of Mission* 105, no. 1 (2016): 5–14.

Malone, Andrew S. *God's Mediators: A Biblical Theology of Priesthood*. New Studies in Biblical Theology 43. Downers Grove, IL: InterVarsity Press, 2017.

McDonald, Brett. "Exile, Suffering, and Holiness: The Use of Psalm 34 in 1 Peter." *Presbyterion* 48, no. 2 (2022): 67–84.

McKnight, Scot. *1 Peter*. The NIV Application Commentary. Grand Rapids: Zondervan, 1996.

Motyer, Stephen. "1 Peter." In *The Baker Illustrated Bible Commentary*, edited by Gary M. Burge and Andrew E. Hill, 1540–50. Grand Rapids: Baker Books, 2012.

Ogden, Greg. *Transforming Discipleship: Making Disciples a Few at a Time.* Rev. ed. Downers Grove, IL: IVP Books, 2016.

Osborne, Grant R. "Hermeneutics." In *Evangelical Dictionary of World Mission*, edited by A. Scott Moreau, 430–32. Grand Rapids: Baker Books, 2000.

Papaioannou, Kim. "1 Peter." In *Andrews Bible Commentary*, New Testament, edited by Ángel Manuel Rodríguez, 1875–90. Berrien Springs: Andrews University Press, 2022.

Putman, Jim. *Real-life Discipleship: Building Churches that Make Disciples.* Colorado Springs: NavPress, 2010.

Sanou, Boubakar. "Biblical Social Justice and Ethical Leadership: A Pastoral Perspective." *Current: Faith Meets Life and Culture* 9 (2021): 37–41.

Sanou, Boubakar. "Exegeting the Bible and the Social Location of the Gospel Recipients: A Case for Worldview Transformation." *Andrews University Seminary Studies* 57, no. 2 (2020): 371–79.

Sanou, Boubakar. "Motivating and Training the Laity to Increase Their Involvement in Ministry in the Ouaga-Center Adventist Church in Burkina Faso." DMin diss., Andrews University, 2010.

Schnabel, Eckhard J. *Paul and the Early Church.* Vol. 2 of *Early Christian Mission.* Downers Grove, IL: InterVarsity Press, 2004.

Schreiner, Thomas R. *1, 2 Peter, Jude.* New American Commentary 37. Nashville: Broadman & Holman, 2003.

Seland, Torrey. "Resident Aliens in Mission: Missional Practices in the Emerging Church of 1 Peter." *Bulletin for Biblical Research* 19, no. 4 (2009): 565–89.

Stenschke, Christoph. "Reading First Peter in the Context of Early Christian Mission." *Tyndale Bulletin* 60, no. 1 (2009): 107–26.

Van Engen, Charles. "Church." In *Evangelical Dictionary of World Mission*, edited by A. Scott Moreau, 192–95. Grand Rapids: Baker Books, 2000.

Vanhoozer, Kevin J. *Hearers and Doers: A Pastor's Guide to Making Disciples through Scripture and Doctrine.* Bellingham, WA: Lexham Press, 2019.

Vanhoozer, Kevin J., Charles A. Anderson, and Michael J. Sleasman, eds. *Everyday Theology: How to Read Cultural Texts and Interpret Trends.* Grand Rapids: Baker Academic, 2007.

Willard, Dallas. *The Great Omission: Reclaiming Jesus's Essential Teachings on Discipleship.* San Francisco: HarperSanFrancisco, 2006.

Wright, N. T., and Michael F. Bird. *The New Testament in Its World: An Introduction to the History, Literature, and Theology of the First Christians.* Grand Rapids: Zondervan Academic, 2019.

Chapter 5

The Role of the Spirit in Mission in 1 Peter

Yimenu Adimass Belay

Introduction

The role of the Spirit in mission is represented in the teaching of the New Testament, beginning with the teaching and the ministry of Jesus Christ. The Gospels and Acts indicate how the Spirit was active in the work of mission in the life and the ministry of Jesus (Luke 4:14; Acts 1:8). As the narrative of Acts indicates, Jesus's apostles continued the ministry. The apostle Peter was one of the first disciples to follow Jesus during Jesus's earthly ministry, and Jesus gave him the authority to preach the good news of Jesus Christ. Since Peter was immersed in the traditions of Jesus, the role of the Spirit in mission can be observed in his first epistle. Therefore, this chapter will focus on selected texts to articulate how the role of the Spirit in mission is portrayed in 1 Peter.

The first part of this chapter interacts with related literature on the role of the Spirit in mission in general and 1 Peter in particular. In the second part, the chapter focuses on the role of the Spirit in mission in first-century Jewish and Christian contexts. In the third part, the chapter focuses on four selected texts of 1 Peter (1:2, 11–12; 3:18–19; 4:14) to argue how the role of the Spirit is connected with the mission of the church. Finally, the fourth part depicts essential lessons for the contemporary church and implications for contemporary Ethiopian contexts and the world. The Ethiopian context is addressed because Ethiopia has been a historic Christian land since the fourth century, contributing to preaching and expanding the work of the gospel until the sixteenth-century Catholic attempts to evangelize Ethiopia and the nineteenth century when the Western missionaries attempted to evangelize Ethiopia. The chapter uses socio-rhetorical analysis as an interpretive framework to argue for the role of the Spirit in mission in the letter of 1 Peter.

Review of Related Literature

The work of mission is not separated from the work of the Spirit in the Old and New Testaments. Even though the Old Testament contains no clear depiction of mission and the role of the Spirit, different texts of the New Testament show the Spirit in the work of mission in different ways, such as empowering a proper Christian life and enabling believers to be witnesses to Christ. James Nkansah-Obrempomg has pointed out how the Spirit brings transformation in the life of Christians, enabling them to fulfill God's moral laws that lead to Christian witness.[1] He pointed out, "The Spirit provides the divine power necessary for Christian living (Rom 8:2–4; Gal 4:6). Living by the Spirit prevents the believers from gratifying the desire of our sinful nature (Gal 5:16)."[2] However, his emphasis is on Paul's Epistles, so he does not address the role of the Spirit in 1 Peter.

Paul J. Achtemeier has argued that the critical theological concepts common in Pauline theology, such as the church as the body of Christ, the work of the Holy Spirit, righteousness by faith, and the tension between church and Israel, are not represented in the letter of 1 Peter.[3] However, even if Peter's presentation is not similar to the Pauline approach, a significant number of texts show the work of the Spirit with the role of mission because the Spirit equips for mission by empowering people for right living and strengthening them in the middle of suffering (1:2; 4:14). Andrew Chester and Ralph P. Martin have discussed the role of the Spirit in 1 Peter, indicating that the Spirit is the base for christological witness that works in the life of believers (1:2) and ministers in the pastoral and practical life of Christian community (4:14).[4] These scholars have further pointed out other functions of the Spirit in 1 Peter, like promoting holiness (1:2, 14–22; 3:15), spiritualization (2:5), heralding the coming of the Messiah (1:11–12) and guaranteeing the new era (4:14).[5]

Dennis R. Edwards has pointed out the place of the Spirit in the opening of 1 Peter, indicating that "the Holy Spirit carries out God's plan of election by setting apart God's people (the technical word is 'sanctify,' *hagiazō*). Peter will elaborate upon the Spirit's work of sanctification throughout the letter (e.g., 1:15–16, 22; 2:5, 9)."[6] Peter H. Davids has argued that the role of the Spirit of God in sanctifying believers shows that he touches believers

---

[1] Nkansah-Obrempong, *Foundations for African Theological Ethics*, 107.
[2] Nkansah-Obrempong, 107.
[3] Achtemeier, *1 Peter*, 17.
[4] Chester and Martin, *Theology of the Letters*, 118.
[5] Chester and Martin, 119.
[6] Edwards, *1 Peter*, 31–32.

in such a way that he enables them to live as the chosen people of God.[7] However, Watson and Callan have argued that the work of the Holy Spirit causes obedience though this obedience is dependent on the individual; the proclamation of the gospel through the Spirit is evident.[8] Christianity was introduced to Ethiopia in the fourth century, so the Ethiopian Orthodox Tewahedo Church has been engaged in mission activity in Ethiopia since ancient times.[9] Even though there has often been little awareness about the role of the Spirit in the early evangelization of the Ethiopian Orthodox Tewahedo Church, the evangelical churches' growth through mission activity is marked by a strong awareness of the power and work of the Spirit.[10] No scholar addresses the role of the Spirit in mission in 1 Peter by focusing on the four selected texts. This chapter intends to analyze these important texts to show the work of the Spirit in a profound way.

The Role of the Spirit in Mission in the First Century

The role of the Spirit in the life and work of Christ is attested in the Gospels, but it is particularly emphasized in the Gospel of Luke and Acts. The Holy Spirit witnessed about Christ in the Old Testament, and Christian missionaries were supported and inspired by the Spirit to bring the good news from Jerusalem to the end of the earth.[11] The birth of the church was not separate from the work of the Spirit, and the day of Pentecost indicates how the Spirit empowered the first disciples to witness to Christ (Acts 2:1–43). The book of Acts reveals how the Holy Spirit enabled followers of Jesus to proclaim the gospel to everyone despite suffering and challenges. The New Testament letters also reveal that the empowerment of the Spirit for the work of mission is manifested in different ways. Luke's presentation indicates that Peter, in his sermon in Acts 2:14–40, connected the baptism of the Spirit and the gospel witness.[12] Keener has argued how the event of Pentecost continued throughout Acts, transforming the lives of many from Jerusalem to the end of the earth.

---

7 Davids, *First Epistle of Peter*, 48.
8 Watson and Callan, *First and Second Peter*, 22, 28–29.
9 Shenk, "Ethiopian Orthodox Church," 8.
10 Binns, *Orthodox Church of Ethiopia*, 31; Esler, *Ethiopian Christianity: History, Theology*, 79.
11 Chester and Martin, *Theology of the Letters*, 119.
12 Keener, *Spirit in the Gospels*, 195.

The Spirit was manifested in the first century by giving different gifts for the edification and the mission of the church. However, the role of the Spirit in Second Temple Judaism needs to be considered because the New Testament theology of the Spirit developed in the context of Judaism, and the first church was predominantly Jewish. In Philo's understanding and interpretation, the role of the Spirit is vital in the interpretation of the Torah.[13] Frederick Dale Bruner has argued not only for the tie between the Spirit and mission in the first century but also for ties to the Pentecostal movement that claims the empowerment of the Spirit is still contributing a significant part to contemporary Christian mission in the world.[14] First-century Christianity is marked by the power and the work of the Holy Spirit, which enabled believers to participate in mission. The apostle Peter was one of the first disciples of Jesus. He experienced both the baptism of the Spirit and the empowering work of the Spirit for the mission that Jesus commanded (Acts 1:8). The ministry of Peter is narrated in Acts 1–12, indicating Peter's experience of both the work of the Spirit and the mission of the church. Beyond the narratives in the Gospels and the book of Acts, the Pauline and General Epistles also reflect the Spirit's role in the mission of the church. The First Epistle of Peter reflects the Spirit's role in the church's mission. The motif of 1 Peter is primarily about standing in the middle of suffering and living according to the will of God. This motif includes the mission activity of the church because it cannot be separated from the life and the practice of the first-century church.

The Role of the Spirit for Mission in Selected 1 Peter Texts

This section provides the exegetical analysis that demonstrates how selected texts of 1 Peter present the role of the Spirit in mission.

1 Peter is understood to be written by the apostle Peter because of the references at the beginning and the end of the letter (1:1–2; 5:1–4). However, the main concern of this section is not to validate the author but to show how the Spirit is portrayed in the mission activity of the church. Therefore, in this section, I will only focus on how 1 Peter has portrayed the church's mission. First Peter 2:9–10 is the center of this argument because it shows that the purpose of believers' transfer to the glorious light is to testify about God's

---

13 Levison, *Spirit in First-Century Judaism*, 192–93.
14 Bruner, *Theology of the Holy Spirit*, 19.

good deeds. The context of 1 Peter can be analyzed by focusing on 2:9–10, which tells about the activity of God both in deed and word; it seems to be the primary intention that governs the message of the letter.[15] Torrey Seland has pointed out that the recipients of 1 Peter are in intense suffering, and in this situation, they are urged to reach out to those in their surroundings and be eager in the mission of the Lord.[16] Seland has also argued that even though modern readers may not understand it correctly, the recipients of Peter's first epistle are a missionary community because they are responsible for showing the goodness of God both in word and deed to their neighboring non-Christ-following community.[17]

Even though there is no explicit explanation about the mission activity of the church in 1 Peter, the interpretation of 1 Peter 2:9–10 is important because it demonstrates the identity of the new community and its role in the world as the called-out community. Paul Akin has argued that the recipients of 1 Peter are advised to have a missional identity and lifestyle that motivates them to share the message of Christ both in verbal and nonverbal ways.[18] Akin also argued that Peter has a clear missiological focus in this letter as the elect exiles in Asia Minor are to have a missional life in the world motivated by the hope of the heavenly inheritance.[19] It is possible to argue that the broader context of the letter affirms the strong framework that the author has in mind, which motivates believers to be witnesses to their fellow inhabitants where they are living as an exilic community for the sake of the Christian calling and witness. Three important texts clearly show how.

The first text is 1:22–25, which shows that the preaching of the word of God has been the source of life for the exiles and encourages them to continue to proclaim the good news through Scripture. In addition, 2:9 demonstrates their calling to proclaim the excellencies of God, who called them into the kingdom of light. Further, 3:15 asks believers to answer anyone who asks them for a reason for their hope and encourages them to proclaim the gospel of Christ to those around them.

The Spirit in 1 Peter 1:2
Peter's use of the Spirit in the introduction is provocative because the role of the Spirit is portrayed in the sanctification of believers (1:2). The Spirit's

---

15 Achtemeier, *1 Peter*, 166.
16 Seland, *Strangers in the Light*, 185.
17 Seland, 185.
18 Akin, "Missiological Motivation," 15.
19 Akin, 19.

work in sanctification is not limited to this text, but a significant number of New Testament texts follow such matters (e.g., Rom 15:16; 2 Thess 2:13; 1 Cor 1:2). Peter's use of this specific text shows that the role of the Spirit is enabling believers to be a missional community because the Spirit has the role of setting them apart. Achtemeier interpreted the phrase "the sanctification of the Spirit" by pointing out that Christians, as God's elect, are enabled by the Spirit for obedience to God.[20] David L. Barrett has pointed out that the role of the Spirit in the life of Christians is to strengthen them toward holiness and sanctify their journey.[21] In the Ethiopic version and the *andəmta* interpretation,[22] the focus of verse 2 is to portray the place of the Trinity rather than merely the role of the Spirit in sanctifying believers.[23]

In general, the missional idea of verse 2 seems clear. The Spirit's role is sanctifying believers, and this sanctification enables them to be light in the midst of a non-believing community. Even though it is a prevalent theme in most of the New Testament letters, the role of the Spirit in sanctifying believers seems to tie together other verses that show the role of the Spirit in the proclamation of the gospel (1:11–12; 3:18–19; 4:14). The Spirit is portrayed as the source of spiritual renewal and transformation in the lives of believers. In 1 Peter 1:2, Peter addressed the recipients of his letter as those who have been "chosen according to the foreknowledge of God the Father, through the sanctifying work of the Spirit, to be obedient to Jesus Christ." Here, the Spirit is identified as the agent of sanctification, purifying and enabling believers to live holy and obedient lives. Through this inner transformation, believers become effective witnesses, shining the light of Christ to others in their missional endeavors.

The Role of the Spirit in Mission in 1 Peter 1:11–12

First Peter 1:11–12 demonstrates the Spirit's missional role in pointing to Christ's suffering, guiding the Old Testament prophets, and revealing Christ so that people may know him. In these two verses, the Spirit is described as the

---

20 Achtemeier, *1 Peter*, 87.

21 Bartlett, "First Letter of Peter," 247.

22 The *andəmta* is an interpretive commentary on the biblical texts in which the commentators use the Ge'ez (Ethiopic) text, patristic authors, and various Greek, Syriac, and Coptic versions of the Bible as well as hagiographies. It is used as a resource for teaching and preaching in the Ethiopian Orthodox Tewahedo Church.

23 Ethiopian Orthodox Tewahedo Church, *Andəmta Commentary*, 208. The Ethiopian Orthodox Tewahedo Church does not give much emphasis to the role of the Spirit in the mission activity of the church.

Spirit of Christ and the Holy Spirit; these terms have no difference.[24] David G. Horrell has pointed out how Peter applied christological hermeneutics, breaking with the Jewish interpretive practice, by claiming that the Jewish prophets were informed about Christ by the Holy Spirit.[25] Horrell insisted Peter was serious about interpreting Jewish Scripture from the Christian perspective, which is that Scripture points to Christ and the Spirit had a role in this.[26] However, Achtemeier has clarified the meaning of the Spirit of Christ, pointing to three possible implications: the Spirit that reveals Christ, the Spirit later revealed in Christ, and the Spirit later revealed in the baptism of Christ.[27] However, Bartlett has argued that the phrase "the Spirit of Christ" depicts and shows Christ who sends the Spirit.[28]

The emphasis is given to the work of the Spirit in 1:11–12, showing that the Spirit works by indicating, testifying, revealing, and bringing the good news through the messengers. This is the role of the Spirit in the broader sense, enabling the believing community for the mission activity of proclaiming salvation in Jesus Christ. The expression "the Spirit of Christ within them was indicating" points out that, through the Holy Spirit, prophets prophesied about Christ, even though they did not know the actual circumstances of Christ Jesus.[29] Ramsey Michaels has pointed out that the term "was indicating" (ἐδήλου) is an imperfect verb referring to the process of renovation that has been practical in the prophetic ministry.[30]

The second reference to the Holy Spirit's work in 1:11–12 is represented by the term "testifying" (προμαρτυρόμενον). The role of the Spirit is to bear witness to Christ, which inspires believers to proclaim the good news of Christ. According to Achtemeier, this indicates the continuity between the prophetic message and the message of the gospel.[31] Watson has pointed out that even though the Messiah's suffering and eventual glorification are not explicit in the Old Testament (Isa 52:13–53:12; 1 Pet 2:21–25), Peter emphasized the role of the Spirit in witnessing the suffering of Christ and his coming glory.[32] Bartlett explained that the same Spirit who inspired the

---

24 Watson and Callan, *First and Second Peter*, 28.
25 Horrell, *1 Peter*, 62.
26 Horrell, 63.
27 Achtemeier, *1 Peter*, 109.
28 Bartlett, "First Letter of Peter," 253.
29 Watson and Callan, *First and Second Peter*.
30 Michaels, *1 Peter*, 43.
31 Achtemeier, *1 Peter*, 111.
32 Watson and Callan, *First and Second Peter*, 28.

prophets also enabled the preachers of the good news to proclaim the saving power of Jesus Christ.[33]

The third term in 1 Peter 1:11–12 that is connected with the work of the Spirit is "revealing" (ἀπεκαλύφθη). Christ's coming, suffering, and glory have been revealed by the Holy Spirit to the Old Testament prophets.[34] Michaels argued that the passive verb ἀπεκαλύφθη shows the activity of God revealing the glorious events and the grace that ministers use in the ministry of the gospel.[35] Achtemeier also portrayed the Spirit's role in revealing future events, showing that the Holy Spirit enabled the Old Testament prophets to see beyond themselves and their contemporaries, focusing on what will happen at the coming of Christ.[36]

The fourth reference to the Spirit is about his role as one sent from heaven (πνεύματι ἁγίῳ ἀποσταλέντι ἀπ' οὐρανοῦ). The Spirit is the one sending good news to the people who need to hear it. According to Michaels, this text indicates that the Holy Spirit, through the announcement of the gospel, was active in consecrating the people of God.[37] Likewise, according to Watson and Callan, "these proclaimers of the gospel came by means of the Holy Spirit sent by God (or Christ; 3:22)."[38] Achtemeier also pointed out, "As the Spirit of Christ informed the message of the prophets, the Holy Spirit impels the proclamation of the gospel."[39]

In general, the role of the Spirit in 1:11–12 is represented by these four essential terms. Each of these terms is strongly tied to the role of the Spirit in mission. The acts of indicating (ἐδήλου, v. 11a), testifying (προμαρτυρόμενον, v. 11b), revealing (ἀπεκαλύφθη, v. 12a), and sending (πνεύματι ἁγίῳ ἀποσταλέντι, v. 12b) are the roles of the Spirit, and his ultimate goal is to manifest and preach the good news of Christ. The general point that Peter communicated is that the role of the Spirit in the mission activity is substantial, essential, and irreplaceable. The Spirit gives believers the power and boldness to proclaim the gospel fearlessly. In verse 12, Peter mentioned that the prophets of the Old Testament "were not serving themselves but, when they spoke of the things that have now been told by those who have preached the gospel by the Holy Spirit sent from heaven."

---

33 Bartlett, "First Letter of Peter," 253.
34 Horrell, *1 Peter*, 62.
35 Michaels, *1 Peter*, 44.
36 Achtemeier, *1 Peter*, 111.
37 Michaels, *1 Peter*, 47.
38 Watson and Callan, *First and Second Peter*, 29.
39 Achtemeier, *1 Peter*, 113.

This highlights the role of the Holy Spirit in inspiring and empowering the proclamation of the gospel. As believers share the message of salvation, the Spirit works through them, opening hearts and minds to receive the truth.

The Spirit in 1 Peter 3:18–19

The role of the Spirit is attested in 3:18–19. It describes how he participated in the resurrection of Jesus Christ and continued after Christ's resurrection by proclaiming Christ's victory. Different interpretations exist about the term πνεύματι: some understand the term as the spiritual state and others understand it as the Spirit. For instance, Watson and Callan argued that the term refers to the spiritual states, pointing out that "flesh in 1 Peter clearly refers to the mortal state, and in this tight contrast, spirit naturally refers to the spiritual state."[40] Bartlett and Michaels have argued in the same way, pointing out that σαρκὶ and πνεύματι indicate two spheres of life, such as the spheres of human limitation and vindicated life.[41] However, Achtemeier has argued against this by pointing out that σαρκὶ and πνεύματι are instrumental rather than adverbial, and they indicate the work of the Holy Spirit as a divine instrument actively working in the resurrection of Jesus Christ.[42] In the same way, Peter Davids views the Holy Spirit as having a role both in the resurrection of Christ and in transporting him to preach his victory amid the spirits.[43] Most of the arguments are identified among one of these two categorical views. However, the latter view seems correct because the immediate context might affirm that Christ went to the midst of the spirits by the power of the Holy Spirit, as the gospel tradition affirms.

In the broader biblical context, the role of the Spirit in different Christian experiences has strong evidence in the Pauline texts such as liberating a Christian life for the Christian life, helping in prayers, giving spiritual gifts, and enabling one to live in Christian happiness (Rom 8:1–4, 26–27; 1 Cor 12:4–7; 1 Thess 1:6). The Spirit's role in the life of Christ is also attested from his birth to resurrection referenced in some specific texts (Matt 1:20; Luke 1:35; Matt 4:1; Luke 4:1; Rom 8:11). Two important texts show that the Spirit is actively working to restore Christ and raise Christ from the dead (Rom 8:11; 1 Pet 3:18). Therefore, the role of the Spirit in 1 Peter 3:18 seems clear. Its use as a dative instrumental shows the work of the Spirit in

---

40 Watson and Callan, *First and Second Peter*, 89.
41 Bartlett, "First Letter of Peter," 293; Michaels, *1 Peter*, 205.
42 Achtemeier, *1 Peter*, 253.
43 Davids, *First Epistle of Peter*, 138.

the resurrection of Jesus Christ. The preceding text and the usage of ἐν ᾧ (1 Pet 3:19a) indicate that Christ has proclaimed through the Holy Spirit to the spirits in prison. Even though scholars are divided on these unclear words, the context seems to affirm that Christ through the Spirit claimed his victory, which is one aspect of the good news that proclaims salvation for humanity and judgment for the evil spirits. ἐν ᾧ implicitly establishes the continuity πνεύματι with the third and second elements beyond making alive Christ, the journey of Christ as well as Christ's preaching in the Spirit. It seems three of the events are continued one after the other while the latter two are strongly tied showing the gospel tradition that states "go and preach" and "go and tell" (Matt 10:7; 11:4; Luke 7:22; Mark 16:10, 15).

The Spirit in 1 Peter 4:14
In suffering, the Spirit is active, enabling the Christian community to stand firm. First Peter 4:14 shows that sharing the suffering of Christ leads to joy because the Spirit empowers those who suffer for the sake of Christ. The expression "the Spirit of glory" might directly show the work of the Spirit, as we have seen in the preceding texts. The Spirit enables believers in different circumstances, which allows believers to witness about Christ in any situation. It seems Christians were under persecution, and unbelievers were mocking them. Watson and Callan have argued for this role of the Spirit in 4:14, pointing to the fact that "elsewhere in the NT the Spirit is mentioned as residing with the Christians in time of suffering (Matt 10:19–20; Luke 12:11–12; John 14:26) and transforming them into the image of Christ's glory (2 Cor 3:8; 4:17; Col 3:4)."[44] Davids also affirmed that the Spirit is promised to those who experience persecution, and the Spirit enables them to witness to the saving power of Christ until death.[45]

The connection between suffering Christians and the Holy Spirit is common in the New Testament. These texts demonstrate that the Holy Spirit comforts believers in different circumstances. Since the Holy Spirit rests upon them, they consider themselves blessed because suffering is a mark of Christianity, and they rejoice with the help of the Holy Spirit. This life is different from others' lives, marking them as light and salt among the unbelieving community. In general, the Spirit sustains believers in times of suffering and persecution. Throughout 1 Peter, the author addressed a group of believers facing various trials and hardships. In 4:14, Peter encouraged

---
44 Watson and Callan, *First and Second Peter*, 111.
45 Davids, *First Epistle of Peter*, 168.

them, "If you are insulted because of the name of Christ, you are blessed, for the Spirit of glory and of God rests on you." Here, the Spirit is depicted as the source of comfort and strength, enabling believers to endure suffering for the sake of the mission.

Summary of the Role of the Spirit in Mission in 1 Peter

The four texts we have discussed are vital because they show how the Spirit works in the mission activity of the church. The place of mission in the context of 1 Peter is straightforward because 2:9–10 shows the calling of Christians to proclaim God's goodness. In addition, the need for preparedness is represented in 3:15. These texts as well as 1 Peter as a whole show the role of mission for the fallen world despite the recipients of this letter experiencing suffering for the sake of their faith in Christ. The centrality of the mission in the letter is attested explicitly and implicitly. This chapter has shown how the role of the Spirit of God is connected with the work of mission specifically in 1 Peter. It has emphasized the role of the Holy Spirit in the individual and corporal mission of the church.

The opening of 1 Peter 1:2 shows the role of the Spirit in sanctifying believers, and this sanctification not only enables believers to live a worthy life in front of God but also to witness to the fallen world to lead people to Christ. The life of holiness can be achieved with the help of the Spirit, and this life is the primary means to proclaim the good news in word and deeds. In addition, Peter's representation of the role of the Spirit in 1:11–12 is also important, showing how the work of the Spirit is tied to the activity of the mission. In these two verses, we have seen four crucial roles of the Holy Spirit: indicating, testifying, revealing, and sending empowered servants to fulfill their service as ones sent by God.

The third point we have argued is the role of the Spirit in 3:18–19. Despite different views on these verses, we have argued that the Spirit here is instrumental in raising Jesus Christ from the dead, and the same Spirit also transported Jesus into the middle of the fallen angels to proclaim his victory, which is one aspect of the gospel. The Spirit in these two texts actively participates in the mission activity of the church because the content and the model of preaching is Jesus Christ. The central message of the good news is Jesus Christ and his victory over sin, Satan, and the fear of death (Heb 2:14–18).

Finally, we argued that the Spirit has a role in the life of those suffering because of their faith, which is portrayed in 4:14. The Holy Spirit is depicted as resting upon these Christians, which is the sign and the mark of true Christianity. The Christian community is not only called to believe in Jesus but also to suffer for the sake of Christ. The Holy Spirit gives power and strength to those who pass through suffering and afflictions because of their faith in Christ. This is a sign of the Spirit's part in mission because Christians, while suffering, rejoice in Christ, and by doing this, they testify about Christ in their words and deeds.

Implications for the Contemporary Ethiopian Church and Beyond
The Spirit has had a substantial role in the contemporary church of Ethiopia and beyond. Through his work in the mission activity of the church, the Spirit has nourished the Ethiopian evangelical church through its history, and the empowerment of the Spirit has significantly contributed to the development of the church both qualitatively and quantitatively.

The work of the Spirit in the contemporary evangelical churches of Ethiopia is essential. As we have seen above, the Spirit sanctifies, indicates, testifies, reveals, enables for service, resurrects, empowers, and rests upon in the life of believers (1 Pet 1:2, 11–12; 3:18–19; 4:14). The Spirit enables believers for the mission of proclaiming the good news for the fallen world. Therefore, the contemporary churches in Ethiopia and beyond can learn from these texts using the role of the Spirit in the mission activity of the church. In this changing world, Christians can be enabled and empowered by the work of the Spirit just as the early church Christians were. The work of the Spirit and the work of mission are united together for the growth of the church.

The importance of mission in the growth of the church is substantial. The church was born by mission activity and cannot live without mission activity. The church will only grow if it works on the mission of the good news for the fallen world. The central activity in the life of the church should be the mission of the good news. The church in Ethiopia has many opportunities to reach the unreached by being a mission-oriented church. First Peter encourages Christians to proclaim the goodness of God as an exilic community despite the suffering they have been experiencing.

The role of the Spirit is to fulfil our mission to communicate the good news about Jesus Christ. In the Ethiopian context, there is a tendency to limit the Spirit to contexts other than the mission of God. The New Testament clearly shows that the Holy Spirit's role in the church's mission is decisive. Therefore, it seems that the importance of the work of the Holy Spirit for Christians goes beyond helping individual Christians with their problems.

When the Holy Spirit indwells the life of the believing community, that community is enabled for the mission of the Christian faith which is edifying the body of Christ and enabling the Church to bring others to Christ.

Conclusion

In conclusion, this chapter has argued that 1 Peter 1:2, 11–12; 3:18–19; 4:14 show how the Spirit works in the life of believers, enabling them to proclaim the good news in any situation. First, we reviewed related literature and considered its contribution toward the theme. In the second section, we established a context by examining how those in the first century understood the role of the Spirit. The third section examined the four selected texts in 1 Peter and argued that the role of the Spirit in mission is evident in 1 Peter. These texts reveal that the mission of the church is fulfilled through the Spirit, which is also affirmed in the broader context of the New Testament. This analysis has implications for the Ethiopian Christian context and beyond in order to strengthen the mission activity of the global church, leading to the proper dependence on the work of the Spirit in mission.

Bibliography

Achtemeier, Paul J. *1 Peter: A Commentary on First Peter*. Hermeneia. Minneapolis: Fortress Press, 1996.

Akin, Paul. "The Missiological Motivation of 1 Peter." *Southern Baptist Journal of Theology* 23, no. 3 (2019): 7–21.

Bartlett, David L. "The First Letter of Peter: Introduction, Commentary, and Reflections." In *The New Interpreter's Bible: A Commentary in Twelve Volumes*, 12: 229–319. Nashville: Abingdon, 1998.

Binns, John. *The Orthodox Church of Ethiopia: A History*. Library of Modern Religion 53. London: I. B. Tauris, 2017.

Bruner, Frederick Dale. *A Theology of the Holy Spirit: The Pentecostal Experience and the New Testament Witness*. Grand Rapids: Eerdmans, 1986.

Chester, Andrew, and Ralph P. Martin. *The Theology of the Letters of James, Peter, and Jude*. New Testament Theology. New York: Cambridge University Press, 1994.

Davids, Peter H. *The First Epistle of Peter*. New International Commentary on the New Testament. Grand Rapids: Eerdmans, 1990.

Edwards, Dennis R. *1 Peter*, edited by Tremper Longman and Scot McKnight. Story of God Bible Commentary. Grand Rapids: Zondervan, 2017.

Esler, Philip F. *Ethiopian Christianity: History, Theology, Practice*. Waco, TX: Baylor University Press, 2019.

Ethiopian Orthodox Tewahedo Church. *Andəmta Commentary on Acts, General Epistles, and Revelation*. Translated by Leeke Lekawint Mehari. Addis Ababa: n.p., 1958.

Horrell, David G. *1 Peter*. New Testament Guides. New York: T&T Clark, 2008.

Keener, Craig S. *The Spirit in the Gospels and Acts: Divine Purity and Power*. Peabody, MA: Hendrickson, 1997.

Levison, John R. *Spirit in First-Century Judaism*. Arbeiten zur Geschichte des antiken Judentums und des Urchristentums 29. Leiden: Boston: Brill, 2003.

Michaels, J. Ramsey. *1 Peter*. Word Biblical Commentary 49. Waco, TX: Word, 1988.

Nkansah-Obrempong, James. *Foundations for African Theological Ethics*. Carlisle: Langham Monographs, 2013.

Seland, Torrey. *Strangers in the Light: Philonic Perspectives on Christian Identity in 1 Peter*. Biblical Interpretation Series 76. Leiden: Brill, 2005.

Shenk, Calvin E. "Ethiopian Orthodox Church: A Study in Indigenization." *Missiology: An International Review* 16, no. 3 (1988): 259–78.

Watson, Duane F., and Terrance Callan. *First and Second Peter*. Paideia. Grand Rapids: Baker Academic, 2012.

Chapter 6

Eschatology and Mission in 1 Peter

Grant LeMarquand

In the middle of the twentieth century, the German historical critic Ferdinand Hahn penned a succinct volume, published in English as *Mission in the New Testament*, in which he devoted only two and a half pages to the topic of mission in 1 Peter. According to Hahn, the theme of 1 Peter is persecution.[1] Hahn believed that this persecution resulted in a situation in which "all missionary activity is denied" to the recipients of 1 Peter. The letter, he said, has an "insistent" eschatological expectation[2] that gave the Christians of "Pontus, Galatia, Cappadocia, Asia, and Bithynia" (1:1) only one option: to give testimony before the gentiles who were persecuting them. They were to be ready to respond to anyone "who calls you to account for the hope that is in you" (3:15). This eschatological expectation "serves to confront the unbelievers and persecutors with their future judge."[3] Therefore, said Hahn, mission can be spoken of only in a "modified way."

> There is no longer any question here of missionary action. Apart from the very indirect function of 3.1f., this Church has no possibility of "missionary service" in the *real* sense. In the passive character of its trials in persecution, and in the testimony that it gives, something of the missionary commission is carried out, in so far as the Church's whole existence is determined by the missionary function.[4]

Hahn was correct to draw attention to the eschatological dimension of the church's testimony in 1 Peter. There are, however, a number of problems with Hahn's exposition of mission in 1 Peter. First, it is not clear that we should speak of the recipients of 1 Peter as persecuted, although it is likely that the letter was written from Rome during a time when persecution had already broken out. Certainly, the recipients of 1 Peter are harassed and suffering, but organized persecution appears still to lie in the future.[5] Second,

---

[1] Hahn, *Mission in the New Testament*, 141.
[2] Hahn, 141.
[3] Hahn, 141.
[4] Hahn, 142, emphasis mine.
[5] Generally, those who assume a late date for 1 Peter might also assume that the letter of the Younger Pliny to Trajan is reflected in 1 Peter. Alternatively, those who hold to an early date for 1 Peter would see Peter's exhortation (especially in 3:15) as an appropriate warning concerning a persecution yet to come. See Knox, "Pliny and 1 Peter," 187–89.

and more important for our purposes, Hahn limited the concept of mission in two ways: (1) Hahn saw mission as a function of the church, and (2) he reduced mission activity to the verbal proclamation of the gospel leading to conversion. In this chapter, I argue that we should approach Peter's first letter with a fuller understanding of mission, that is (1) mission is primarily God's mission and only secondarily the mission of the church, and (2) mission is not only a matter of evangelism—as crucial and important as that is—but also of witness to the lordship of Christ, by word and deed, in every aspect of life.[6] With this fuller understanding of mission, we can achieve a broader understanding of how Peter's eschatology relates to his missionary exhortation in this letter.

Eschatology

In order to approach the eschatology of 1 Peter, we must first examine the Old Testament (and Second Temple Jewish) understanding of "the end" in which Peter lived and moved and had his being.[7] Early Christian writers and audience were aware that the Christian life was eschatological, that is, lived in hope, in the reality of the last things inaugurated by the incarnation, death, and resurrection of Jesus the Messiah. Christ's appearing was seen by the early church as the fulfillment of a cluster of Old Testament promises, images, and ideas. Fundamentally, eschatology was a corollary to two other Old Testament convictions: monotheism and election. The Old Testament canon affirmed that there is one God, the creator and Lord of all. Israel also affirmed that this one God had chosen Israel to be his people. These two foundational beliefs raised the question, "If there is one sovereign creator God and if this one God has chosen Israel, then why is Israel suffering?" Eschatology addresses this fundamental question with the conviction that suffering must be temporary because the God of Israel will come to save his people.[8]

---

6 In 1 Peter, "no sphere of life is to be exempted from obedience to Christ." Köstenberger and Alexander, *Salvation to the Ends*, 97.

7 In this essay, I refer to the author of 1 Peter as "Peter." Opinions about authorship vary widely, but I will not give the space here to argue the issues that are easily found in the major commentaries.

8 This paragraph owes much to Wright. See, for example, his *New Testament and the People*, especially ch. 9. He said belief in monotheism and election "committed any Jew who thought about it for a moment to a further belief: YHWH … was irrevocably committed to further action of some sort in history, which would bring about the end of Israel's desolation and the vindication of his true people. Monotheism and election lead to eschatology" (247).

The Old Testament prophets and Psalms, and the Jewish writings of the Second Temple period give much attention to how and when God will come to rescue his people. A seminal text is the warning in Deuteronomy 30. After promising that those entering the promised land would be blessed if they obeyed his commands, God warned Israel of the consequences of disobedience. "But if your heart turns away and you do not hear, but are led astray to bow down to other gods and serve them, I declare to you today that you shall perish; you shall not live long in the land that you are crossing the Jordan to enter and possess" (Deut 30:17–18).[9] Obedience leads to blessing in the land; disobedience leads to exile. The prophetic tradition repeatedly warned of the possibility of exile due to Israel's immorality and idolatry, and the judgment of expulsion from the land finally happened—in 733 BC for Israel (the northern kingdom) at the hands of the Assyrians and in 597–586 BC for Judah (the southern kingdom) at the hands of the Babylonians. In spite of the people's disobedience, God remained faithful and the prophets and Psalms are full of promises that God will restore them. The promises associated with this restoration reminded Israel that God the creator can bring a new creation, and the God of the deliverance at the Red Sea can effect a new exodus.

The new life that the prophets and Psalms anticipated contained a number of elements, many of which were picked up in apocalyptic discourse in Jewish literature of the Second Temple period,[10] including the following themes:[11]

- The people will return from exile and receive back their "inheritance" ("whoever takes refuge in me shall possess the land and inherit my holy mountain," Isa 57:13b; cf. 58:11; 60:21; 65:9; Ezek 36:12; 47:14, 22–23);

- The return from exile will be like the dead being given new life (Ezek 37; cf. Isa 40:1–5; 43:1–7);

- A period of suffering for God's people, often called "the messianic woes," will precede the coming of a deliverer (Dan 12:1–2; cf. *T. Mos.* 8 and 10; *1 En.* 1; 1QM 1.11–12);

---

9 Bible references are NRSV unless otherwise noted.

10 On "apocalyptic discourse" and literature designated as "apocalypses," see Carey, "Introduction: Apocalyptic Discourse," 1–17; Hansen, "Apocalypses and Apocalypticism," 1:279–82; Collins, *Apocalyptic Imagination*; and Collins, "Introduction: Towards the Morphology," 1–20.

11 The biblical and extra-biblical references included here are merely a sample.

- A messianic figure empowered by the Spirit will come not only to restore the Davidic kingdom but also to bring a new creation even better than Eden (Isa 11; 65:17–25);
- Sins, the cause of the exile, will be forgiven (Dan 9:14–15, 24–25; Isa 40:1–2; 43:25);
- God will pour out his Spirit on all flesh (Joel 2:28; cf. Ezek 36:27; 37:9–10; 39:29);
- The temple will be rebuilt or descend from heaven, or the community itself is conceived of as a temple (Hag; Mal; Ezek 40–48; cf. *T. Benj.* 9.2; *Jub.* 24.32; 4QFlor; 1QS 8.4ff.; 11.3ff.);
- The rebuilt temple of Zion will be a magnet drawing the nations to serve Israel and worship Israel's God (Isa 2:1–5; 19:16–25; 60:1–14; Pss 65–67; 97–100);
- There will be a final judgment and an end to death and suffering (Dan 12:1–3; Isa 25:6–8).

Peter's first letter notices all of these Old Testament eschatological and apocalyptic themes. In fact, many identify eschatology as central to this letter. It is "inflamed by an eschatological fire,"[12] said Johannes Schattenmann. "A strong eschatological component flavors the entire epistle,"[13] said Köstenberger and Alexander. "The End is at hand, which will bring destruction to their enemies and, if they stand firm, everlasting glory to themselves" said J. N. D. Kelly.[14] Similarly, Robert Webb said, "Apocalyptic discourse may be identified throughout 1 Peter, to such an extent that it could be said that an apocalyptic perspective pervades and penetrates the very heart of this letter."[15] Examples of this consensus that "the end" is a key theme in 1 Peter could be multiplied.[16]

Even a cursory reading of 1 Peter easily unearths multiple eschatological themes. For example, the word "hope" appears five times (1:3, 13, 21; 3:5, 15); "glory" is mentioned ten times, several with a clearly eschatological meaning (1:7, 11; 4:13; 5:1, 4, 10); Peter looked forward to the "revealing"

---

12 Schattenmann, "Little Apocalypse of the Synoptics," 193.
13 Köstenberger and Alexander, *Salvation to the Ends*, 92.
14 Kelly, *Commentary on the Epistles*, 1.
15 Webb, "Intertexture and Rhetorical Strategy," 79.
16 It should be noted that 1 Peter also makes use of gospel traditions, including Jesus's eschatological teaching. See Miller, *Echoes of Jesus*.

of Jesus (1:5, 7, 13, 20; 4:13; 5:1); "salvation" is often a future reality in 1 Peter (1:5, 9, 10; 2:2); the "end" of the ages or all things is anticipated (1:20; 4:7; cf. 4:17); the time of "judgment" is near (1:17; 2:12 ["the day of visitation"], 23; 4:5, 6, 17); the "resurrection" anticipated in the prophets has happened in Christ (1:3; 3:21); Christians have received the promised Spirit (1:2, 11, 12; 4:6, 14); the community of believers is the newly rebuilt temple (2:4–10); and the anticipated movement of gentiles to Zion is fulfilled in a surprising way (2:9–10).

It is clear from this quick survey that 1 Peter shares with the rest of early Christianity the assurance that the end times are already present. The Messiah has come; he has risen from the dead; the Spirit has been poured out on all flesh; Jews and gentiles together are being built into a new temple. On the other hand, some aspects have not yet occurred: Christ is raised, but the general resurrection has not yet happened; although there is forgiveness, sin and suffering and "exile" continue; judgment and final glory are still in the future, but are beginning to be experienced already; hope is still necessary; the final "revelation" of Christ is yet to come. Eschatology, in other words, has been bifurcated. The readers of 1 Peter already live in the end but still look forward to the final end.[17]

Having briefly sketched Peter's eschatological ethos, we turn now to what this letter says about mission.

Mission

The idea of mission also has two senses. Although many limit the notion of mission to human activity and then confine it even further to the realm of verbal proclamation (evangelism), I contend that the idea of mission is actually much broader. Most importantly, mission is not primarily an anthropocentric idea. Mission is first of all theocentric; it is about God himself. Mission begins in the heart of God. Although the phrase "the mission of God," or the *missio Dei*, is sometimes used in an unhelpful way, we should not shy away from it.[18] Rightly understood, the notion of the "mission of God" asserts that God himself is outward focused. Although self-sufficient, God created the world out of love. When his good world fell into sin and evil and death, God did not abandon his creation but instead created a people, Israel

---

17 The classic statement of this bifurcated early Christian eschatological perspective is found in Cullmann, *Christ and Time*.

18 For the history of this term's use, see Bosch, *Transforming Mission*, 398–402. For a thoroughly biblical and evangelical use of the term, see Wright, *Mission of God*.

(Gen 12:1–3), to whom he revealed himself and through whom he sent a deliverer (John 3:16), not only to rescue all nations (Matt 28:16–20) but to renew the whole cosmos (Col 1:15–23; Eph 1:10). Among many other things, the mission of Jesus reveals the heart of the missionary God.[19]

Secondarily, mission involves the church, God's people. The mission of the church, the *missio ecclesia*, follows from the *missio Dei*. Because those who trust in Christ are followers and worshipers of a missionary God, God's people are necessarily missional people. The church's outward-focused work of proclaiming and living out the gospel is a corollary of belonging to a God who loves his world (John 3:16).

We have seen that 1 Peter has a strong eschatological ethos. Given this, it should be evident that 1 Peter also has a missional ethos. Old Testament and Jewish eschatology anticipated God's future rescue of Israel and the creation from the decay of sin, evil, and death. Eschatology, therefore, is the expectation of God acting to judge and to save, the assurance that the God who had come in the past will once again act decisively. In other words, eschatology is inherently missional. Old Testament and Jewish eschatology expected, indeed longed for, God's missionary action. The presumption of Hahn, mentioned at the beginning of this essay, which reduced mission to human activity and therefore saw little mission theology in 1 Peter, is reductionistic. If we recognize that the Bible narrates the story of a missional God, we will recognize "mission" as a theme that pervades the eschatological atmosphere of 1 Peter. Eschatological ideas had real-life missiological consequences for the writer and readers of 1 Peter. Christ's first coming to die and rise from the dead and second coming at the judgment reveal that God's mission—his plan to rescue the world from sin and death—has come to a climax. The church's mission is to bear witness by word (in proclamation) and deed (especially in honorable behavior and in suffering) until the coming judgment.

Several Petrine passages help us to discern the contours of what could be called 1 Peter's "missional eschatology." We will examine two passages that highlight *God's mission*, before looking at two sets of passages that emphasize *the mission of the church*.

---

[19] I have discussed this more thoroughly in LeMarquand, "From Creation to New Creation," 9–34.

God's Mission, Part 1: Petrine Christians as Recipients of God's Mission (1:1-12)

First Peter's letter opening follows a familiar Hellenistic letter structure, adapted by early Christian writers.[20] The author begins with a self-identification, followed by a description of the recipients of the letter and a greeting. In Hellenistic letters, this opening is followed by a health wish. In most early Christian letters, the health wish is transformed into a prayer or prayer report. In 1 Peter, the prayer opens in a typically Jewish fashion: "Blessed be God."[21]

The epistolary outline of 1 Peter 1:1–12 therefore looks like this:

- Sender (1a)
- Receivers (1b–2a)
- Greeting (2b)
- Blessing prayer (3–12)

Peter adapted the basic Hellenistic letter form to signal the message of the letter as a whole. The recipients, therefore, are not just Christians living in regions of Asia Minor, but are "chosen and destined by God" (NRSV) or, perhaps better, "elect exiles of the dispersion" (ESV). Although some have argued that the recipients were literally "exiles" and "sojourners," that is, not native to Asia Minor,[22] it seems more likely that Peter employed this language metaphorically. No matter where they live or whatever their earthly citizenship, these believers should consider themselves strangers in this fallen world.[23] To be an exile is to be vulnerable. Peter conveyed from the start that his readers are people in a potentially dangerous situation. But, although at risk in the world, they have already been "chosen" (*eklektos*) and "sanctified" (*hagiasmos*). Using language employed by the Septuagint to describe the people of Israel, Peter asserted that these dispersed Christians

---

20 On epistolary structure see Doty, *Letters in Primitive Christianity*; Jervis, *Purpose of Romans*; O'Brien, *Introductory Thanksgivings*; and Weima, *Paul the Ancient Letter Writer*. Although most New Testament epistolary critics have focused on Paul, the lessons learned can easily be transferred to other early Christian letters.

21 Most of Paul's prayer reports open with *eucharistō*, but 2 Corinthians and Ephesians, like 1 Peter, both begin *eulogeō*.

22 Elliott has argued this position in several publications; see especially his *Home for the Homeless* and *1 Peter*. He has been followed by, among others, McKnight, *1 Peter*.

23 Compare Paul, a Roman citizen, speaking of believers as citizens of heaven (Phil 3:20).

are already rescued from the world by the blood of Christ.[24] Already we can see that Peter's purpose is to inform his readers that they are living in an eschatological tension. They are in a sinful, broken world, but they are God's chosen people who have already been rescued by the blood of Jesus: they live in the reality of one rescue while anticipating another.

Peter reinforced this message in his prayer report in vv. 3–12. The prayer itself is permeated with eschatological and apocalyptic language: hope (v. 3), resurrection (v. 3), inheritance (v. 4), kept in heaven (v. 4), salvation ready to be revealed in the last time (*en kairō eschatō*) (v. 5), for a little while (v. 6), your faith—tested by fire—may be found to result in praise and glory and honor when Jesus Christ is revealed (v. 7), though you do not see him now (v. 8), the outcome of your faith, [is/will be] the salvation of your souls (v. 9), the prophets prophesied and inquired about this coming salvation (vv. 10–11), things that angels longed to see, were revealed to the prophets (v. 12). Peter assures the Asian Christians that the God who promised salvation through the prophets has now acted in Jesus Christ. They have been given a "new birth" (v. 3) because of the death (vv. 2, 10) and resurrection (v. 3) of Jesus Christ. That Jesus has risen from the dead signals to the readers that the end time has come (Ezek 37; Dan 12). This good news has been announced to them (1 Pet 1:12), and they have already received mercy (v. 2). On the other hand, the perfect "end" has not yet come: "now for a little while you have had to suffer various trials" (v. 6). Suffering will continue for some time, but they are assured that future salvation is coming (vv. 5, 9, 10) at the revelation (*apokalypsis*) of Jesus Christ (vv. 5–7).[25] In this in-between time, believers are guarded (v. 5) while their inheritance is protected in heaven (v. 4). In other words, the recipients of Peter's letter are participants in the drama of God's mission. God's plan that the prophets and angels anticipated has now been put into action in Christ. Because of God's missional action, these believers have heard and received the gospel message (v. 12) and been born anew (v. 2). They now wait in a foreign world, expecting a renewed world, their future inheritance and salvation, to be received at the revelation of Jesus Christ at the last day.

---

24 On Peter's language of blood sacrifice for African Christians today, see Mbuvi, "Christology and *Cultus*," 151–54.

25 A fine, detailed study of Peter's eschatology as founded on the eschatological program of Zechariah 9–14 can be found in Liebengood's *Eschatology of 1 Peter*. Liebengood argued that 1 Peter contains numerous echoes of Zechariah's prophecy, which provide "the substructure of 1 Peter's eschatological programme" (215). The emphasis of this current chapter is less on the origin of Peter's eschatological thought and more on how Peter uses eschatological themes to encourage his readers to live in the present overlap of the ages.

We should note that immediately following Peter's prayer report in 1:3–12 comes the letter body itself. It continues the eschatological emphasis: "Therefore prepare your minds for action; discipline yourselves; set all your hope on the grace that Jesus Christ will bring you when he is revealed" (v. 13). Although he moved from prayer to encouraging his readers to ethical living, the basis of ethics is their future hope—the Petrine Christians are to wait in hope for grace that will be revealed at Christ's coming.

God's Mission, Part 2: The Cross, Resurrection, and Ascension of Christ (3:18-22)

Peter reiterates the mission of God in Christ which opens the letter in 3:18–22, a section often considered one of the most difficult passages in the New Testament. Elliott summarized the difficulties and issues:

> This complex passage has long challenged scholars and poses a host of questions concerning the syntax and structure of these verses, their sources and conceptual background, their coherence and meaning, their relation to 4:1–6, their rhetorical function, and their relation to the concept of Christ's "descent into hell," despite the fact that neither "descent" nor "hell" is mentioned here.[26]

I will not argue my position at length against other interpretations.[27] I will, rather, try to describe how this passage contributes to thinking eschatologically about the mission of God in Christ. This passage follows a section (which we will examine a bit later) in which Peter encouraged his readers to be prepared to give a defense of their hope in Christ if they were called to account (3:15). He warned that they may have to suffer for their faith (3:17). In 3:18–22, he supported his exhortation (as in 1:3–12) by recounting the story of *God's mission* in Christ.

> For Christ also suffered for sins once for all, the righteous for the unrighteous, in order to bring you to God. He was put to death in the flesh, but made alive in the spirit, in which also he went and made a proclamation to the spirits in prison, who in former times did not obey, when God waited patiently in the days of Noah, during the building of the ark, in which a few, that is, eight people, were saved through water. And baptism, which this prefigured, now saves you—not as a removal of dirt from the body, but as an appeal to God for a good conscience,

---

26 Elliott, *1 Peter*, 638.
27 On the many interpretative possibilities see Bauckham, "Spirits in Prison," 6:177–78; Dalton, *Christ's Proclamation*; and Reicke, *Disobedient Spirits and Christian Baptism*.

through the resurrection of Jesus Christ, who has gone into heaven and is at the right hand of God, with angels, authorities, and powers made subject to him.

Verse 18 begins the narrative at the crucifixion. Whether the original text said "suffered" or "died" (ancient manuscripts are divided), it is clear that the cross is in mind. Christ's death achieved reconciliation between God and the believer ("in order to bring you to God"). The last part of the verse is more controversial: being put to death "in the flesh" is likely another way of referring to the crucifixion—but what does it mean that Christ was "made alive in the spirit"? Several possibilities have been suggested. There is a long tradition that says that this alludes to the time between Christ's death and resurrection. The "spirit" in that case would be Christ's human spirit (note the lowercase *s* in the NRSV). This would mean that Christ died bodily at the cross but was still alive "spiritually." It is more likely, however, that Christ's "being made alive" is a way of talking about the resurrection and the "Spirit" (capital *S*) is the agent of the resurrection. Therefore, it is likely that dative case (*pneumati*) should be understood as instrumental, "by the Spirit" rather than "in the spirit." Verse 18, therefore, tells the story that Christians have always told: Christ died for our sins to bring us to God and was raised from the dead. Peter reinforced that "being made alive" in verse 18 is resurrection language when he says in verse 21 that baptism "saves ... through the resurrection of Jesus Christ."[28]

If verse 18 is about the cross and resurrection, then verse 19 does not refer to Christ's descent into hell when it says that "he went and made a proclamation to the spirits in prison." Rather, this proclamation was made during his ascension. His "going" was going up rather than down. Having been raised from the dead (v. 18), Christ now ascends triumphantly (v. 19), proclaiming his victory to the "spirits." These spirits are not the human spirits[29] of those disobedient people who died during the days of Noah (v. 20), but rather the spiritual beings ("sons of God," Gen 6:2) who violated God's created order (Gen 6:1–4).[30] That the ascent is in view is emphasized in verse 22, where Peter told his readers clearly that "Christ has gone into heaven and is at the right hand of God" and, importantly, that "angels, authorities, and

---

28 Cf. Wright, *Resurrection of the Son*, 467–69.

29 In the Second Temple period, referring to dead human beings as spirits would be highly unusual. For a different view appealing to African tradition about the living dead, see Mbuvi, "Christology and *Cultus*," 155–59.

30 These verses, therefore, are similar to the narrative underlying Ephesians 4:8–10.

powers subject to him." The Old Testament and Second Temple Judaism looked forward to the coming of a Messiah who, empowered by the Spirit (Isa 11:1–5; note "by the Spirit" in 1 Pet 3:18) would triumph over God's and Israel's enemies. This eschatological hope, said Peter, is now fulfilled in the cross, resurrection, and ascension of Jesus. God's mission to save, not just Israel but the world, has been accomplished. Just as God saved Noah's family from the flood, so believers are now saved by the death and resurrection of Jesus, signified in baptism (vv. 20–21).

In the context of 1 Peter as a whole, Christ's proclamation to the spiritual powers serves to comfort and encourage Christians who are still oppressed by worldly powers. Knowing that Christ has triumphed over the "spirits" (3:19) and reigns over all "angels, authorities, and powers" (3:22) assures Peter's readers that their suffering is temporary because the end-time events are already unfolding. Their hope, therefore, is secure.

The Mission of God's People, Part 1: Worship and Ethics (2:1-12)

Having examined two passages in which Peter dealt primarily with the eschatological nature of God's mission, we turn now to passages that focus on the mission of God's people. Crucial to Peter's letter is his message in 2:1–12 that those who believe in Jesus have inherited the promises and, indeed, the identity of Israel. Although most of his readers are probably gentiles (v. 10), Peter uses a variety of Old Testament texts to explain that they are now "God's people" (vv. 9, 10) because they are born anew (2:2; cf. 1:3), have "tasted the kindness of the Lord" (2:3), and have "received God's mercy" (2:10). They are "a chosen race, a royal priesthood, a holy nation" (2:9; cf. Exod 19:6). Peter "transfers to the Christian community a string of honorific titles which in the original applied to Israel."[31] They are God's temple, "living stones" who are being built into a "spiritual house" (2:5). The Old Testament, as we have seen, expected a new temple to be built after the exile. Some Jews, especially the Qumran community, interpreted this hope as fulfilled not in a physical structure but in themselves as God's community. Early Christians, including Peter in this text, interpreted Old Testament promises of a new temple as fulfilled in their community.[32]

---

31 Kelly, *Commentary on the Epistles*, 96.

32 Among other texts see 1 Corinthians 3:16–17; 2 Corinthians 6:16; Ephesians 2:11–22. On the implications of the temple motif for mission, see Beale, *Temple and the Church's Mission*. On this particular text, see Mbuvi, *Temple, Exile and Identity*.

But Peter's point goes beyond asserting that believers have the honor and privilege of being God's people and receiving his kindness (2:3) and mercy (2:10). In addition to looking forward to God's salvation (2:2; cf. 1:5, 9, 10), they also inherit responsibilities. That is, they not only receive the benefits of God's rescue mission in Christ, but they also become participants in mission for the sake of the world. Peter taught that they are to engage in mission in two ways: through their worship and through their ethical behavior.

As God's "holy priesthood," they are to "offer spiritual sacrifices" (2:5). Since this new spiritual house is not an architectural structure but a community, the spiritual sacrifices to be offered are metaphorical. Two kinds of offerings are in mind: "In 1 Peter, as in Hebrews [13:15–16], the 'spiritual sacrifices' are first of all something offered up to God in worship … and, second, a pattern of social conduct."[33] The Godward direction of the community is reinforced in 2:9, where the Petrine readers are told that they are called to be God's people, "in order that you may proclaim the mighty acts of him who called you out of darkness into his marvelous light." An Old Testament text stands behind Peter's words here. Isaiah 43:21 says that God chose Israel to "declare my praise." Worship, praise, was to be Israel's *raison d'être*. As believers, both Jew and gentile, inherit Israel's promises and responsibilities at the end of the ages, praise is their purpose. This praise, however, is missional as well as doxological. Or, we might say, the church's doxology has a missional dimension. Worship is not "a private affair between God and the worshipers, but it spills out into the public arena as one of the means by which God draws the nations to himself."[34] The Old Testament eschatological expectation of the pilgrimage of the nations to Zion is enacted in the church's declaration of praise.

In addition to praise and worship, God's renewed Israel also participates in mission through their ethical behavior. In 2:12, Peter charged his readers to "Conduct yourselves honorably among the Gentiles."[35] The purpose of this honorable conduct is to win over those who do not yet believe so that they too would join in the eschatological pilgrimage to the new Zion, to "the cornerstone chosen and precious" (2:6). If non-believers witness the good conduct of believers, they can be won for Christ: Christians act ethically so that they may "glorify God when he comes to judge" (2:12). Because the end

---

33 Michaels, *1 Peter*, 101.
34 Wright, *Mission of God's People*, 250.
35 Note that since all Christians, Jew and non-Jew, are now "Israel," Peter uses the word "gentile" to mean non-Christian.

has begun in the death and resurrection of Jesus, Peter was assured that the final judgment cannot be far behind. If God is coming to judge the world, the church's witness must invite those who have not yet "tasted the kindness of the Lord" (2:4) to also "come to him" (2:3). One way of giving that invitation is by living lives whose "honorable deeds" (2:12) are attractive. Here Peter echoed the teaching of Jesus: "Let your light shine before others, so that they may see your good works and give glory to your Father in heaven" (Matt 5:16). "Peter means that seeing and recognizing good deeds will lead some of those Gentiles who formerly slandered them [the Petrine Christians] to praise God instead. Such a change of heart can surely include the possibility of a genuine conversion to Christianity."[36]

The Mission of God's People, Part 2: Suffering and Submission (2:13-3:2; 3:13-17; 4:12-19)

Persecution and suffering are not the main theme of 1 Peter, but they are still a major issue. Leonard Goppelt said it well,

> This issue [Christian suffering] was not its theme; it was rather the occasion for composition and a consequence of its theme. In 1:1–2:12, readers were addressed not as persecuted but as "[chosen] exiles of the Dispersion" or as "aliens and exiles." The letter addressed them in terms of their situation in society. Consequently, its theme was the question that is discussed today throughout ecumenical Christianity: Christian responsibility in society.[37]

The purpose of 1 Peter is to encourage the Christian church in Asia Minor in their mission to live as God's people in a foreign environment, in a world that does not understand God's ways and, therefore, may become hostile. In the midst of this reality, Christians should "not be surprised at the fiery ordeal that is taking place among you to test you, as though something strange were happening to you" (4:12). Until the final revelation of Christ, suffering, and perhaps persecution, will be the norm for believers who are aliens in the world.

There is a kind of suffering that comes on those who do evil. Christians should not put themselves in situations that cause them to suffer for doing wrong: "Let none of you suffer as a murderer, a thief, a criminal, or even as a mischief-maker" (4:15). But there is another kind of suffering. To suffer

---

36 Marshall, *1 Peter*, 82.
37 Goppelt, *Theology of the New Testament*, 164.

for being a Christian does not bring shame (4:16); indeed, to suffer for the name of Christ brings blessing, "because the spirit of glory, which is the Spirit of God, is resting on you" (4:14). In fact, such suffering is a sharing of Christ's own suffering (4:13) and has eschatological consequences, for the Christian who suffers for Christ will "be glad and shout for joy when his glory is revealed" (4:13).

This theme of suffering for Christ is woven through the letter. Peter explained that there are numerous situations in which Christians are in real danger and therefore must act with wisdom as they live as followers of Jesus. In 2:13–3:2, Peter records his version of a Christian household code (*Haustafel*). A *Haustafel* is a common literary form in the Greco-Roman world. Several are found in the New Testament (Col 3:18–4:1; Eph 5:21–6:9). In Christian versions, members of the household (wives, husbands, parents, children, slaves, masters) are instructed concerning how to live Christian lives in their various stations. In Peter's version, the whole household is addressed in 2:13–17. Then two groups receive most of his attention: household servants (*oiketai*) in 2:18–25 and wives in 3:1–6 (Christian husbands receive a short admonition to be gentle with their wives in 3:7).

The two groups singled out for instruction are both vulnerable. Although Peter addressed "household servants" rather than "slaves" (*douloi*), these synonyms probably describe a similar reality of precarious existence in the Roman world. Peter opened with a word that is perhaps shocking to modern readers. Slaves are to submit (*hupotassō*). Peter was aware of the insecurity of living as a slave: they may endure pain and suffer unjustly (2:19); they may be beaten (2:20); they may be reviled (2:23). Peter held up Christ's crucifixion as the example to follow, perhaps implying that such punishment was a possibility for slaves.[38] As Peter warned every Christian that there is shame for suffering for doing wrong (4:15), so he also warned slaves in particular: "If you endure when you are beaten for doing wrong, where is the credit in that?" (2:20a). Christian slaves are to live exemplary lives in situations that may seem intolerable: "But if you endure when you do right and suffer for it, you have God's approval" (2:20b). Slaves are to show respect to their earthly masters, even those who are harsh (2:18). The purpose of such behavior is missiological. As Peter said to the whole church, good conduct will silence the foolish (2:15), and may convert some so that they give glory to God on the last day (2:12). Until that day, all

---

38 On crucifixion as an execution for slaves, see Hengel, *Crucifixion: In the Ancient World*.

Christians, including slaves, trust God who will judge justly (2:23). This trust follows the example of Christ (2:21) who, though sinless (2:22), suffered without reviling or threatening (2:23).

Christian wives of non-Christian husbands (those who are "disobedient to the word," 3:1) are similarly vulnerable. In the ancient world, the normal pattern was for the woman to follow the religion of her husband. Although Peter instructed wives to be submissive, such submission does not include conversion away from Christ. Wives are to live pure and reverent lives, adorning "the inner self with the lasting beauty of a gentle and quiet spirit, which is very precious in God's sight" (3:4). The purpose of such good deportment is evangelistic: the husband may be "won over without a word" by the wife's conduct (3:1; cf. 1 Cor 7:16a). This wordless evangelism is eschatological: faithful wives of unbelieving husbands live in "hope," said Peter, just as the holy women in the Old Testament lived in hope (3:5).

In 3:13–17, Peter envisioned the possibility that his readers may be "called to account" (*logon peri*, v. 15). Edward Selwyn noted that this Greek phrase is used in Plato's *Politics* to mean "a rational account of" and therefore has a "juridical flavour."[39] When required, Christians should be ready to give a "defense" (*apologia*). Peter may or may not have had a formal court scene in mind. Whatever situation is in view, Christians may be called to "suffer for doing what is right" (vv. 13, 17).[40] This suffering must be borne "with gentleness and reverence" (v. 15) and with a clear conscience (v. 16)—and, possibly, with an evangelistic purpose: "those who abuse you for your good conduct in Christ may be put to shame" (v. 16). Although Peter did not state that this shame will lead to repentance and conversion, this is a possible inference. Wayne Grudem, for example, suggested that this shame may lead to them "subsequently ... considering and believing the gospel,"[41] an inference made possible by 2:12, 15. As with his advice to slaves, Peter pointed to Christ as the exemplar in any situation of suffering (3:18).

---

39 Selwyn, *First Epistle of Peter*, 193–94.

40 Most scholars assume that Peter's statement about it being better to suffer for good in 1 Pet 3:17 is a generalization of his address to slaves in 2:20. However, Peter possibly referred to eschatological judgment in 3:17. Michaels argued that 3:17 is similar to the dominical saying in Matthew 10:28, that the disciple should not fear the one who can kill the body but rather the one who can destroy both the body and the soul in hell. See Michaels, "Eschatology in 1 Peter 3:17," 394–401; and Michaels, *1 Peter*, 191–93. This argument overlooks the similarity of vocabulary between 2:20 and 3:17 and assumes that Jesus was talking about God in Matthew 10:28.

41 Grudem, *First Epistle of Peter*, 154.

And, once again, the eschaton is in view. The defense of the gospel given when accused is an account of the Christian's "hope" (*elpis*, 3:15). Mission, said Peter, is always done with an eye toward God's future action.

Conclusion

Peter's first letter is thoroughly eschatological, as virtually all readers of the letter can agree. This vision of future hope, now inaugurated in the ministry, suffering, death, resurrection, and ascension of Jesus is a missiological hope in two senses. God has come to rescue his world in Christ, fulfilling his promises to Israel; and God calls his people to follow Christ, witnessing to him through their suffering, their exemplary behavior, and sometimes their words so that those now unbelieving may one day "glorify God when he comes to judge" (2:12). Peter's first letter, therefore, is thoroughly missiological because it is eschatological.

Bibliography

Bauckham, Richard. "Spirits in Prison." In *Anchor Yale Bible Dictionary*, 6: 177–78. New Haven: Yale University Press, 1992.

Beale, G. K. *The Temple and the Church's Mission: A Biblical Theology of the Dwelling Place of God*. Downers Grove, IL: InterVarsity Press, 2004.

Bosch, David J. *Transforming Mission: Paradigm Shifts in Theology of Mission*. Maryknoll, NY: Orbis Books, 1991.

Carey, Greg. "Introduction: Apocalyptic Discourse, Apocalyptic Rhetoric." In *Vision and Persuasion: Rhetorical Dimensions of Apocalyptic Imagination*, edited by Greg Carey and L. Gregory Bloomquist, 1–17. St Louis: Chalice, 1999.

Collins, John J. *The Apocalyptic Imagination: An Introduction to the Jewish Matrix of Christianity*. New York: Crossroad, 1984.

Collins, John J. "Introduction: Towards the Morphology of a Genre." *Semeia* 14 (1979): 1–20.

Cullmann, Oscar. *Christ and Time: The Primitive Christian Conception of Time and History*. Translated by Floyd V. Filson. London: SCM, 1951.

Dalton, William Joseph. *Christ's Proclamation to the Spirits: A Study of 1 Peter 3:18–4:6*. Analecta Biblica 23. Rome: Pontifical Biblical Institute, 1965.

Doty, William G. *Letters in Primitive Christianity*. Guides to Biblical Scholarship New Testament. Philadelphia: Fortress, 1973.

Elliott, John H. *1 Peter: A New Translation with Introduction and Commentary*. Anchor Bible 37B. New York: Doubleday, 2000.

Elliott, John H. *A Home for the Homeless: A Sociological Exegesis of 1 Peter, Its Situation and Strategy.* Philadelphia: Fortress, 1981.

Goppelt, Leonhard. *Theology of the New Testament*, Vol. 2, *The Variety and Unity of the Apostolic Witness to Christ.* Translated by John E. Alsup. Grand Rapids: Eerdmans, [1976] 1982.

Grudem, Wayne. *1 Peter*. Tyndale New Testament Commentaries 17. Grand Rapids: Eerdmans, 1988.

Hahn, Ferdinand. *Mission in the New Testament.* Translated by Frank Clarke. Studies in Biblical Theology 47. London: SCM, 1965.

Hansen, Paul D. "Apocalypses and Apocalypticism: The Genre, Introductory Overview." In *Anchor Yale Bible Dictionary*, 1:279–82. New Haven: Yale University Press, 1992.

Hengel, Martin. *Crucifixion: In the Ancient World and the Folly of the Message of the Cross.* London: SCM, [1976] 1977.

Jervis, L. Ann. *The Purpose of Romans: A Comparative Letter Structure Investigation.* Journal for the Study of the New Testament Supplement Series 55. Sheffield: JSOT Press, 1991.

Kelly, J. N. D. *A Commentary on the Epistles of Peter and Jude.* London: A&C Black, 1969.

Knox, John. "Pliny and 1 Peter: A Note on 1 Pet 4:14–16 and 3:15." *Journal of Biblical Literature* 72, no. 3 (1953): 187–89.

Köstenberger, Andreas J., and T. Desmond Alexander. *Salvation to the Ends of the Earth: A Biblical Theology of Mission.* 2nd ed. New Studies in Biblical Theology 53. Downers Grove, IL: IVP Academic, 2020.

LeMarquand, Grant. "From Creation to New Creation: The Mission of God in the Biblical Story." In *Waging Reconciliation: God's Mission in a Time of Globalization and Crisis*, edited by Ian Douglas, 9–34. New York: Church Publishing, 2002.

Liebengood, Kelly. *The Eschatology of 1 Peter: Considering the Influence of Zechariah 9–14.* Society for New Testament Studies Monograph Series 157. New York: Cambridge University Press, 2013.

Marshall, I. Howard. *1 Peter*. IVP New Testament Commentary. Downers Grove, IL: InterVarsity Press, 1991.

Mbuvi, Andrew M. "Christology and *Cultus* in 1 Peter: An African (Kenyan) Appraisal." In *Jesus without Borders: Christology in the Majority World*, edited by Gene L. Green, Stephen T. Pardue, and K. K. Yeo, 141–61. Carlisle, UK: Langham, 2015.

Mbuvi, Andrew M. *Temple, Exile and Identity in 1 Peter.* Library of New Testament Studies 345. New York: T&T Clark, 2007.

McKnight, Scot. *1 Peter.* NIV Application Commentary. Grand Rapids: Zondervan, 1996.

Michaels, J. Ramsey. *1 Peter.* Word Biblical Commentary 49. Waco, TX: Word, 1988.

Michaels, J. Ramsey. "Eschatology in 1 Peter 3:17," *New Testament Studies* 13, no. 4 (1967): 394–401.

Miller, Timothy E. *Echoes of Jesus in the First Epistle of Peter.* Eugene, OR: Pickwick, 2022.

O'Brien, Peter T. *Introductory Thanksgivings in the Letters of Paul.* Eugene, OR: Wipf & Stock, 2009.

Reicke, Bo. *The Disobedient Spirits and Christian Baptism A Study of 1 Pet. 3:19 and Its Context.* Acta Seminarii Neotestamentici Upsaliensis 13. Copenhagen: Ejnar Munksgaard, 1946.

Schattenmann, Johannes. "The Little Apocalypse of the Synoptics and the First Epistle of Peter." *Theology Today* 11, no. 2 (1954): 193–98.

Selwyn, Edward Gordon. *The First Epistle of St. Peter: The Greek Text with Introduction, Notes, and Essays.* Grand Rapids: Baker Books, [1947] 1981.

Webb, Robert L. "Intertexture and Rhetorical Strategy in First Peter's Apocalyptic Discourse: A Study in Sociorhetorical Interpretation." In *Reading First Peter with New Eyes: Methodological Reassessments of the Letter of First Peter*, edited by Robert L. Webb and Betsy Bauman-Martin, 72–110. Library of New Testament Studies 364. London: T&T Clark, 2007.

Weima, Jeffrey A. D. *Paul the Ancient Letter Writer: An Introduction to Epistolary Analysis.* Grand Rapids: Baker Academic, 2016.

Wright, Christopher J. H. *The Mission of God: Unlocking the Bible's Grand Narrative.* Downers Grove, IL: InterVarsity Press, 2006.

Wright, Christopher J. H. *The Mission of God's People: A Biblical Theology of the Church's Mission.* Grand Rapids: Zondervan, 2010.

Wright, N. T. *The New Testament and the People of God.* Christian Origins and the Question of God 1. Minneapolis: Fortress, 1992.

Wright, N. T. *The Resurrection of the Son of God.* Christian Origins and the Question of God 3. Minneapolis: Fortress, 2003.

Part 2
The Missionary Message of 1 Peter

Chapter 7

Salvation and Judgment as Missionary Message in 1 Peter

Markus T. Klausli

Introduction

As this present volume demonstrates, the five chapters of 1 Peter provide a rich and unique repository for crafting mission theology.[1] Recent scholarship has accurately noted how Peter carefully adapted his missionary message to address the various levels of persecution his readers were experiencing.[2] For some, persecution meant social ostracization (3:1; 4:5–6); for others, slander in the public arena (2:13–16; 4:6).[3] Whatever the cause, the result was that mission has been made more difficult.[4] Yet rather than call for a "siege mentality,"[5] Peter encouraged these early Christians to boldly share their faith using a subversive strategy:[6] they must actively live out God's will[7] while being ready to share their faith with those who ask (3:15–16). To help them in this endeavor, Peter structured his letter to inform their actions and words should the opportunity present itself.[8]

This chapter examines one piece of this missionary message, namely, 1 Peter's rich presentation of God's salvation in light of the reality of God's judgment. First, I will explore how Peter described God's marvelous saving

---

[1] Hahn groups 1 Peter with the Pastoral Epistles and 2 Thessalonians. *Mission in the New Testament*, 140–42.

[2] For a summary of introductory matters similar to my own positions, see Schreiner, *1 & 2 Peter and Jude*, 3–38.

[3] For a thorough discussion of the extent of suffering in 1 Peter see Williams, *Persecution in 1 Peter*.

[4] Hahn, *Mission in the New Testament*, 141.

[5] Senior and Stuhlmueller, *Biblical Foundation for Mission*, 299.

[6] Cf. Köstenberger, who sees mission here as "more defensive than, … the Great Commission at the end of Matthew." "Mission in the General Epistles," 205. I prefer "subversive" since Peter still calls for active witness done in a careful manner. See also Brunk who uses the term "low profile mission." "Missionary Stance of the Church," 71.

[7] See Hahn, *Mission in the New Testament*, 141. On the importance of good deeds in witness, see Boyley, "1 Peter: A Mission Document?," 85; and Köstenberger, "Mission," 192.

[8] See Joseph, "Background and Implications," 330. On the function of this theological knowledge, see Akin ("Missiological Motivation," 11) who helpfully points to Schnabel, *Paul and the Early Church*, 1525.

acts as a rescue from future judgment. Second, I will show how he unpacked the implications of this rescue for his readers in view of their current accountability to God's present judgment. Since my approach is mainly biblical-theological, the findings are based on the exegesis of relevant texts and presented in a logical structure.

God's Salvation from Future Judgment

First Peter's portrayal of God's salvation is best observed within a salvation-historical framework.[9] In this section, we will first see how Peter presented God's redemption in terms of his work in eternity past, Christ's coming, and the preaching of the gospel. Next, we will explore his description of present benefits and, finally, the culmination at Christ's future return.

The clearest statement of God's saving action in eternity past is found in 1:19–20, where Peter presented Christ as the "unblemished and spotless lamb ... [who] was foreknown before the foundation of the world but was manifested in these last times for your sake."[10] The Greek word translated here as "foreknown" does not simply mean that God knew about Christ before his incarnation.[11] Instead it emphasizes how God both anticipated and even predetermined the role Christ would play as the sacrificial lamb that he would offer for humanity's sin.[12]

The terminology of "new birth" (1 Pet 1:3, cf. v. 23) highlights the necessity of such a costly sacrifice as it implies humanity's deadness toward God. Every person is "disobedient to the gospel" (4:17; cf. 2:8; 3:20; 4:1), has gone "astray" from God's ways (2:25), and is bound to "evil urges" (1:14) leading to sinful behavior (1:18; see 4:3). Thus, before their Creator, every person is "unjust" (3:18) and "ungodly" (4:18), and as a result, in danger of condemning judgment.

For a relatively short letter, 1 Peter discusses the idea of judgment surprisingly often, sometimes to warn of a final reckoning and other times to motivate ethical behavior. Our focus will be on the final reckoning before we discuss ethical behavior in the second half of the article. The most direct

---

9 Similarly, Green, *1 Peter*, 200–1. For a more recent discussion, see Green, *Vox Petri*, 316–26.
10 Unless otherwise stated, all Bible quotations are from *The New English Translation*, 2nd ed.
11 Silva, "προγινωσκω," 139.
12 See Achtemeier, 131. See also Naseri who connects this verse with "the election of the Petrine Christians" in 1:2. "Mission of Jesus as Purposed," 360.

statements of final eschatological judgment can be found in 4:5 and 17–18.[13] In 4:5, Peter assured his readers that those who persecute them for refusing to engage in evil behavior will "face a reckoning before Jesus Christ who stands ready to judge the living and the dead."[14] In 4:17–18, Peter spoke of the "judgment ... begin[ning]" with God's people[15] that will culminate against "those who are disobedient to the gospel of God"—something he illustrated by citing Proverbs 11:31 (LXX) in 4:18. In contrast, believers now participate in God's mercy (2:10), and at Christ's return they will not only receive praise (1:7) and grace from God (1:13) but also the "salvation of (their) souls" (1:9).[16]

Though God's saving acts began with Israel, even Israel's prophets knew that the nation itself was not its culmination. Instead, they anticipated a future Messiah who would suffer and be glorified to make it possible (1:10–11).[17] As both Peter and the readers were aware, these prophecies have now been fulfilled in the person of Jesus of Nazareth.

Peter portrayed Jesus's death as the centerpiece of God's redemption. Not only did he die bodily on a cross (lit. "on the tree," 2:24a)—a historical event fulfilling Old Testament prophecy (1:11)—he did so as "an innocent sufferer" (2:23; Isa 53:9),[18] implying that his death functions as a "vicarious" or "substitutionary" sacrifice able to atone for sin.[19] For example, in 1:18–19 Peter described Christ's death using Passover imagery from Exodus 12:5–7 as the "unblemished and spotless lamb" whose "precious blood ... ransomed [them] ... from [the] empty way of life inherited from [their] ancestors."[20] Elsewhere, we find assertions such as "He himself bore our sins in his body" (2:24) or "Christ also suffered once for sins, the just for the

---

13 The reference to the "day of visitation" (ESV) is another possibility (see Jobes, *1 Peter*, 172), though see Green (*Vox Petri*, 333) who understands it as God's salvation.
14 For the inclusion of "Jesus" here, see Green, 331.
15 For reasons why this refers to the final judgment, see Dubis, *Messianic Woes in First Peter*, 143–44. See the discussion in the second half of the chapter for my disagreement with his position connecting judgment to Christian persecution.
16 "Souls" here is better understood as "lives." See Davids, *A Theology of James*, 127n120.
17 See Schreiner, *1 & 2 Peter, Jude*, 71–72 for arguments that "prophets" should be taken as Old Testament rather than New Testament prophets.
18 See Davids, *Theology*, 166.
19 See Green, *Vox Christi*, 352; and Davids, *Theology*, 166. Davids also noted that Peter "quotes or alludes to Isa 53:9, 4, [12], 5, and 6 (in that order), probably using a preformed tradition of the community, perhaps a credal formula" (166).
20 Scripture references here and to the end of the paragraph come mainly from Green, *Vox Christi*, 349–53, 355.

unjust" (3:18). These references point to the fulfillment not only of the Old Testament sacrificial system (Lev 5:5–11; 6:18, 23; 14:19; 16:3–5) but also of the prophecy of the suffering servant from Isaiah 53. Currently, believers participate in this atonement as they have been "set apart by the Spirit for obedience and ... sprinkling with Jesus Christ's blood" (1:2). This covenant language from Exodus 24:1–8 marks the readers' "entr[y] into [the] new covenant through their pledge of obedience to the gospel (1 Pet 1:22) and the blood of Christ (1:19)."[21] Finally, Jesus's death serves not only as the means to rescue believers from sin's penalty but also its power. Christ died "that we may cease from sinning and live for righteousness" (2:24b; 4:1), even as it provides an example of enduring suffering (2:21). In summary, Christ's death is the path by which sinners are truly "healed" (2:24c; Isa 53:5), as it brings wandering "sheep" back to the "shepherd and guardian of [their] souls" (1 Pet 2:25; Isa 53:6).

In addition to his death, Christ's resurrection is also of central importance for believers' salvation. Not only does it provide them a firm hope of an eternal inheritance (1 Pet 1:3, 21), but it also is the occasion for the Holy Spirit to be "sent from heaven," empowering evangelists to proclaim the gospel to the readers (1:12; 4:6). Further, now that Christ is risen and in God's presence, he reigns supremely over the heavenly powers (3:21–22).[22] This means that believers need not fear the attacks of the devil (5:8). Finally, Christ's resurrection means that he cares for his earthly people by holding church leaders accountable for their spiritual care (5:1–4).

Belonging now to God, believers participate in three main benefits that transform their difficult circumstances into opportunities for fruitful witness: a restored relationship with God, a new identity and sense of purpose, and help in trials.

When they heard and embraced the gospel message (1:12, 25b), believers were restored to a relationship with God (1:21). Peter spoke of how they "obey[ed] the truth" (1:22) and were "born anew" (1:23; cf. 1:3), enabling them to "see [Christ's] value" (2:7) and "make the pledge of a good conscience to God" in baptism (3:21). This resulted in their "ransom" from sinful actions (1:18, 24; 4:4) and rescue from God's judgment (4:17–18). Having this "freedom" (2:16), they are now no longer obligated to sin (2:24;

---

21 Green, 349.

22 Though disputed, Christ's victory over evil powers seems to be the most likely subject of 3:19. For a readable overview of the issues involved, see Schreiner, *1 & 2 Peter and Jude*, 208–16.

4:1) but have received enablement to live for God (2:24b; 4:1–2, 6) and to serve the community with the gifts God has given them (4:10–11).

Connected to God, the readers' identity is as God's holy and elect people. In 1:1 Peter addressed them as "chosen sojourners of the diaspora"[23] and in 2:9 as "a chosen race." In both cases, "chosen" seems not intended to explain *how* they entered into this position but instead to describe their connection to Israel through Christ, whom God selected out of Israel to accomplish his plan of salvation (2:4, 6).[24] Borrowing language from Hosea 2:23, he described them as "God's people" in contrast to their earlier status as "not a people" (1 Pet 2:10).[25] Not only are they God's "obedient children" (1:14), they are now tasked with worship (2:6) and mission (2:9)[26] as a "royal priesthood" and a "holy nation," serving as God's dwelling place made up of "living stones" even as they follow Christ, "a living stone" and "chosen and precious cornerstone" (2:4–7).

Despite the privilege of this priestly status, Peter clarified that his readers would encounter trials in the form of persecution. These persecutions are attacks of the devil intended to drive them away from God (5:8), are difficult (4:12), cause sadness and come in various forms (1:6), and include the struggle against temptation (2:11). One form these sufferings take is the pilgrim status believers have in this world. This can be seen in the "chosen sojourners" paradox in 1:1–2 that is reiterated in 1:17. Though verses 1–2 and verse 17 use different terminology (παροικία and παρεπίδημος), they are finally brought together in 2:11, where readers are addressed "as strangers and sojourners."[27]

This tension can be seen in how their association with Christ (4:16) causes them to be "malign[ed] as evildoers" in the public square (2:12, cf. 15), "insulted for the name of Christ" (4:14), and "vilif[ied]" by former friends (4:4). Wives live in fear toward unbelieving husbands (3:1–6) as do slaves who "endur[e] hardships" at the hand of "perverse" masters (2:18). Further, as Jobes stated, some of the readers "may have been found

---

23 My translation. See Liebengood, "Participating in the Life of God," 78–79, who suggests "elect–sojourners."

24 See also Achtemeier, *1 Peter*, 163.

25 See Ok, *Constructing Ethnic Identity*, 61 and Hall, "Christian Mission in the Contemporary World," 121, who address the concerns of some recent interpreters who view negatively the appropriation of language intended for Israel for gentile first-century believers.

26 See Köstenberger "Mission," 203; and Schnabel, *Paul and the Early Church*, 1522.

27 My translation. For a helpful analogy that understands this foreign status as a kind of suffering, see Ok, "Always Ethnic, Never 'American,'" 583–95.

wanting, whether by popular opinion or by official action" (4:6).[28] Making this situation even more difficult is that they were not allowed to assimilate into the larger culture.[29]

To help them cope with these trials, Peter demonstrated how they serve God's sovereign plan because they align with what Christ endured to bring about their salvation. For slaves who "endure" suffering unjustly, he reminds them that they were actually "called" to this "since Christ also suffered for [them], leaving ... an example to follow in his steps" (2:20b–21)." He spelled out this example in 2:22–25 using a series of allusions to Isaiah 53: (1) Christ suffered innocently, i.e., not for doing anything wrong (1 Pet 2:22; Isa 53:9); (2) Christ suffered in a non-retaliatory way in that he "committed himself to God who judges justly" (1 Pet 2:23; Isa 53:7); and (3) Christ suffered to bring about salvation, as he "bore our sins in his body on the tree" (1 Pet 2:24; Isa 53:4). As believers "follow in his steps" (2:21), they can be assured of "God's favor" (1 Pet 2:19). For the present, this means bearing the distinction of one who has "shared in the sufferings of Christ" (4:13; 2:4–5, 7). For the future, it means that God will ultimately vindicate them from their enemies (4:4–5), even as he vindicated Christ in his resurrection and glorification (3:21–22). At that time, they will receive praise from Christ (1:7; 4:13), God will restore the years they have suffered (5:10), and their enemies will be forced to glorify God—on account of their works (2:12).[30] For now, however, he reminded them that "those who suffer according to the will of God [should] entrust their souls to a faithful Creator as they do good (4:19)."

Peter further encouraged them in God's sovereignty by connecting their experience with past and future saints.[31] For example, when Christian wives "do what is good and have no fear in doing so," they take up the mantle of "Sarah," Abraham's wife, "who obeyed [her husband], calling him lord" (3:6). And should believers think of themselves alone in their suffering, Peter admonished them to join their "brothers and sisters throughout the world [who] are enduring the same kinds of suffering" as they "resist [the devil]" who attempts to bring them away from their faith (5:8–9).[32]

---

28 See Jobes, *1 Peter*, 271. Elliott further clarified that this "statement ... represent(s) the position of the Gentiles that the physical death of the believers was actually a proof of their condemnation." *1 Peter*, 737.
29 Ok, "Always Ethnic," 591.
30 See our discussion above of the "day of visitation." Statements in 2:15; 3:1, 16 suggest that a form of God's vindication could take place in the present.
31 See Ok, who discusses Peter's use of "a theological and emotional narrative to [help readers] interpret their suffering." Ok, "Always Ethnic," 588.
32 For this explanation of 5:8, see Dubis, *Messianic Woes*, 183.

Finally, God's sovereignty can be seen in how suffering functions as an important part of their salvation. First, it "show[s] the proven character of [their] faith" (1:7), implying that God will not allow them to suffer any more than his will requires (1:6; 3:14, 17)[33] and that these sufferings ultimately lead to their eternal inheritance (1:3–5). Second, suffering shows the presence of the Holy Spirit (4:14). And third, suffering contributes to their sanctification by helping them be "concerned about the will of God and not human desires (4:2)."[34]

From certain statements, the future consummation of salvation is not as far off as expected. For example, he told his readers in 4:7: "The culmination of all things is near," and referred to the first coming of Christ as part of the "last times" (ἐπ'ἐσχάτου τῶν χρόνων, 1:20), which give way to "a salvation ready to be revealed in the last time" (ἐν καιρῷ ἐσχάτῳ, 1:5). Regardless of the timing, however, it is Christ's return (his "revelation," 1:7, 13; 4:13) that initiates final salvation. At this time, believers will experience three benefits. First, they will be rescued from future judgment (1:9), even as they receive a perfect "inheritance" (1:4, cf. "blessing" in 3:9), which is the final installment, so to speak, of God's grace (1:13; 5:12).[35] Second, having now been saved from God's judgment, believers can look forward to participating in Christ's glory. This eternal praise seems mainly related to overcoming suffering (1:7; 4:13; 5:1, 10),[36] though Christ will also give recognition to church leaders who have faithfully fulfilled their duties (5:4). Finally, future salvation will ensure the eternal vindication of faithful believers who have endured suffering for Christ (1:7–9; 4:13).

A Worthy Response to God's Salvation in Light of Present Judgment

In the previous section, we surveyed Peter's description of salvation and judgment in his missionary message to help believers fully understand and explain the extent of God's work in their own lives. Yet, similar to other New Testament writers, Peter saw God's salvation not merely in terms of what believers should *know* but, more importantly, what they should *do* now that they have embraced that knowledge.[37] This is no mindless legalism.

---

33 See Grudem, *1 Peter*, 67.
34 See Jobes, *1 Peter*, 265 and Achtemeier, *1 Peter*, 280.
35 Jobes, *1 Peter*, 110 refers to it as a "realiz[ation]."
36 In 1:7, it is unclear whether the praise is directed toward believers or Christ.
37 Joseph, "Background Implications," 323.

Believers have become participants in God's grace (5:12) and can look forward to its future consummation (1:13).[38] For this reason, every God-pleasing action provides not only a worthy response to this grace but also allows them to fulfill their mandate as God's chosen people in this world who "proclaim the virtues of the one who called [them] out of darkness into his marvelous light" (2:9). Thus, the heart of Peter's missionary message is that a pleasing response to God's grace has the potential to awaken interest in the gospel and provide believers with the opportunity to explain God's saving acts.[39] In the following section we will explore how this response is portrayed in terms of the pursuit of holiness and, once again, in light of the accountability of God's judgment.

Pursuit of Holiness

Peter admonished his readers to pursue holy lives based on two Old Testament passages. In 1:15–16, he first summarized and then cited Leviticus 19:2: "Like the Holy One who called you, become holy in all your conduct." Later, in 3:10–12 he cited Psalm 34:12–16 (33:13–16 LXX) from which he constructed a pathway to holiness based on the admonition to "turn away from evil and do good" (3:11a), terminology he repeated throughout the epistle (e.g., 2:15, 26; 3:6, 17).

Holy Behavior

By "doing good," Peter meant that readers should act according to godly standards and not the "empty way of life inherited from [their] ancestors" (1:18). For this reason, he admonished them to avoid evil desires and the actions resulting from them, using expressions such as "do not comply with" (1:14), "get rid of" (2:1), and "keep away from" (2:11). He encouraged them instead to practice specific behaviors that demonstrate a new life, both in public and private spheres (2:12, 20; 3:1–2). This new way of life begins with right desires such as "set hope" (1:13), "yearn … for pure, spiritual milk" (2:2), and being "devoted to good" (3:13). The person who now lives for God should be "concerned about the will of God and not human desires" (4:2) and manifest this through "self-control" (4:7), caring relationships built on love (1:22; 2:17; 4:8, 14a), service to those in the church (4:9; 5:2–3), bold yet respectful witness (2:9, 13–17; 3:15–16), and humility toward others (4:9; 5:5–6).

---

38 Grace (χάρις) in 1 Peter appears ten times and describes God's salvation from various perspectives (1:2, 10, 13; 2:19–20; 3:7; 4:10; 5:5, 10).

39 Seland noted the role of both "works" and "good works." Seland, "Resident Aliens in Mission," 566.

Holiness as Submission

One specific, though difficult, way his readers must "do good" is to be subject to those in authority. This is not a demand for blind submission.[40] Rather, it is an appeal for them to consider voluntarily how best to represent Christ in difficult situations.[41] Believers who submit to "human institutions" shame those intending to slander them before human rulers (2:14–15). Christian slaves who submit to a master causing them suffering (2:18) earn God's favor as imitators of Christ (2:19–21). Christian wives who submit to unbelieving husbands have the opportunity to win them to the gospel "without a word" (3:1).[42] Younger men in the church who submit to the "elders" who have been placed there by Christ himself, as well as those who live humbly with others, have the prospect of Christ's later exaltation (5:5–6).

Holiness and Persecution

While "doing good" plays a central role in living out the reality of God's salvation, Peter's most significant contribution is connecting doing good with enduring persecution. As a rule, upright behavior should not cause them any problems (3:13), especially before human "governors" whom God has set in place "to punish wrongdoers and praise those who do good" (2:14). Yet, many of the readers experienced various forms of persecution even though they only sought to please God and respect the social order. For this reason, Peter reminded them that as "foreigners and exiles" (2:11), they must be prepared to suffer unjustly (2:20) because they are "Christian[s]" (4:16). In this way they "share in the sufferings of Christ" (4:13; cf. 2:4, 7; 5:1) and "follow in his steps" (2:21; see also 4:1). Despite these challenges, however, Peter wanted them to know that the path through suffering also presents them with two important opportunities. The first is to experience eschatological joy in the present, the second is to bear witness for Christ.

Joy in Suffering

For some of Peter's readers, the idea of experiencing joy in suffering is nothing new (1:6–8).[43] Yet, he wanted this to be the norm so that rather than being "astonished" when persecutions come, they choose instead to "rejoice in the degree that [they] have shared in the sufferings of Christ"

---

40 See Horrell, "Fear, Hope, and Doing Good," 422.
41 See Köstenberger and Alexander, *Salvation to the Ends*, 95.
42 See Fleming, "Won Over without a Word," 59.
43 Dubis noted that the present tense verb ἀγαλλιᾶσθε (rejoice) in 1:6 can be either indicative with a present meaning or future meaning or imperative. *1 Peter*, 10.

(4:12–13). As Karen H. Jobes noted, "This does not mean that [they] should enjoy suffering per se, but undeserved suffering because of Christian faith is evidence of future eschatological deliverance."[44] By practicing this attitude now in anticipation of future glory, they will have even greater joy at Christ's return (4:13).

Bearing Witness

Most importantly for his missionary message, Peter reminded his readers that God is able to use persecution as a means for sharing Christ with others.[45] While Peter gave concrete examples of this kind of evangelistic suffering in the experience of believing slaves and believing wives (2:18–3:6),[46] the clearest statement is found in 1 Peter 3:14–16. Should believers find themselves "slander[ed] for their good conduct in Christ" instead of being afraid (3:16), he reminded them to "always be ready to give an answer to anyone who asks about the hope [they] possess."[47] Despite the challenges of this kind of witness, the fact that they found Christ through evangelists empowered by the Holy Spirit (1:12) should have assured them that the same Holy Spirit dwelling in them (4:14) would enable them for this task. Ideally, this witness will have two outcomes: first, those observing the situation will conclude that the believer has been falsely accused and the accusers put to shame (3:16; cf. 2:15), and second, all might be exposed to the hope of the gospel and receive it for themselves.[48]

God's Judgment as Motivation to Holiness

Since "good behavior" precedes witness,[49] Peter also warned his readers against the negative effects of "doing evil" (e.g., 1 Pet 3:17) and set before them a series of warnings that their actions will be held accountable before God's present judgment. In 1:17, believers are reminded that just because

---

44 Jobes, *1 Peter*, 287.
45 Fleming, "Won Over without a Word," 66. For a further discussion of the connection between suffering and mission in 1 Peter, see Köstenberger and Alexander, *Salvation to the Ends*, 96–97.
46 Horrell, "Fear, Hope, and Doing Good," 420.
47 Though the Greek word ἀπολογία translated in the NET as "give an answer" is used in the New Testament to describe situations where a defense in formal (i.e., "judicial") settings is required (Acts 22:1; 25:16), it is also used in informal settings, such as where Paul defends his actions before the Corinthians (1 Cor 1:9) or they before him (2 Cor 7:11). See Achtemeier, *1 Peter*, 233 who believes the latter is more likely here.
48 For a similar reading on the role of hope, see Feldmeier, "Die Außenseiter Als Avantgarde," 176, 178.
49 See Fagbemi, "Transformation, Proclamation and Mission," 219.

they address God as "Father" does not imply that he will ignore their evil deeds.[50] God is an "impartial" judge, and they should expect to be held to the same standard as those who do not know God, especially, now that they have been "ransomed" with the "precious blood of Christ" (1:18–19).

A further example is the citation of Psalm 34 in 1 Peter 3:10–12.[51] Here believers are admonished to "bless" rather than take revenge (3:9) since pure speech is the way to "see good days" (3:10).[52] More specifically, he entreated Christian husbands to treat their wives considerately so that "nothing will hinder [their] prayers (3:7)," something that seems to fit well with the warning in 3:12 that "the Lord's face is against those who do evil."[53] Finally, the summary at the end of 3:13–17 implies both reward and judgment aspects mentioned in the psalm: "For it is better to suffer for doing good, if God wills it, than for doing evil."

The most specific statement where Peter linked the necessity of a holy life to divine accountability is in 4:17–18. On the one hand, believers must no longer fear the final judgment coming on the "ungodly and sinner" because they are obedient "to the gospel of God" and now function as "the house of God."[54] Yet with this new status comes responsibility, since the final judgment is not simply a future day of reckoning but has now entered into the present and "begins" with them![55]

Outside of the warning to Christian husbands in 3:7, the nature of this judgment is left mostly undefined. Some interpreters understand it in terms of the persecution believers face.[56] These sufferings, as some argue, point to the unfolding of the "messianic woes"—the period of suffering expected before the return of Christ.[57]

The main problem with equating persecution with God's judgment is that it fails to address the warning function of the judgment statements we have seen above. Of the nine passages in 1 Peter where Christians are described

---

50 See Davids, *Theology*, 180.
51 Not all interpreters agree, however, that the judgment aspect in this passage should be applied to Christians. For example, Schreiner, *1 & 2 Peter, Jude*, 190–91.
52 See Carson, "1 Peter," 1037.
53 See also Achtemeier, *1 Peter*, 227 n. 90.
54 A likely reference to the imagery introduced in 2:5; see Achtemeier, *1 Peter*, 316.
55 See Köstenberger "Mission," 192–93.
56 Marshall, *1 Peter*, 156.
57 Jobes, *1 Peter*, 293. For an extensive discussion of this topic, particularly a treatment of 4:17, see Dubis, *Messianic Woes*, 142–62. For a full treatment of the problems in describing suffering in 1 Peter in terms of the messianic woes, see Klausli, "The Question of the Messianic Woes."

to be on the receiving end of divine judgment (1:7, 17; 2:18–20; 3:7; 3:10–12; 4:13; 5:4, 5), the majority are linked to ethical admonitions to do good. Thus, to connect God's judgment to persecution would put believers in an impossible situation since the good they do to avoid God's judgment would be what leads to the persecutions that are now revealed to be his judgment!

Some interpreters try to avoid this conundrum by seeing the persecution-judgment idea as the means God uses to identify true believers in the community.[58] Yet, the judgment in 4:17 seems primarily intended to secure God-honoring behavior and effective witness in the present, especially as it relates to the admonition in 4:15–16.[59] Further, to view this judgment in terms of the messianic woes falters primarily on the discrepancy between the sufferings described in 1 Peter and the sufferings depicted in many of the background texts.[60] As Kelly D. Liebengood commented: "Curiously, we find none of this language in 1 Peter. Instead, the suffering in 1 Peter is paradigmatically framed as fiery πειρασμοί."[61]

Conclusion

In this chapter, we have briefly explored how God's salvation and judgment lie at the heart of 1 Peter's missionary message. Because of potential persecution, Peter focused on equipping his readers to engage the surrounding culture not only by proclaiming the gospel but also by living a holy life. So that they will know what to say when they have the opportunity to witness, Peter provided them with a compact survey of God's gracious provision of salvation. He explained how God, in eternity past, planned for Christ to be the sacrifice for humanity's sin and then brought it to completion by fulfilling in Christ the message of Israel's prophets and sending out evangelists through the Holy Spirit. Peter then focused on the benefits of this salvation enjoyed by believers, which include a restored relationship to God, a new identity, help in suffering, and the hope of salvation's final consummation.

Yet, in 1 Peter's missionary message, the opportunity to share about this salvation will most likely come when outsiders respond either positively or negatively to the way believers live out their faith. For this reason, Peter spent a significant amount of time clarifying a worthy response to all that God has done. This response consists of orienting oneself toward God's

---

58　This is Jobes's solution to the conundrum noted above. See *1 Peter*, 293–94.
59　See the comment on ὅτι in 4:17 in Dubis, *1 Peter*, 153–54.
60　See Liebengood, *Eschatology of 1 Peter*, 121.
61　Liebengood, 122.

grace and pursuing a holy life, not only in terms of avoiding evil but also in terms of doing the good that God requires.

On both sides of the salvation message, judgment plays a prominent role. First, Peter helped them understand how Christ's sacrifice rescues believers from the prospect of standing before God on the last day. Second, he sought to motivate them to be godly witnesses by making them aware of the impartial Judge who even now holds them accountable for their present actions.

This dual focus of salvation and judgment in 1 Peter's missionary message is as important as ever for today's global church. First, it calls all Christians to eschew a focus on either knowledge or action and to contemplate how to bring both of these aspects of salvation into balance to help the gospel progress. Second, it brings a new awareness of the greatness of God's grace that saves us from condemnation even as it motivates his children toward a holy life and fruitful witness.

Bibliography

Achtemeier, Paul J. *1 Peter*. Hermeneia, ed. Helmut Koester, et al. Minneapolis: Augsburg Fortress, 1996.

Akin, Paul. "The Missiological Motivation of 1 Peter." *Southern Baptist Journal of Theology* 23, no. 3 (2019): 7–21.

Boyley, Mark. "1 Peter: A Mission Document?" *Reformed Theological Review* 63, no. 2 (2004): 72–86.

Brunk, George R., III. "The Missionary Stance of the Church in 1 Peter." In *Mission Focus: Current Issues*, edited by Wilbert R. Shenk, 70–81. Scottdale, PA: Herald Press, 1980.

Carson, D. A. "1 Peter." In *Commentary on the New Testament Use of the Old Testament*, ed. G. K. Beale and D. A. Carson, 1015–47. Grand Rapids: Baker Academic, 2007. Accordance Version.

Danker, Frederick W., Walter Bauer, William F. Arndt, and F. Wilbur Gingrich. *Greek-English Lexicon of the New Testament and Other Early Christian Literature*. 3rd ed. Chicago: University of Chicago Press, 2000.

Davids, Peter H. *A Theology of James, Peter, and Jude*. Biblical Theology of the New Testament, edited by Andreas J. Köstenberger. Grand Rapids: Zondervan, 2014.

Dubis, Mark. *1 Peter: A Handbook on the Greek Text*. Baylor Handbook on the Greek New Testament, edited by Martin M. Culy. Waco, TX: Baylor University Press, 2010.

Dubis, Mark. *Messianic Woes in First Peter: Suffering and Eschatology in 1 Peter 4:12–19*. Studies in Biblical Literature 33. New York: Lang, 2002.

Elliott, John H. *1 Peter. A New Translation with Introduction and Commentary*. Anchor Bible 37B. New York: Doubleday, 2000.

Fagbemi, Stephen Ayodeji A. "Transformation, Proclamation and Mission in the New Testament: Examining the Case of I Peter." *Transformation* 27, no. 3 (2010): 209–23.

Feldmeier, Reinhard. "Die Außenseiter als Avantgarde: Gesellschaftliche Ausgrenzung als missionarische Chance nach dem 1. Petrusbrief." In *Persuasion and Dissuasion in Early Christianity, Ancient Judaism, and Hellenism*, 161–78. Contributions to Biblical Exegesis & Theology 33. Leuven: Peeters, 2003.

Fleming, Dean. "'Won Over without a Word': Holiness and the Church's Missional Identity in 1 Peter." *Wesleyan Theological Journal* 29, no. 1 (2014): 50–66.

Green, Gene L. *Vox Petri: A Theology of Peter*. Eugene, OR: Cascade Books, 2020.

Green, Joel B. *1 Peter*. Two Horizons New Testament Commentary, ed. Joel B. Green and Max Turner. Grand Rapids: Eerdmans, 2007.

Grudem, Wayne A. *1 Peter: An Introduction and Commentary*. Tyndale New Testament Commentaries, ed. Leon Morris. Downers Grove, IL: InterVarsity Press, 1988. Logos Version.

Hahn, Ferdinand. *Mission in the New Testament*. Translated by Frank Clarke. Studies in Biblical Theology 47. Naperville, IL: Allenson, 1965.

Hall, Joshua D. "Christian Mission in the Contemporary World: A Dialogue between 1 Peter and Postcolonial Critics." *Horizons in Biblical Theology* 43, no. 2 (2021): 119–45.

Horrell, David G. "Fear, Hope, and Doing Good: Wives as a Paradigm of Mission in 1 Peter." *Estudios Bíblicos* 73, no. 3 (2015): 409–29.

Jobes, Karen H. *1 Peter*. Baker Exegetical Commentary on the New Testament. Grand Rapids: Baker Academic, 2005.

Joseph, Abson Prédestin. "The Background and Implications of the Language of New Birth in 1 Peter." *Journal of Theological Interpretation* 15, no. 2 (2021): 318–32.

Klausli, Markus T. "The Question of the Messianic Woes in 1 Peter." PhD diss., Dallas Theological Seminary, 2007.

Köstenberger, Andreas J. "Mission in the General Epistles." In *Mission in the New Testament: An Evangelical Approach*, edited by William J. Larkin Jr. and Joel F. Williams, 189–206. American Society of Missiology 27. Maryknoll, NY: Orbis Books, 1998.

Köstenberger, Andreas J., and T. Desmond Alexander. *Salvation to the Ends of the Earth: A Biblical Theology of Mission.* 2nd ed. New Studies in Biblical Theology 53, edited by D. A. Carson. Downers Grove, IL: IVP Academic, 2020. Logos Version.

Liebengood, Kelly D. *The Eschatology of 1 Peter: Considering the Influence of Zechariah 9–14.* Society for New Testament Studies Monograph Series 157. Cambridge: Cambridge University Press, 2014.

Liebengood, Kelly D. "Participating in the Life of God: Exploring the Trinitarian Foundation of 1 Peter's Missional Identity." *Midwestern Journal of Theology* 15, no. 2 (2016): 74–90.

Marshall, I. Howard. *1 Peter.* IVP New Testament Commentary, ed. Grant R. Osborne. Downers Grove, IL: InterVarsity Press, 1991.

Naseri, Christopher. "The Mission of Jesus as Purposed by God in 1 Peter 1:18–20 and Its Resonance among African Christians." In *A Biblical Approach to Mission in Context: A Festschrift in Honor of Sr. Prof. Teresa Okure, SHCJ*, edited by Michael Ufok Udoekpo, 352–65. Eugene, OR: Wipf & Stock, 2022.

Ok, Janette H. "Always Ethnic, Never 'American': Reading 1 Peter through the Lens of the 'Perpetual Foreigner' Stereotype." In *T&T Clark Handbook of Asian American Biblical Hermeneutics*, edited by Uriah Y. Kim and Seung Ai Yang, 583–95. London: T&T Clark, 2019.

Ok, Janette H. *Constructing Ethnic Identity in 1 Peter: Who You Are No Longer.* Library of New Testament Studies 645. London: T&T Clark, 2021.

Schnabel, Eckhard J. *Paul and the Early Church.* Vol. 2 of *Early Christian Mission.* Downers Grove, IL: InterVarsity Press, 2004.

Schreiner, Thomas R. *1 & 2 Peter and Jude.* Christian Standard Commentary 37. Nashville: Holman Reference, 2020.

Seland, Torrey. "Resident Aliens in Mission: Missional Practices in the Emerging Church of 1 Peter." *Bulletin of Biblical Research* 19, no. 4 (2009): 565–89.

Senior, Donald, and Carroll Stuhlmueller. *The Biblical Foundation for Mission.* London: Orbis Books, 1983.

Silva, Moisés, ed. *New International Dictionary of New Testament Theology and Exegesis.* 2nd ed. 5 vols. Grand Rapids: Zondervan, 2014.

Williams, Travis B. *Persecution in 1 Peter: Differentiating and Contextualizing Early Christian Suffering.* Supplements to Novum Testamentum 145. Leiden: Brill, 2012.

Chapter 8

The Missiological Message of Hope in 1 Peter

Sarah Lunsford

As Jurgen Moltmann said in his highly influential *Theology of Hope*, "Christianity is eschatology, is hope… the passionate suffering and passionate longing kindled by the Messiah."[1] First Peter presents this very picture of hope—passionate suffering and passionate longing. The enigmatic hope Peter presents, a hope that thrives in and through suffering, is a thoroughly missiological concept.

For many New Testament scholars, the missiological implications in 1 Peter are limited to 3:15, where he said to be "ready at any time to give a defense to anyone who asks you for a reason for the hope that is in you."[2] However, Peter pointed his readers to a much larger doctrine of hope through his numerous references and allusions to the Old Testament, a hope that is richly missiological and brings a depth and coherence to the epistle's various elements.

In this chapter, we will explore Peter's message about the missiological nature of our hope in the covenantal promise of God for a blessing, a people, and a land as a key aspect to the *missio Dei*; the confident assurance of our faith-like hope in the accomplished work of Christ; and our missional identity as exiles. We will then discuss the testimony of our hope including the missiological purpose for our continued suffering; the ways that our hope is made visible through our ethical conduct, our praise, and our community of faith; and the missiological account we can offer the world for the hope we have, even amid our suffering.

The Missiological Nature of Our Hope

Peter wrote his first epistle to discuss the reality of Christian suffering while anchoring the subject in a biblical understanding of hope.[3] He described the suffering that comes from direct persecution against Christians, as well as the suffering we often face at the hands of society's power structures—

---

1 Moltmann, *Jurgen Moltmann*, 9.
2 All Scripture quotations are taken from the CSB version.
3 Köstenberger and Goswell, *Biblical Theology*, 637.

governments, masters, and husbands. As a result of the fall of man, there are no perfect power structures. A cursory view of world history will show the vast suffering caused by most governments through wars, dictatorships, genocides, injustice, nepotism, exploitation, and oppression of the weak and marginalized. While governments are meant to protect the rights of their citizens (2:14), even the best can be negligent of or blind to certain causes. Likewise, masters and employers are often (if not usually) prone to exploit workers for personal gain, including child labor, sweatshops, slave trafficking, and excessive working hours with unlivable wage compensation.[4] Similarly, most husbands throughout global history would be categorized as abusive to their wives and children by modern standards.[5] The world at large has generally considered domestic violence to be an insignificant issue,[6] with many cultures and religious teachings worldwide encouraging violence as a proper means of maintaining household authority over the already weak and vulnerable members of the family.[7] Each of these authority structures are meant to serve, to protect, and to provide justice (2:13), but in this sin-cursed world, most authority figures fail to protect their citizens, particularly the most vulnerable, from suffering.

Even as Peter addressed some of the most common sources of suffering in this world, he enigmatically pointed his readers to godly living standards and hope, despite the most hopeless environments. Peter's moral code of holy living is not separate from his theme of hope in suffering. The persecution, injustice, false condemnations (2:12), beatings (2:20), and fear (3:6) that power figures can inspire in us is the kind of hope Peter described.

The Covenantal Promise of God and the Missio Dei
First Peter interacts with the Old Testament more than any other New Testament book of its size, other than possibly Revelation.[8] Rather than give

---

[4] See for instance the 2022 report on "Global Estimates of Modern Slavery."

[5] For example, family and domestic violence is a common problem in the United States (a nation that largely holds to a Judeo-Christian ethic), affecting an estimated 10 million people every year (Huecker, King, Jordan, et al. "Domestic Violence"). As many as one in four women in the USA will experience severe physical violence by an intimate partner in their lifetime (Leemis, Friar, Khatiwada, et.al."National Intimate Partner and Sexual Violence").

[6] Much domestic abuse globally is not even considered "abuse" by many cultural standards and is considered too low of a priority to garner thorough analysis and research (See the UN call for further research on global domestic violence, "Examining Domestic Violence").

[7] Fortune and Enger, "Violence against Women."

[8] Vanhoozer, *Dictionary for Theological Interpretation*, 583.

a thorough Pauline-type treatise on the nature of our hope, Peter pointed the reader back to rich, foundational teachings. There are significant ties to Isaiah 54, Ezekiel 36, and Psalm 41, wherein the Lord encourages his suffering people that his protection and blessings will vindicate them.[9] Peter referenced Old Testament narrative typology, sharing lexical and plot parallels, in a way that clearly pointed his readers to the covenantal promise of God as their source of hope.

In the creation mandate, God promised a blessing, a fruitful lineage or seed, and a land or inheritance (Gen 1:28; 2:17). This is repeated in the covenants with Noah (Gen 9:1–2, 7) and with Abraham (Gen 12:1–3).[10] Throughout the grand narrative of Scripture, from creation and fall to redemption and consummation, we see that God has a clear and purposeful trajectory toward fulfilling this tri-part promise.[11] In fact, the movement of God throughout history to fulfill this promise is the *missio Dei*.[12]

The missiological nature of the Abrahamic covenant is well known: "that the nations might be blessed" (Gen 12:3).[13] God blessed Abraham and Israel, his chosen people and kingdom of priests, so that they would serve as a light of testimony and an avenue of blessing to the nations (Exod 19:5–6). The promised blessing relates to glory and honor, which we see in the glorification of Christ as a guarantee of our own future glory. This glorification of Christ (1 Pet 1:21) refers to the resurrection (1:11; cf. 5:1, 4, 10; also Luke 24:26; 1 Cor 15:40–43; Phil 3:21) as well as the correlated honor (cf. 1 Pet 1:7–8; 2:12; 4:11, 16).[14] Our present blessing is spiritual (Eph 1:3) in our salvation through Christ, but our ultimate blessing is eschatological as we await the glory that comes with the return of Christ.[15]

Christ also fulfills God's promise of fruitful lineage as he is the promised seed. Peter said in 1:3 that the Father has *birthed us* into a living hope, a new family, a new community, and new people. "Just as biological generation

---

9 Joseph, "Background and Implications," 318–32.

10 Postell, Bar, and Soref, *Reading Moses*, 23, 26.

11 Bird, *Evangelical Theology*, 274.

12 See Köstenberger and Goswell, *Biblical Theology*, 108–10 for a more complete position on the three-fold promises of God, and see Wright, *Mission of God*, for a comprehensive argument for the *missio Dei* as the backbone for the Grand Narrative of Scripture.

13 See Kaiser, "Israel's Missionary Call," 10–16 as an early treatment on the missional blessing of Abraham. See Wright, *Mission of God's People*, 63–81; and Wright, *Mission of God*, chs. 6, 7, 14 for a more complete exploration.

14 Keener, *1 Peter*, 110.

15 Mbuvi, *Temple, Exile and Identity*, 128.

brings biological life, so regeneration from an immortal seed (1:23), thus becoming the Father's children (1:14), brings new eternal life."[16] When we are birthed into God's family, we are connected to an ancient heritage with a shared history and a common hope to sustain us.[17] In this family of God, birthed into a living hope while living as exiles and pilgrims, we receive both the suffering and the promise common to his people.[18]

In this new family of promise, we have God as our Father, which includes his provision, protection, and justice.[19] It is God the Father who judges (1:17; also 2:23; 4:5, 17–18): "The father by whose power the audience is being guarded (1:5) is the just judge into whose hands Jesus entrusted his life (2:23) and the faithful and trustworthy creator to whom the audience is urged to commit their lives for safekeeping (3:17; 4:19)."[20]

This world is cruel and painful, unfair and hopeless. Peter offers us the hope that our suffering will end soon when Christ returns and ushers in the coming judgment. When Christ comes to judge the living and the dead, we the believing household of God will be saved, as the ark of Noah saved his believing household from judgment (3:20). Not only will we be saved through the secured work of Christ, but we will finally receive justice. Peter offered hope that those who have mistreated believers in their quest for self-aggrandizement, whether intentionally or as a negligent consequence of their selfish pursuits, will be held accountable (4:5). When we are born into the family of God, our Father-Judge, we have hope that our suffering will be vindicated.

Being born into the family of God includes the promise of a sure inheritance (*klēronomia* 1:4). This inheritance is the land that God promised to Israel (Num 32:19; Deut 2:12; 12:9; 25:19; 26:1; Josh 11:23; Ps 105:11; Acts 7:5), but "we also see in the NT that the language of inheriting the kingdom is another way of saying that believers will receive eternal life (cf. Matt 19:29; 25:34; Mark 10:17; Luke 10:25; 18:18; 1 Cor 6:9–10; Gal 5:21)."[21] The early church was likely discouraged that the long-awaited

---

16 Keener, 65.
17 Kaalund, *Reading Hebrews and 1 Peter*, 120.
18 "Violent separations characterize diasporas… . These fissures, often economically motivated, demonstrate the far-reaching effects of the power dynamics that accompany the creation of diasporas. However, such separations did not destroy family; they simply redefined family." Kaalund, 52.
19 Joseph, "Background and Implications," 325.
20 Joseph, 325.
21 Schreiner, *1 & 2 Peter and Jude*, 54.

hope for the promise of God was still a distant reality. Peter established their hope in the missiological nature of the promise of God by pointing their eyes to their future inheritance (1 Pet 1:4) and to their future glory in the coming kingdom (1:21–23; 3:22; 4:13; 5:10). Just as Abraham understood the promise to refer most fully to the heavenly city (Heb 11:13–16), so also Peter pointed to believers' eschatological hope for inheritance (see Gal 3:18; 4:30; Eph 1:11, 14; 5:5; Col 1:12; 3:24) and to a new heaven and new earth (see 2 Pet 3:13; Rev 21:1–22:5).

Our Faith-like Hope in the Work of Christ

In 1 Peter 1:3, Peter wrote that God the Father "has given us new birth into a living hope through the resurrection of Jesus Christ from the dead." Only a living God, the Creator God and the resurrected Messiah, can offer us a living hope.[22] This living hope (*zōsan*) stands in contrast with the dead or futile hope of this world (cf. Eph 2:12; 1 Thess 4:13).[23] In 1 Peter 1:13, he said, "Set your hope completely on the grace to be brought to you at the revelation of Jesus Christ,"[24] and in 1 Peter 1:21, he argued that since God raised Jesus from the dead and gave him glory, "your faith and *hope* are in God." Peter was a firsthand witness to both the resurrection (5:1) and the glory of the transfiguration of Christ (2 Pet 1:16–18). It is through this trustworthy testimony that our hope is assured in Christ. Clearly, Peter grounds our hope in Christ. "The vindication and glorification of Christ after his sufferings (see Isa 52:13) is the paradigm for believers. As God's exiled people they suffer now, but their future hope is resurrection and glorification."[25]

The resurrection of Christ anchors our hope from a wishful dream (hope) to an assured expectation (faith-hope). While Peter used the common New Testament Greek word for hope (*elpis*), many scholars have noted that Peter used hope (*elpis*) in a way that is nearly synonymous with faith (*pistis*)[26]

---

22 Vanhoozer, *Biblical Theology*, 306. Vanhoozer continued, "All promises made in the name of other gods will fail (Jer. 14:22)."

23 "In Greek thought, the despair of this life is followed only by the unending night of death.... . This Greek thought is not unlike the existentialist and materialistic philosophy apparent today." Jobes, *1 Peter*, 91. Jobes noted that in *Oedipus* 121a.15, Sophocles says that it is best not to be born at all or to die at birth, and in *Fifth Epigram* 4–6, Catullus writes that our lifetime of sunrises and sunsets leads us only to one endless night of sleep.

24 Keener summarized the three commands in this verse: (1) keep ready or gird your minds, (2) be disciplined or watchful (cf. 5:8), and (3) hope, which is the main imperative. "They could function as three related commands, but much more likely, one expresses hope by keeping ready and disciplined." Keener, *1 Peter*, 93.

25 Schreiner, *1 & 2 Peter*, 71.

26 For example: Vanhoozer, *Dictionary*, 306; and Schreiner, *1 & 2 Peter*, 71.

because of the level of assurance we have in the future reality. As Moltmann described it,

> Hope is nothing else than the expectation of those things which faith has believed to have been truly promised by God. Thus, faith believes God to be true, hope awaits the time when this truth shall be manifested; faith believes that he is our Father, hope anticipates that he will ever show himself to be a Father towards us; faith believes that eternal life has been given to us, hope anticipates that it will sometime be revealed; faith is the foundation upon which hope rests, hope nourishes and sustains faith.[27]

Our Missional Identity as Exiles

When Peter repeatedly referred to his readers as "exiles" (*parepidēmos* in 1:1, cf. 1:17; Heb 11:13; *paroikos* in 2:11; cf. Acts 7:6, 20; Eph 2:19), he was making a purposeful connection to the repeated stories of exile in the Old Testament[28] and was thus pointing toward the dominant theme of the promise of God in the Old Testament. Peter likewise referred to believers as "living stones" in the new temple of God, connecting the missiological nature of the New Testament church to the Old Testament promise of blessing for the nations.[29]

Peter set his teaching on hope in the most hopeless of contexts. In the ancient world, the inheritance of land was the primary means for increasing one's wealth, security, and social status. To be in exile or diaspora is to be stripped of your honor (blessing), separated from your people (lineage), and impoverished by the loss of your land.[30] Peter's Jewish readers remembered that Israel had been "ravished, defiled, and defaced successively by the Assyrians, Babylonians, Persians, Ptolemies, Seleucids, and Romans"[31] They understood that his references to exile pointed to God's promise and its relationship to both faith and hope.

---

27 Moltmann, *Collected Readings*, 12.
28 Consider another example: "And if we consider the principle of 'deeds of the fathers as a sign to the sons' (*ma'asei avot, siman l'banim*), Adam's story *never was intended* to warn Israel from following in Adam's footsteps... . Rather, Adam's story *is intended to be* a prophecy that Israel will follow in Adam's footsteps." Postell, Bar, and Soref, *Reading Moses*, 26. Emphasis in original.
29 1 Peter 2:5, 9.
30 Jobes, *1 Peter*, 92.
31 Jobes, 92.

The Old Testament accounts always connect the promise of God with the faith of his people. Adam was offered blessing, fruitful lineage (seed), and land, but as a consequence of his sin, he was exiled from the garden. Under Abraham and Moses, we see God's people living under a worldly system (Egypt) and being expelled because their faith set them apart. The exodus from Egypt was meant to elicit a faith response from Israel (Exod 14:31; 19:9; Num 14:11; 20:12; Deut 1:32; 9:23). Moses often predicted the future exiles of Israel that would come about as a result of their lost faith.[32] Peter's allusions to the Old Testament teachings about our faith in the promises are described more explicitly in Hebrews 11:9–10, where the author reflected on how Abraham understood the promise of God to be a heavenly hope.[33] "By faith Abraham, when he was called, obeyed and set out for a place that he was going to receive as an inheritance.... By faith he stayed as a foreigner in the land of promise, living in tents as did Isaac and Jacob, coheirs of the same promise. For he was looking forward to the city that has foundations, whose architect and builder is God." Abraham lived in the promised land as an exile because he anticipated that God's blessing, fruitful family, and land/inheritance ultimately represented a future reality in the next life. His faith was in an eschatological hope.

Peter's abundant Old Testament allusions and references ground our present hope in the promises of God. Though we suffer as foreigners under a corrupt regime in this world, we have hope in the blessing, the family, and the inheritance. The redemption and consummation of this fallen creation into a glorified family of God ruling over a new heaven and new earth is the *missio Dei*, the grand uniting theme of all Scripture. The nature of our hope is our assurance in Christ that God's mission to fulfill his promise is a certain future reality.

---

32 Postell, Bar, and Soref, *Reading Moses*, 26.

33 Hebrews and 1 Peter share a multitude of parallels due to a shared reliance on the Old Testament, a similar audience with a strong understanding of the Old Testament, and a related historical context of persecution. They share several key Greek words that are used nowhere else in Scripture and contain numerous parallels in thought and argument. While Peter alluded to Old Testament lessons, the author of Hebrews argued the same points more explicitly. For this reason, while Peter alluded to this argument through literary analogy, we can look to Hebrews for a more directly argued position on the way Abraham's faith in the promises played out in his choice to live as an exile in the promised land.

The Missiological Testimony of Our Hope

The Missiological Purpose for Our Shared Suffering with Christ
As Peter wrote to build believers' hope in the promises of God accomplished through the work of Christ (the *missio Dei*), he frequently pointed to their shared suffering with Christ (2:21–24; 3:18; 4:1–2, 13–19). How does suffering with Christ build our hope or provide us with a defense when we are called to account for our hope? How is his suffering a comfort? There are several levels to this answer. The most apparent is that we are comforted that we are not alone in our temptations and challenges (cf. Heb 4:15). We also see in 1 Peter 3:17 that it is better to suffer for doing good because Christ suffered with the same purpose (3:18) and because following his example is the path to victory.[34] A third reason that suffering with Christ brings us hope is because it disproves the common philosophy that suffering is the direct judgment of God against us as Job's friends assumed. Christ was perfect and without sin, and yet he suffered. Therefore, if we are suffering for doing good, our suffering does not reflect God's judgment upon us. Another point of comfort is that Christ's suffering led to his victory over death and that now all authorities and powers have been made subject to Christ (3:22). "The same word for the subjection of hostile powers is used to urge slaves and wives to submit" (2:18–3:6).[35] Thus we can hope in our shared sufferings with Christ because they portend a shared victory; we can submit to injustice and suffering, knowing that those same powers are subject to Christ.

While all these reasons to take hope in our shared suffering with Christ are significant, there remains the vital missiological element of our shared *purpose* for suffering with Christ. If Christ's suffering was meant to secure our promises, then why do we still suffer? Why do we continue in exile when the promises have been won? We find that Peter gave a direct answer to this question in his second epistle: "The Lord does not delay his promise, as some understand delay, but is patient with you, not wanting any to perish but all to come to repentance" (2 Pet 3:9; cf. 3:15).

We share in Christ's mission to bring the nations to repentance, to share the promises of God with the lost, dying, and hopeless. His suffering was salvific, but it was also a light of testimony in the way he willingly submitted to live among us and to suffer along with us, experiencing every temptation.

---
34 Jobes, *1 Peter*, 217.
35 Vanhoozer, *Dictionary*, 582.

He is Immanuel, God-with-us, the God who tabernacles among his people. In the same way, we are the living stones of a spiritual house (2:5) bearing testimony to the name of God amid the nations.

Paul said in Colossians 1:24, "Now I rejoice in my sufferings for you, and I am completing in my flesh what is lacking in Christ's afflictions." Our sufferings do not add to the redemption wrought by Christ, but rather, our sufferings are a living and present witness to our ministry as a holy priesthood, bearing testimony to the promises secured in Christ (cf. 2 Cor 1:5–6).[36] Just as God called (*kalesanta*) us "out of darkness into his marvelous light" (2:9), he also calls us to suffer with patience and meekness, following the example of Christ (2:21; 3:9; 5:10). In so doing, we serve as his kingdom of priests, bearing witness to the light in the darkness.

Our Hope Made Visible

We have said thus far that the object of our hope is missiologically grounded in the promises of God, and we are called to share in the sufferings of Christ, participating in his mission to bring the nations to repentance. This brings us back to the key verse, 1 Peter 3:15, which says that we must be "ready at any time to give a defense to anyone who asks you for a reason for the hope that is in you." Why would anyone ask about someone's hope? How would they see evidence of a person's internal frame of mind, and why would it draw attention? How is our hope revealed? Peter demonstrated that our hope, which shines brightest in the darkness of suffering, is seen through our ethics, our praise, and our community.

Peter urged believers to respond to suffering and injustice with humility and respect.[37] This kind of response to mistreatment is startlingly out-of-alignment with this world's values and draws attention to itself. The natural human response is either despair and hopelessness or vengeance, returning evil for evil (3:9). When believers continue to do good and to show respect even to their oppressors, their hope is revealed, shining like a light of testimony. Peter said that submission offers a nonverbal testimony that might lead others to salvation (3:1). This is why Peter urges us to operate from a clear conscience, so that our submission to suffering is not mistaken for submission to a well-deserved penalty, and thus our testimony is made known.[38]

---

36 Piper, "Why God Appoints Suffering," 91–110.
37 Jobes, *1 Peter*, 212.
38 Jobes, 212.

It is important to note that submission to injustice can be done in a way that undermines our missiological testimony to hope. If we place our hope completely in the future eschaton and lay down in apathetic resignation toward the sin and injustice of this world, we reflect the sin of hopelessness rather than the testimony of hope in the kingdom of God.[39] Christ died to overcome the effects of the fall, and God's judgment against mistreatment, oppression, and abuse are severe. God forbid that we submit to all powers and authorities in a manner that enables evil to thrive.[40] "Hope is discontent with the present, personally and structurally, unwilling to remain wounded and wounding. The remedy includes corporate, personal, and cosmic dimensions, all integral to God's salvation (Rom 8:19, 22). Hope derives from the Messiah's cumulative work and thus experiences the tension between present and future blessings."[41]

Rather, we suffer all the more because we side with God in opposition to the reign of sin and death, in battle against the effects of the fall.[42] "Hopeful Christians should be diligent servants in the world, manifesting the gospel's hope in their vocations. As new creations foreshadowing the new creation, Christians should be means of gracious change to the communities and structures of the age, calling others to join in mercy and justice now and hope for the culminative justice and renewal."[43]

Our hope is also revealed through our testimony of praise. In 1 Peter 2:5, we are called the living stones of a spiritual house and a holy priesthood for the purpose of offering up spiritual sacrifices. Christopher Wright argued that Peter is talking about spiritual offerings of praise—"so that you may proclaim the praises of the one who called you out of darkness into his marvelous light" (2:9). The word that Peter used for "proclaims" (*exangellō*) is also used in Psalm 9:14, "so that I may declare all your praises" and is always used in the context of public worship (Pss 71:15; 73:28; 79:13; 107:22).[44] "And Isaiah, like Peter, envisaged such praise as the responsibility of God's people *with the clear intention of drawing other people to do the same.*"[45] In this way, our testimony of hope, as seen through our sacrifice of praise

---

39 Moltmann, *Collected Readings*, 14.
40 Kaalund, *Reading Hebrews and 1 Peter*, 125–27.
41 Vanhoozer, *Dictionary*, 306.
42 Moltmann, *Collected Readings*, 13.
43 Vanhoozer, *Dictionary*, 307.
44 Wright, *Mission of God's People*, 250.
45 Wright, 250, emphasis his.

through suffering, leads the nations to likewise praise. Live such good lives among the nations that "when they slander you as evildoers, they will observe your good works and will glorify God on the day he visits" (1 Pet 2:12).[46]

Our inner hope is revealed through our ethical behavior, our praise, and our community of faith. When Peter said to give a defense for the hope that is in you, he used the plural form of "you," meaning something more like "the hope that is *among* you." We will be asked to explain the shared hope that is apparent within the community of faith.[47] In the household of faith, we are motivated to bring honor rather than dishonor upon our family name.[48] Peter told believers living in shared exile[49] to live lives of *love* (1:8, 22–23; 2:1; 4:8; 5:14), seek peace and pursue it (3:10–11), be hospitable (4:9), and serve one another for the glory of God (4:10–11).[50] As Jesus said in John 13:35, our love for one another bears testimony to our bond in the family of God and to our shared hope in his promises.

The Missiological Account for Our Hope

When Peter told believers to give a defense for our hope, he began with another missiological allusion. He said not to be afraid or intimidated by false accusations or hurtful authority figures but instead "in your hearts regard Christ the Lord as holy," a phrase which refers to Isaiah 8:13, "You are to regard only the Lord of Armies as holy. Only he should be feared."[51] Wright said that we are called to be witnesses, just as Israel was, testifying "to the truth of the biblical story of redemption, with its warning of judgment and hope of glory."[52]

In a world that is buried in hopelessness and despair, we are called to be a beacon of hope, shining a light in the darkness. When our behavior reveals that light of hope within us, and we are asked to explain it, then we point to the object of our hope guaranteed in Christ. We share the story of God's mission to redeem and restore a fallen and rebellious world through the

---

46 Similarly, Jobes says, "Doxology provides the context for Christians' new life in Christ (1:3–5) because both their experience of suffering grief in trials (1:6–7) and their present and ultimate salvation is the goal not only of their faith but also of the plan of God as revealed to the prophets (1:8–12)." *1 Peter*, 86.
47 Keener, *1 Peter*, 260; and Jobes, *1 Peter*, 211.
48 Kaalund, *Reading Hebrews and 1 Peter*, 128.
49 Vanhoozer, *Dictionary*, 582.
50 Köstenberger and Goswell, *Biblical Theology*, 639.
51 Keener, *1 Peter*, 260.
52 Wright, *Mission of God's People*, 279.

death and resurrection of Christ. To those who suffer under the cruel weight of injustice and neglect at the hands of their government, their employer, or their own family, we offer the hope of forgiveness and justice. To those who are alienated from their people and homeland, we present the hope of a Father and a people who willingly live in exile for the sake of welcoming the refugee into a new home. To those who endlessly pursue glory and honor but feel the sting of shame, we offer our respect for the Lord's sake and describe the blessing that can be theirs in Christ. To those who are weary in their work to build their wealth and to those who have everything, we offer an eternal inheritance and all the security that comes with being adopted into the family of God. We willingly and eagerly give a defense for the hope within us so that perhaps we can save them from giving a defense before the Judge on the day of judgment.[53]

Conclusion

Peter tells us to be prepared to give an account for the hope that is in us. The hope we have is rooted in the mission of God to bring us into his promised blessing, family, and inheritance, secured for us through the mission of Christ and revealed in us through our ethical response to suffering and injustice, our sacrifices of praise, and our loving community of faith. Therefore, "with your minds ready for action, be sober-minded and set your hope completely on the grace to be brought to you at the revelation of Jesus Christ." (1:13) This is a reference to pulling up a robe in order to facilitate acts of service (Eph 6:14) like in urgent prophetic missions (2 Kgs 4:29; 9:1; Jer 1:17) and in an exodus context (Exod 12:11)[54]. Thus, Peter is telling us, as those in exile, to gird our minds with hope in Christ's coming and in the ultimate fulfillment of God's promises, ready to run with our role in the mission of God. We speak our hope into a hurting and suffering world that is hungry for a blessing, a people, and a home. We speak it because this promise is the heart of the mission of God, assured in Christ, to which he has called us to serve as priests to bear a light of witness in the darkness and to be a living example of the Immanuel God who suffers for the sake of redeeming the lost.

---

53 Cf. 3:15 and 4:5. Both use the same word (*logos*) to describe the defense believers give for their hope and that unbelievers give at the final judgment. See Keener, *1 Peter*, 260, 308.
54 Keener, *1 Peter*, 92.

Bibliography

Bird, Michael F. *Evangelical Theology: A Biblical and Systematic Introduction*. 2nd ed. Grand Rapids: Zondervan Academic, 2020.

Fortune, Marie M., and Cindy G. Enger. "Violence Against Women and the Role of Religion." National Online Resource Center on Violence Against Women. https://vawnet.org/material/violence-against-women-and-role-religion.

Huecker, Martin R., Kevin C. King, Gary A. Jordan, and William Smock. "Domestic Violence." Updated April 9, 2023. https://www.ncbi.nlm.nih.gov/books/NBK499891/.

International Labour Organization. "Global Estimates of Modern Slavery: Forced Labour and Forced Marriage." September 12, 2022. https://www.ilo.org/global/topics/forced-labour/publications/WCMS_854733/lang--en/index.htm.

Jobes, Karen H. *1 Peter*. Baker Exegetical Commentary on the New Testament. Grand Rapids: Baker Academic, 2005.

Joseph, Abson Prédestin. "The Background and Implications of the Language of New Birth in 1 Peter." *Journal of Theological Interpretation* 15, no. 2 (2021): 318–32.

Kaalund, Jennifer T. *Reading Hebrews and 1 Peter with the African American Great Migration: Diaspora, Place and Identity*. Library of New Testament Studies 598. New York: Bloomsbury, 2018.

Kaiser, Walter C. "Israel's Missionary Call." In *Perspectives on the World Christian Movement: A Reader*, 4th ed., ed. Ralph D. Winter and Steven D. Hawthorne, 10–16. Pasadena: William Carey Library, 2009.

Keener, Craig S. *1 Peter: A Commentary*. Grand Rapids: Baker Academic, 2022.

Köstenberger, Andreas J., and Gregory Goswell. *Biblical Theology: A Canonical, Thematic, and Ethical Approach*. Wheaton, IL: Crossway, 2023.

Leemis, Ruth W., Norah Friar, Srijana Khatiwada, May S. Chen, Marcie-jo Kresnow, Sharon G. Smith, Sharon Caslin, and Kathleen C. Basile. "The National Intimate Partner and Sexual Violence Survey: 2016/2017 Report on Intimate Partner Violence." National Center for Injury Prevention and Control Centers for Disease Control and Prevention. Atlanta, GA: October 2022. https://www.cdc.gov/violenceprevention/pdf/nisvs/nisvsreportonipv_2022.pdf.

Mbuvi, Andrew M. *Temple, Exile and Identity in 1 Peter*. Library of New Testament Studies 345. New York: Bloomsbury, 2007.

Moltmann, Jurgen. *Jurgen Moltmann: Collected Readings*. Edited by Margaret Kohl. Minneapolis: Fortress Press, 2014.

Piper, John, and Justin Taylor, eds. *Suffering and the Sovereignty of God*. Wheaton, IL: Crossway, 2006.

Postell, Seth D., Eitan Bar, and Erez Soref. *Reading Moses, Seeing Jesus: How the Torah Fulfills Its Goals in Yeshua.* 3rd ed. Bellingham, WA: Lexham, 2017.

Schreiner, Thomas R. *1 & 2 Peter and Jude.* Christian Standard Commentary 37. Nashville: B&H Publishing, 2020.

United Nations: Academic Impact. "Examining Domestic Violence around the World: The Cost of Doing Nothing." https://www.un.org/en/academic-impact/examining-domestic-violence-around-world-cost-doing-nothing.

Vanhoozer, Kevin J., ed. *Dictionary for Theological Interpretation of the Bible.* Grand Rapids: Baker Academic, 2005.

Wright, Christopher J. H. *The Mission of God: Unlocking the Bible's Grand Narrative.* Downers Grove, IL: InterVarsity Press, 2006.

Wright, Christopher J. H. *The Mission of God's People: A Biblical Theology of the Church's Mission.* Biblical Theology for Life. Grand Rapids: Zondervan, 2010.

Chapter 9

Mission to the Dead and the Resurrection of Jesus

1 Peter 3:18-22 and Ancestor Christology in Africa

Rudolf K. Gaisie

Introduction

The significance of the suffering, death, and resurrection of the Lord Jesus Christ in 1 Peter 3:18–22 is quite clear. In the passage, the author concluded a discussion on suffering for doing the right thing before God. Jesus's efficacious death not only dealt with the sins of the living, but it also brought a message for the dead. The relevance of Jesus for both "the living and the dead" is recaptured in 1 Peter 4:5–6, where the author reiterated the preaching of the gospel to the dead, assuring his audience that accountability will come for unbelieving gentiles who are not living for the will of God.

The place of ancestors and their perceived role in the affairs of the living are manifested in many societies around the world. This presents religious and cultural challenges on many fronts to contextual Christian mission and thought. Ancestor Christology in Africa has been pursued largely because of valuing what the living does with the memory and perceived influence of ancestors in various societies. Most traditional societies in Africa amid globalization, or non-African influence, continue to be influenced by the place of the ancestors in traditional thought. Christian mission in such African societies needs to continually work out the uniqueness and superiority of Jesus Christ in relation to ancestral activities (Ancestor Christology). From an Akan reading of 1 Peter 3:18–22, this essay highlights some aspects of a functional Ancestor Christology for the Akan context and beyond.

The resurrection of Jesus Christ is not only foundational to Christianity but is also the point of departure of all subsequent explorations in Christology. The recollected stories about Jesus of Nazareth and the impact of his life and ministry in the New Testament were from the standpoint of his being raised from the dead. In Peter's first public address, following the coming of the Holy Spirit on the day of Pentecost, he mentioned God raising Jesus from the dead twice (Acts 2:24, 32). For the apostle, "the resurrection of the Christ

[Messiah]" had been foretold (Acts 2:25–31).[1] The reason and effect of Jesus's suffering, death, and resurrection are functionally retold in different ways in the New Testament. It is in 1 Peter that we find commentary on the three-day period between the death and resurrection of Jesus.

Among other concerns that the epistle addresses, the author underscored the significance and function of the resurrection of Christ. The resurrection offers clues to why Christ died and what his death achieved for humankind. This chapter highlights the theme of resurrection in the epistle and how it functionally informs the missional role of Ancestor Christology particularly in Africa. I argue that it is the resurrection that ratifies the image of ancestor for and the ancestorship of Jesus, as it does for all other images in Christology. I draw attention to some Old Testament texts on death and resurrection before discussing the theme in 1 Peter, focusing on selected texts and paying attention to the Akan (Twi) mother-tongue readings. This attempt highlights some insights from this Petrine epistle for the missiological pursuit of a mother tongue (Akan) Ancestor (Nana) Christology.

Old Testament Ideas on Death and Resurrection

If the ministry and destiny of Jesus correlate with the tradition of the Old Testament, just as Jesus taught and the early Jewish believers apprehended, then his death and resurrection give a clearer understanding of the life and death intimated in the Old Testament. God (Elohim) is the source of the animating breath of human life (2:7), and it is from him that the word תוּמ ("death" or "die"), one of the two main Hebrew words for "death," first appears (Gen 2:17) to describe the consequence if the first human couple ate the fruit of the tree of knowledge of good and evil. Life and death are, therefore, realities originating from God. Certainly, the sense of death at this time in the Genesis narrative is closely linked to the absence, or the leaving, of the breath (from God) from a person's body. When Adam had lived for 930 years, he died (תוּמ) (Gen 5:5). Adam's death seems natural due to old age, unlike his son Abel who was murdered by his brother Cain (Gen 4:8). Sometimes God is the cause of people's death (Exod 13:29). Other times death is caused by a destroyer from God (Exod 12:23), an angel of death or an angel of the Lord (2 Kgs 19:35), or animals (1 Kgs 13:24).

---

[1] Unless otherwise noted, all Scripture quotations in this chapter come from the ESV, and the Akan version used is the New Revised Asante Twi.

Those who die continue to exist or live on in another realm, a fact that can be deduced from the reference to joining or going to "your fathers [ancestors]" as captured in the LORD's assurance to Abram (Abraham) concerning his descendants in the future (Gen 15:15). The order of the wording in this verse is significant. Abraham will *first* join his fathers in peace (שָׁלוֹם) then *his body* shall be "buried in a good old age." The place where Abraham's deceased fathers dwell must be a place of peace since the LORD assured Abraham he would go when he had finished his course in their covenant relationship. The physical burial place is not necessarily the place of the fathers. Though Jacob had requested (while still alive in Egypt) to be buried with his fathers in the land of Canaan (Gen 49:29), Joseph was content to be buried first in Egypt and then later have his bones be carried along when God brought his kin into the land promised to their ancestor Abraham (Gen 50:24–26).

Death (מָוֶת) is juxtaposed to life (חַי) in Deuteronomy 30:15. The psalmist cries to the LORD to deliver "my life [נֶפֶשׁ]" for there is no remembrance or praise of the LORD in death [מָוֶת] (Ps 6:4–5). In Psalm 6:5, death is synonymous with Sheol, which in some contexts refers to the grave (Ezek 32:26–27) or the pit (Ps 30:3). The reference to the ground opening "its mouth" and swallowing people so that "they go down alive to Sheol" (Num 16:30–33) suggests that "death" or Sheol is a place under the earth. The dead are sometimes regarded as fallen asleep (Job 14:12; Dan 12:2). From the activities of the prophets, particularly Elisha and Elijah, we see instances where people who were declared dead for a while were brought back to life through prayer or some physical contact (e.g., 2 Kgs 4:31–37; 13:21). These people would eventually die again, and these examples are different from the later understanding that "many of those who sleep in the dust of the earth shall awake, some to everlasting life, and some to shame and everlasting contempt" (Dan 12:2). Death as an enemy to life from God will ultimately be defeated by the true source of life himself, God (Isa 25:8).

The Suffering, Death, and Resurrection of Jesus Christ and Mission to the Dead

Jesus's suffering and eventual death was a shock and disappointment to his disciples, even though the narratives indicate that he consistently foretold this to them.[2] The news of Jesus's resurrection was similarly received with

---

2 Mark 8:31–33; 9:30–32; 10:32–34.

doubt among some of the disciples.³ The commission to go "make disciples of all nations, baptizing them in the name of the Father and of the Son and of the Holy Spirit" (Matt 28:19), the assurance of "power" from the Holy Spirit to be Jesus's witnesses (Acts 1:8), and the signs accompanying those who believe (Mark 16:17–18) were all from the words of the resurrected Jesus. The disciples worked from the experience and understanding that God raised Jesus who was "crucified and killed by the hands of lawless men" (Acts 2:24). The experience of being "filled with the Holy Spirit" (Acts 2:4) was understood as a result of the exaltation of Jesus as "both Lord and Christ" (Acts 2:36), who after his resurrection has received that promise from the Father and "has poured out" (Acts 2:33) the Spirit upon his disciples. For Peter, this followed the testimony of the patriarch David (Acts 2:25–35).

In 1 Peter, the word ἀναγεννάω ("resurrect") appears twice (1:3; 3:21) and ἐγείρω ("awaken" or "raise up") once (1:21). The death and resurrection of Jesus Christ, at this early point in the epistle, have immediate relevance for the present as well as the future. God, the Father of Jesus Christ, in his great mercy or compassion, has caused a new beginning or birth (ἀναγεννάω, in Twi: *awo foforɔ*) into a living hope through the ἀνάστασις of Jesus Christ from the dead. The "living hope" or *anidasoɔ a emu wɔ nkwa* ("a hope that has life in it") is linked to an "inheritance that is imperishable (ἄφθαρτον), undefiled (ἀμίαντον), and unfading (ἀμάραντον)," which is "kept in heaven" (1:4).⁴ This is the "salvation ready to be revealed" at the end of time (καιρός) to those who believe in Jesus and the work of God through him, for such are "being guarded [watched over] through faith" by God's power (1:5). God has thus "chosen to redeem [humankind] by giving new birth"⁵ through the death and resurrection of Jesus Christ, and this is given to faith.

The outcome of genuine faith in and love for Jesus guarantees the salvation of the person (ψυχή) at the revelation of Jesus Christ (1:6–10). Peter acknowledged the exercise of faith among his audience. Unlike them, Peter had the opportunity to see Jesus while he was alive and to encounter him after his resurrection. Peter's faith in Jesus was based on physical interactions. This encouragement is suitable for fellow believers who "have been grieved by various trials" that test the genuineness of their faith.

---

3 Mark 16:14; Matthew 28:17.

4 The three alpha-privative adjectives used here are noted to apparently emphasize the eternal nature of the inheritance devoid of any stain, respectively, via death, evil, and time. See Jobes, *1 Peter*, 85–86.

5 Jobes, 82.

Furthermore, they are to continue in the faith to obtain its outcome of a salvation, which remained a mystery until Jesus came and completed God's plan of redemption through the resurrection. This is also a salvation of grace (χάρις), which will be brought at the revelation of Jesus Christ (1:13), that is, to be "fully realized at some future time [or moment]."[6]

In the epistle, the centrality of Jesus Christ seems taken for granted. It is through Jesus, for Peter, that his audience became believers in God, "who raised (ἐγείρω) him from the dead and gave him glory" so that their "faith and hope are [ultimately] in God" (1:21). The resurrection of Jesus Christ, which has secured the "new birth" of a living hope and inheritance toward a salvation by grace, is the work of God in his great mercy. In other words, it was God's will in his eternal purpose to have Jesus, as "a lamb without blemish or spot," to suffer and die, shedding his "precious blood" to ransom people from "the futile ways inherited" from their ancestors (πατροπαράδοτος) (1:18–19). Such "futile ways" include malice, deceit, hypocrisy, envy, and slander (2:1). Obedience to the truth of God in Jesus Christ through faith and the attendant action of love are the imperatives to avoid such "futile ways" and to be able to "grow up into salvation" (2:2). Believers in Jesus Christ are like "living stones" just like Jesus, who is "chosen and precious" in God's sight even though rejected by people (2:4). Through faith and obedience, believers are "built up as a spiritual house, to be a holy priesthood, to offer spiritual sacrifices acceptable to God through Jesus Christ" (2:5). Through Jesus Christ, God has accepted the gentiles in faith, and like Jewish believers, they offer all things back to God through Jesus Christ. Believers are, thus, to see their present experiences in the light of, or through the reality of, the resurrected Christ. Jesus is the exemplar and encouragement for believers in their trials of suffering for righteousness' sake (2:21–23; 3:14–17). Thus, it is understandable that the theme of the suffering and death of Jesus is seen as the starting point for three christological passages in 1 Peter: 1:18–21; 2:22–25, and 3:18–22. The apparent ministry of Christ in the spirit world is of particular interest to people in African societies where the "spirit world" indeed pervades the "physical world" without any expressed dichotomy.

For Christ "suffered once (ἅπαξ, *prɛko*) for sins" being "the righteous for the unrighteousness" (3:18). Christ's suffering was definitive and not in vain; it achieved an eternal purpose, and this should be an example for his followers in their suffering. In their case it is a testing of the genuineness

---

6 Jobes, 84.

of their faith (1:7). Christ suffered in the flesh as "a lamb without blemish" for the unrighteous, to bring those who believe to God. Though Jesus was put to death in the flesh (σάρξ), bearing "our sins in his body on the tree" (2:24), he has been made "alive in [the] spirit" (πνεῦμα) and in this living spiritual state "went and proclaimed to the spirits in prison" (3:19). The parallels between verses 18 and 19 ("death in the flesh" and "alive in spirit"; "in which also" and "at which time also") have lent much to various exegetical positions across the centuries. Karen H. Jobes concluded her analysis of the "three basic interpretations" of the two verses by indicating that the contrast between the nouns σάρξ and πνεῦμα refers more "to two aspects of the redemptive event: Christ's death and subsequent resurrection." When this is linked to the reference to Christ's ascension in 3:22 it "completes the redemptive sequence: crucifixion ("put to death"), resurrection ("made alive"), and ascension ("gone into heaven")."[7]

The question of what transpired and where it happened within the three days between the death and resurrection seems inevitable and legitimate in any cultural understanding of and response to Jesus Christ. The various proponents of the three basic interpretations of these verses have opined largely from their cultural and pre-Christian religious orientations. Culture and language are key in exegesis and translation, and these subtly contribute to the "difficulties" associated with the verses under consideration and indeed the entire passage of 3:18–22. The first interpretation that "Christ preached through Noah to Noah's generation" was in the teaching of Saint Augustine who, as Jobes intimated, took this position in reaction to his contemporaries' teaching that "Christ descended into hell between his death and resurrection."[8] Augustine sought to avoid the "theological problem of possible postmortem conversion (people being saved after death)."[9] Augustine operated in Latin and was apparently less interested in the use of Greek, so he could not so much accommodate the view of the descent to hell (*descensus ad inferos*). On the other hand, Clement of Alexandria and Origen were well versed in Greek language and culture, so they identified with the idea.[10] The second interpretation of proclamation in hell was not originally from the 1 Peter passage, but the "theological questions" it sought to address resonate, for example, with Akan traditional religious thought

---

7   Jobes, 241–42.
8   Jobes, 239.
9   Jobes, 239.
10 Jobes, 239, 241.

as highlighted in a section below: "(1) How would the saints of the Old Testament times [ancestors] be redeemed by Christ, since they lived before his time? (2) Where was Jesus Christ and what was he doing between his death and resurrection?"[11]

The third interpretation, which is predominate among contemporary interpreters, sees the "flesh-spirit contrast" not in terms of Jesus's body and soul[12] but in "his two states of existence"—his earthly existence before his death and "his glorified state of existence after the resurrection."[13] This sense is not foreign to Akan traditional thinking. The "glorified state" of a person in this case, however, is in their entry into *asamando* (the abode of the spirits of the deceased) when they have lived a "good life" and died a "good death" without any disgrace to self, or family or community. Jesus, then, through his life, death, and resurrection, has something to do with the idea of an ancestor (*nana*) among the Akan. Jesus's death and resurrection do not disqualify him from being designated a *nana* (ancestor). While his death gives him a right or opportunity to be an ancestor, his resurrection ratifies him as a *nana* among the living and *nananom nsamanfo* (those in *asamando*).

Baptism (by water)—which corresponds to the rescue of the believing, obedient Noah and his family through or by water—is effective "through the resurrection of Jesus Christ" in appealing "to God for a good conscience" (3:21). In his resurrection, Jesus Christ went into heaven exalted "at the right hand of God" with "angels, authorities, and powers having been subjected to him" (3:22). Verses 19 and 22 point to the movement (πορεύομαι) of Christ in two domains of the spirit realm: the "spirits in prison" and "into heaven." With the assumption that heaven, God's "perfect" domain, is for "obedient or obeying spirits," the reading of hell (the domain of disobedient spirits) and heaven respectively in verses 19 and 22 seems *natural* in the flow of thought. As African commentator Sicily Mbura Muriithi intimated, "death separated Christ's spirit from his body" and he "was enabled to go to preach in the spirit world (3:19)," adding that "while not all spirits will benefit from such preaching, each is accountable for the life lived on earth."[14] If God in Jesus is "ready to judge the living and the dead" (4:5),

---

11 Jobes, 241.
12 The cultural influence of "Greek Platonic dualism" is linked to the development of the understanding of 3:18 as pointing to a body-soul dichotomy. See Jobes, 241.
13 Jobes, 239.
14 Muriithi, "1 Peter," 1522.

then the ministry of Jesus in both the physical (earth) and spiritual realms is easily recognizable in a primal religious context that is mindful of the traffic between the physical and spiritual, that is, the physical being "sacramental of the spiritual."[15] Because of Christ's resurrection over both the living and dead, his lordship bears missiological importance.

Nana Yesu and an Akan Reading of 3:18-19 and 4:5-6

The author of the epistle and his immediate audience obviously shared some cultural and religious assumptions with the foundation of the Hebrew Scriptures and the (oral) teachings of Jesus Christ. While Jobes acknowledged that 3:18–22 "assumes a familiarity with images and traditions alien to modern [Western] culture,"[16] the story might be different for African Christians in touch with the primal or traditional religious realities of their contexts. When people read these verses, especially in their mother tongues, they are largely guided by translators' choice of words in addition to their own traditional and contemporary cultural and religious assumptions.

Jesus taught that God is "not God of the dead but of the living" as he responded to the issue of "the dead being raised" (Mark 12:26–27). There is life beyond death and virtually every human society in history has held a view of that. Such views on the afterlife have informed the various rites and practices that honor the memory of deceased relations. The attitude toward the deceased is also linked to traditional views about the nature of the human being. I demonstrate this with the example of the Akan of Ghana.

In Akan thought, the human being has both material and immaterial components. The material components include the body (*nipadua* or *honam*) and blood (*mogya*), which are considered as coming from the mother. The immaterial components are ɔkra ("soul"), ntorɔ ("fatherhood-deity"), *sunsum* ("spirit"), and *honhom* ("breath of life"). The ɔkra comes from God, the spark that gives life to a person; it is considered the bearer of destiny (*nkrabea*), identified as the "soul" or "spirit" of a person or distinct from the person and returns to God at death, which is seen as the separation of the ɔkra from the body. The *sunsum* is thought to come from one's father and is generally responsible for an individual's personality. It is regarded with the ɔkra as "constitutive of a spiritual unit,"[17] which means you cannot have

---

15 Turner, "Primal Religions of the World," 32.
16 Jobes, *1 Peter*, 236.
17 Gyekye, *Essay on African Philosophical Thought*, 98.

one without the other in a person. Since the body and blood do not survive death, that which lives on after death in Akan understanding is that which constitutes the ɔkra and *sunsum*, which is called *saman* ("ghost" or "spirit of a deceased").[18] The *saman* is apparently able to speak the language of the living and that of those in *asamando*,[19] making it possible for the Akan to convey (libation) requests to Onyankopɔn (God).

The sense of family (*abusua*) among the Akan is fundamental. Since each person belongs to a family, death and funerals are usually not a private affair. The extended family is usually significantly involved in the planning and execution of funerals and hence the Akan proverb *Abusua do funu* ("The family loves a corpse"). The *nsamanfo* are able to "participate" in the affairs of the living and so are usually invited or recognized during communal gatherings and special rites. For example, there is the *adae* ceremony usually for the royal *nsamanfo*, which essentially is for "renewing the spiritual and political bonds that allow for the continued participation of the dead in the affairs of the living."[20]

In keeping with the witness of the Synoptic Gospels, for the Akan, the human Jesus would thus have the animating ɔkra ("soul"), *sunsum* ("spirit"), and *ntorɔ* ("fatherhood-deity") from the Holy Spirit of God, and his body and blood would come from his mother. In Akan thinking, since Jesus died as a human and though his body was buried in the tomb, his *saman* continued to *asamando*. In his death, his *sunsum* would have been involved in the activities hinted at in the 1 Peter texts. Though in Akan thought his violent and premature death (and no wife and children) may deny him at least immediate entry to *asamando*, a case can be made for the sacrificial nature of his death as a good or righteous man before God who has done good for the community. The Christian dimension here is that by virtue of being the only sinless person to die, he is unique in the world of the dead. In this sense, he has a message for those in *asamando*. Thus, if 1 Peter communicates a sense of Christ giving a message to those in *asamando*, leaving a mark, and then coming back from *asamando* (*owusɔre*, resurrection) to live forever in Onyankopɔn (God), a typical Akan mind would not struggle with this sense. Thus, an Akan Christian can readily work with such an interpretation of 3:18–22 and 4:6.

Jesus's resurrection, then, transformed his body to function materially and immaterially.[21] His resurrection informs Akan ancestors that there is

---

18 Gaisie, *Jesus Christ as Logos Incarnate*, 88–89.
19 Opoku, *West African Traditional Religion*, 36.
20 Nketia, *Role of Traditional Festivals*, 1.
21 Evidence of this includes the fact that the disciples could touch and feel his wounds (John 20:27), see that he ate (John 21:13, 15), and see that he ascended into the heavens in their

another reality yet to be experienced and that their state in *asamando* is not the final one. Through his resurrection, Jesus has become an ancestor of the ancestors, a *nana* of the *nananom nsamanfo*. Jesus the *nana* has gone to heaven and has authority and power over "angels, authorities, and powers" so that these, as the Akan (Twi) translation goes, *abrɛ wɔn ho ase ama no* ("humble themselves before him") (3:22). Such authorities and powers in Akan thought would include the *abosom* ("tutelary deities"), *sasabonsam* ("a fearful being residing usually in the forest"), as well as the terror of the *nsamanfo* ("spirits of the deceased"). Thus, proclaiming Nana Yesu, the son of *Onyankopɔn* (God), enforces Jesus's superiority and power over all entities under *Onyankopɔn* in the Akan spiritual universe. Thus, an Akan Nana (Ancestor) Christology can draw from 1 Peter to reiterate the significance of the resurrection of Jesus and his redeeming message to the spirit world of deities and ancestors. For, indeed, Jesus did not go to the realm of the ancestors and deities as one of them but rather as their Lord, assuming "all their powers and cancels any terrorizing influence they might be assumed to have upon us."[22]

Proponents of Ancestor Christology in Africa have considered the incarnation and resurrection of Jesus within the pervasive nature of ancestors in traditional societies.[23] Jesus not only embodies the whole concept of the ancestor, but he can be explained and appropriated through the image of the ancestor. Jesus's death qualifies him as an ancestor and the fact of his resurrection ratifies his ancestorship. If Jesus was not resurrected from the dead, his ancestorship would continue to remain potential. For Peter K. Sarpong, it is the resurrection of Jesus that gives the Asante (Akan) "an indication that he was an ancestor."[24] According to Charles Nyamiti, it is through the work of the Holy Spirit in the birth, life, ministry, death, and resurrection of Jesus that his ancestorship "begins to be, operates, grows,

---

presence (Acts 1:9).
22 Bediako, *Jesus in African Culture*, 18–19.
23 "When the Incarnation is understood in African ancestral terms, the Logos' becoming flesh and all his redemptive activity (the analogous parallel to the African ancestral mediatory function)—together with the descendantisation of his members through grace (the analogous parallel to the African descendants' loving and respectful sacred communication with their ancestor)—must be considered as inseparable constitutive elements of the Incarnation. At the same time, this implies also that all the Christological items found in the New Testament teachings on Christ's mode of being and salvific activity are particular dimensions of his Incarnation understood in the African ancestral sense." Nyamiti, *Jesus Christ, the Ancestor*, 59.
24 Sarpong, *Dear Nana*, 153.

reaches its full maturity, and is factualised."[25] Jesus is Messiah and Lord because of the resurrection. The resurrection justifies his passion, or sacrificial death, for the larger family of the world. Jesus qualifies and is an Akan *nana* because of his death and resurrection. His death took him to *asamando*, and his resurrection has given hope to those in, and who will go to, *asamando*, of the resurrection to transformed bodies like that of Christ. All these are given to faith, and in that sense, one could even submit that the concept of ancestor is in effect a preparation for the resurrection.

An Akan *Nana* (Ancestor) Christology enables the demonstration of the lordship of Jesus Christ, the paradigmatic *Nana*, over the Akan material and immaterial world. Preaching *Nana Yesu*, as the one who suffered and died for our salvation and who proclaimed God's salvation in *asamando* and was raised back to life to give hope to the living and the dead, has implications for members of the Akan community and leaders, both living and dead, who bear the title of *nana*. The Akan now have a reference point in *Nana Yesu*. Those living can look to him and follow his example of complete obedience to God to become a true or real *nana* (ancestor). Those in *asamando* who have believed in God in obedience can also look to Jesus for the next creative stage of their existence, the resurrection to transformed bodies like Jesus.

It is in our experience of Christ, in the never-ending growth in fellowship with him, that our christological insights find meaning and clearer expression. Who Jesus is or becomes to you may not immediately make sense when compared with another's experience. However, if the experience is genuine and of him, others may at some point express the same reality of the experience in Jesus. The charge is to grow in the knowledge and grace of the Lord Jesus (2 Pet 3:18), that is, grow in your experience of Jesus. Christology, then, becomes the fruit of your growing experience of Jesus. In other words, Christology is an intricate by-product of the process of conversion. The goal is to imitate Jesus in his fellowship with the Father. What we say of Jesus during the process is always germinal, and there is room for clarity or improvement.

Conclusion

The understanding from 1 Peter is that the message of the gospel is for both the living and the dead. The one who is going to judge the living and the dead has ensured that prior to the resurrection the message of the gospel was proclaimed to both realms of existence. For the Akan mind, this implies

---

25 Nyamiti, *Jesus Christ, the Ancestor*, 158. Accordingly, the event of Pentecost "completes" Jesus Christ's "messianic work and factualises his Ancestorship."

those in *asamando* have received the witness of the gospel. What the dead in *asamando* do with the witness of the gospel is quite another matter beyond the focus of this chapter. The resurrection of Jesus Christ, however, demonstrates to the Akan that there is the reality of rising from the dead awaiting those in *asamando*. This also means for the Akan that *asamando* is not the ultimate destination. What is important, nonetheless, for the living Akan person is for him or her to experience the reality of the risen Lord Jesus Christ through the agency of the Holy Spirit from heaven, by whom Peter reminded his audience they heard the gospel from those who proclaimed it (1:12).

The idea of the resurrection is key to understanding the missiological import of the epistle. Christ sacrificially died and has been raised from the dead. This is hope for the living and the dead. Without the resurrection of Jesus Christ, everything seen and said of him remains potentially true. The resurrection has ratified God's eternal purpose of the salvation of humankind, both living and dead, through Jesus Christ. All things are now pointing toward the resurrection at the appearance of Jesus Christ. For both the immediate audience of 1 Peter and us, Christ has won the victory in his death and resurrection and thus becomes the example, focus, and key in all Christian experiences of suffering, persecution, prosperity, sacrifice, and even relative peace. Indeed, it is Jesus who gives the power, grace, and peace to people to live a life worthy of God and worth remembering by the living when they are dead. For "the God of all grace" is faithful, who calls people to "his eternal glory in Christ," and after his people "have suffered a little while" he "will himself restore, confirm, strengthen and establish" them (5:10).

Bibliography

Bediako, Kwame. *Jesus in African Culture: A Ghanaian Perspective*. Accra: Asempa Publishers, 1990.

Bediako, Kwame. *Jesus in Africa: The Christian Gospel in African History and Experience*. Theological Reflections from the South. Akropong: Regnum Africa, 2000.

Campbell, D. N., and Fika J. van Rensburg. "A History of the Interpretation of 1 Peter 3:18–22." *Acta Patristica et Byzantina* 19, no. 1 (2008): 73–96. https://doi.org/10.1080/10226486.2008.11745788.

Dalton, William J. "Interpretation and Tradition: An Example from 1 Peter." *Gregorianum* 49, no. 1 (1968): 11–37.

Fagbemi, Stephen Ayodeji A. "Transformation, Proclamation and Mission in the New Testament: Examining the Case of 1 Peter." *Transformation* 27, no. 3 (2010): 209–23.

Gaisie, Rudolf K. *Jesus Christ as Logos Incarnate and Resurrected Nana (Ancestor): An African Perspective on Conversion and Christology*. African Christian Studies Series 19. Eugene, OR: Pickwick, 2020.

Gyekye, Kwame. *An Essay on African Philosophical Thought: The Akan Conceptual Scheme*. Rev. ed. Philadelphia: Temple University Press, 1995.

Jobes, Karen H. *1 Peter*. Baker Exegetical Commentary on the New Testament. Grand Rapids: Baker Academic, 2005.

Muriithi, Sicily Mbura. "1 Peter." In *African Bible Commentary: A One-Volume Commentary Written by 70 African Scholars*, edited by Tokunboh Adeyemo, 1517–24. Nairobi: WordAlive, 2006.

Nketia, J. H. Kwabena. *The Role of Traditional Festivals in Community Life*. Legon: Institute of African Studies, University of Ghana, n.d.

Nyamiti, Charles. *Jesus Christ, the Ancestor of Humankind: An Essay on African Christology*. Studies in African Christian Theology 2. Nairobi: CUEA Publications, 2006.

Opoku, Kofi Asare. *West African Traditional Religion*. Accra: FEP International Private Limited, 1978.

Sarpong, Peter K. *Dear Nana: Letters to My Ancestor*. Takoradi: Franciscan Publications, 1998.

Turner, Harold W. "Primal Religions of the World and Their Study." In *Australian Essays in World Religions*, edited by Victor C. Hayes, 27–37. South Australia: Bedford Park, 1977.

Part 3
The Missionary Methods of 1 Peter

Chapter 10

Missional Hospitality

Responding to Physical and Spiritual Alienation

Tricia Stephens

Introduction

In the context of Christian mission, hospitality presents a biblically mandated means of welcoming migrants as a response to God's hospitality to us. These migrants represent an unprecedented local opportunity for global mission in communities undergoing demographic revolutions. Christian organizations and churches in Canada and the US are looking to formulate responses to the growing presence of diasporic communities from across the planet.[1] This new reality has increased discussions on the nature of diaspora mission with sincere attention to the power paradigms attached to traditional mission.[2] Enoch Wan's work on diaspora mission among international students suggests that traditional missiological paradigms have viewed the Great Commission (Matt 28:19–20) with a Westernized focus on programs and management.[3] This, in Wan's estimation, has led to mission preoccupied with doing rather than being, which has left behind the essentially relational nature of the triune God's mission.

Hospitality, inherently relational and connected to the alien and stranger, can thus become a key component in mission to migrants. Two recent works on diaspora mission from Ross Langmead and Darren Cronshaw and others have centralized the role of hospitality. Langmead's work on a theology of mission to refugees considers hospitality a central metaphor that expresses God's divine hospitality multidimensionally.[4] At the same time, Langmead's

---

[1] Belz, "Survey: Today's Evangelicals More Likely."

[2] See Langmead, "Refugees as Guests and Hosts," 9–47; Cronshaw, et al., "Mission as Hospitality with Refugees," 150–76; Smither, *Mission as Hospitality*; Smither, "Missional Hospitality in Hebrews, 71–86; and Wan, "Diaspora Missiology," 10–49.

[3] Wan, 11. Wan distinguishes between diaspora missions and traditional thoughts about local evangelism by incorporating geography or territory. Wan suggests that traditional models consider local outreach as evangelism and international outreach as missions. However, the reach is global in diaspora missions, while the action is local (34). The NIV Bible was used unless otherwise directly indicated.

[4] Langmead, "Refugees as Guests and Hosts," 29, 36.

ethics of welcome recognizes that hospitality can also be subject to power differentials that can lead to "a tendency to indoctrinate" or dominate.[5] Langmead proposed that people in power adopt a strategy that leads to an awareness of power dynamics, but he offered no concrete approach. However, Cronshaw and his colleagues, in their response to Langmead's article, explored some of the practical considerations in developing a strategy, including recognizing others' cultural location, making room for liminality, and accepting their unique differences.[6] While that work offers some important considerations, it only tangentially introduces the role of identity in those power paradigms. This is where I propose that 1 Peter challenges traditional host-guest power dynamics by shaping a powerful Christian identity as aliens and strangers.

Building on these discussions, this chapter argues that 1 Peter offers a transformative perspective on hospitality in mission, particularly in challenging traditional power dynamics between host and guest. By framing Christians as strangers and aliens, 1 Peter reorients from the host-centric view of traditional Christian hospitality to a Christ-centered position of Christians as hosts and guests. Additionally, the chapter explores how 1 Peter's eschatological perspective infuses hospitality with a sense of future hope and purpose, aligning mission with God's ultimate plan.

Greco-Roman Hospitality

Hospitality was a central social practice in Greco-Roman life and tied to the ideas of moral virtue, sacred duty, privilege, and relationship in the ancient world.[7] In the context of the provinces of Galatia and Asia Minor named in 1 Peter, both Christians and non-Christians would have relied on private hospitality as much as possible because the public hotels (*hospitium*) and inns (*stabula*) had reputations for their low quality, filth, robbery, and prostitution.[8] Private hospitality, which was widespread and highly valued across the Roman Empire, increased in importance as the importation of goods and food led to expanded commercial and trade networks.[9] Hospitality was the grounds for hosts to encounter and evaluate strangers. Strangers

---

5 Langmead, 45.
6 Cronshaw et al., "Mission as Hospitality," 166–68.
7 Matthews, "Hospitality and the New Testament, 66–70. See also Arterbury, *Entertaining Angels*; and Aristotle, *Poet*.
8 O'Gorman, "Discovering Commercial Hospitality," 48; Keener, *1 Peter*, 318.
9 O'Gorman, "Discovering Commercial Hospitality," 44.

were vulnerable to the threat of danger or robbery, but they also posed a threat of danger, warfare, or disease. Every stranger had the potential to be an esteemed friend or an enemy (Aelian, *Var. hist.* 4.9).

Hospitality was encouraged in the ancient world on moral grounds, being considered a philanthropic act of generosity (Cicero, *Off.* 2.64; Acts 28:7).[10] Strangers who became guests could expect protection from their host because violating hospitality was an impiety or even a crime.[11] There is even precedence for offering hospitality to the stranger as a means of paying homage "to the divine as the protector and avenger of the stranger" (Tacitus, *Ann.* 15.52 [Jackson, LCL]; 2 Macc 6:2). Strangers regularly carried a token of hospitality or letter conveying they were worthy of the status of a guest-friend (Euripides, *Med.* 613; Plautus, *Poen.* 958). With or without such a letter, a host could still expect to receive, welcome, and feed their guest before asking any questions about identity and news. Once the guest was received and the host's treatment granted, a mutually beneficial relationship called balanced reciprocity could be established, obliging even future generations to honor the relationship (Cicero, *Verr.* 2.2; Livy, *Hist.* 25.18.4–5).

Private Hospitality and Reciprocity

Although hospitality was considered a sacred duty, it still operated within a system of reciprocity.[12] There was generalized reciprocity, which operated within kinship communities where altruism and repeated exchanges were common.[13] However, 1 Peter 4:9 speaks of *philoxenia*, a Greek term that refers to hospitality to aliens and strangers.[14] This hospitality involved a type of reciprocity known as compactual reciprocity, which included things like peace-making, friendship agreements, hospitality, and gift-giving.[15] Compactual reciprocity reflected balanced relationships between equals, as well as unequal exchanges such as patronage, but it demonstrated that hospitality functioned in a context of social status, influence, material resources, and honor (Cicero, *Off.* 2.64).[16]

---

10 Blomberg, *Contagious Holiness*, 86.
11 O'Gorman, "Discovering Commercial Hospitality," 45.
12 Arterbury, *Entertaining Angels*, 27.
13 Sahlins, *Stone Age Economics*, 191–95.
14 Artebury, *Entertaining Angels*, 107–8.
15 Cook, "Homeric Reciprocities," 95–96.
16 Donlan, "Reciprocities in Homer," 143–50.

So, the stranger was a guest, who was also a potential ally, patron, client, or obligation. Plato detailed four types of strangers and the appropriate care for each, from the "inevitable immigrant" to be received in public spaces to the highest tier that should be hosted by the "rich and the wise."[17] Yet there was nuance as Plutarch suggested that pleasure was more important in dining companions than family, wealth, or position (Plutarch, *Mor.* 618a). In any case, the host would hope to receive favorable treatment from former guests when they themselves traveled, so the status and wealth of the guest impacted reciprocity (Aelian, *Var. hist.* 4.9). There was also gift-giving in hospitality that often entailed obligation and served to remind participants of having the right connections.

The New Testament writers clearly encouraged hospitality but set new expectations. Being hospitable is commended among believers and attributed to the good character of elders and widows (Rom 12:13; Heb 13:2; 1 Tim 3:2; 5:9–10; Tit 1:8). First Peter 4:9, similarly, exhorts its readers to be hospitable without grumbling. So it is important to examine how the letter strategically challenged the model of Greco-Roman hospitality and thus shaped how we approach hospitality on mission.

The Social Condition of the Readers of 1 Peter: Aliens and Strangers

As 1 Peter weaves a thematically and theologically rich discourse, using the imagery of nationhood, belonging, peoplehood, otherness, and relationship, one of the most interesting commentaries is about Christian alienation. As Peter employed paronyms of strangers and aliens, he developed a theological treatise on alienation and suffering for Christ's sake. The readers were repeatedly called aliens and strangers, living distinctly from the society around them that is marked by anti-Christian sentiment (1:1, 17; 2:11; 4:3). Joel B. Green noted that their allegiance to Christ's lordship "has won for them animosity, scorn and vilification," which paints them as "misfits worthy of contempt."[18] They are living with the complex identity of "members of the household of God" who are marginalized outsiders and foreigners to the surrounding cultures (4:3). Rahel Jaeggi proposed the provocative idea

---

17 Plato (*Leg.*, 12:952d–53e [Bury, LCL 192]) details four types of immigrants, beginning with the summer tourist, who should be engaged to the least extent possible. He calls the second type an inspector who sees all and who should be heard, seen, and received by temple priests. The third type must be welcomed and received by public officials, and the fourth must be noble and over fifty years of age, who should be received by those who are rich and wise and have been honored.

18 Green, *1 Peter*, 169.

that "alienation is a relation of relationlessness," which is not the complete absence of relation but rather the experience of deficient ones.[19] This type of alienation will be familiar to believers who experience difficulties with or even lose their work or relationships with family or friends after conversion. However, it is not limited to only this type of scenario. Missionaries working in a new cultural context, whether within the same society or country, international students, and other displaced peoples, can experience the same sense of alienation stemming from diminished social relationships.

Another aspect of being an alien and stranger is the absence of a community that shares the features of heritage, language, origin, etc. This imposes a type of marginalization that is difficult to overcome. Samuel Escobar's work "Migration: Avenue and Challenge to Mission" speaks of the specific conditions for migrants as they transition into life in a new country or part of the world.[20] His work recognizes that migrants, like many displaced people, are in transition and experiencing alienation with the loss of familial roots. Each suffers from a type of homelessness individually, but worldwide such marginalization happens on a massive scale.

Interpretation of Resident Aliens and Strangers: Legal Status

When 1 Peter describes Christian readers as chosen strangers living scattered among gentiles, the Greek terms resident alien (*paroikos*) and visitor (*parepidēmos*) introduce the language of alienation (1:1, 17; 2:11; 4:3). The term *paroikos* generally refers to foreigners, but John H. Elliott has already argued that it more frequently captured a "technical, political-legal meaning" of resident aliens who lacked the rights of a citizen or those native born.[21] The prevalence of this sociopolitical usage of the term in ancient writings convinced him that a literal reading best describes Peter's usage.[22] In this case these young Christians are resident aliens, who through the forces of migration and scattering have come into the diaspora with a legal and social status dependent on the goodwill and acceptance of societies that were not their own.

---

19 Jaeggi, *Alienation*, 3. Jaeggi's treatment of alienation from the perspective of social philosophy views alienation as fundamentally an "inability to establish a relation to other human beings, to things, to social institutions and thereby also—so the fundamental intuition of the theory of alienation—to oneself" (3).

20 Escobar, "Migration: Avenue and Challenge," 19–20.

21 Elliott, *Home for the Homeless*, 67. Tabbernee, *Early Christianity in Contexts*, 25. For an example of a general use of foreigner, see Philo, *Virtues* 107; Plutarch, *Pyrr.* 10.3; and Diodorus, *Bibliotheca Historica* 20.84.2.

22 Elliot, *Home for the Homeless*, 25.

The legal status of aliens was often vulnerable in many Roman cities. They could be subject to higher taxes, disenfranchisement, and ridicule, among other responses.[23] Dio Chrysostom wrote that "to the disenfranchised life seems with good reason not worth living, and many choose death rather than life after losing their citizenship" (*De gloria i* (Or. 66.15) [Crosby, LCL]). The reality was that resident aliens enjoyed varying levels of participation in society depending on a variety of factors, and they were often a cultural litmus test revealing societal values and notions toward acceptance and hospitality. Thus, Julius Caesar could refer to the *paroikon* Jews as friends and confederates (Josephus, *J.W.* 14.213). The *paroikos* and *parepidēmos* could often be seen as sources of commercial opportunity, future threats, or alliances.[24]

Interpretation of Resident Aliens and Strangers: Metaphorical

Although some adopted Elliott's perspective regarding their literal social alienation, the predominant view has been that Peter most likely applied the terms metaphorically.[25] These Christians may have been native to the regions where the letter circulated but were still experiencing forms of socio-cultural alienation including persecution and exclusion (4:4). First Peter 2:11 opens with an exhortation urging these beloved believers, as aliens and strangers, to abstain from fleshly desires with exemplary behavior so their gentile neighbors will glorify God. It would be unlikely that Peter was asserting a connection between a legal status as literal foreigners and their testimony to the God of their salvation (3:1–2, 15). Rather, these believers now appear as aliens and strangers to the gentiles around them (4:3). These believers have a new strangeness related to their God-glorifying behavior that is foreign to the surrounding culture as much as it is observable (2:12; 4:3–4; cf. 3:16). The new social status of these converts, perhaps comparable to Jewish proselytes, engenders hostility and ostracism because of their new religious identity.[26] They have become cultural outsiders alienated from society at large.

---

23 Keener, *1 Peter*, 46. Elliott cites inscriptional evidence that there were differences in the treatment of the *paroikoi* but notes that their general economic condition is not well understood. Elliott, *Home for the Homeless*, 27.

24 Plutarch, *Lives. Pyrrhus* 10.3; and Diodorus, *Bibliotheca Historica* 20.84.2.

25 Phillips, "Use of the Psalms in 1 Peter," 220. See Seland, "Resident Aliens in Mission," 565–89.

26 See Seland, "Resident Aliens in Mission," 565–89.

Alien and Stranger as a Multivalent Topos

From this discussion, it follows that Peter's use of the alien-stranger topos has multiple meanings.[27] The letter employs different aspects of this identity to comment on their relationship to the world, each other, and God. By calling these Christians aliens and strangers, there is an identity formation that emphasizes their distinctiveness within the Roman cultural milieu. This strategy is recognizable in other early Christian texts such as the Shepherd of Hermas and the Epistle to Diognetus that "paradoxically use a language of alterity" to develop an insider identity.[28] This rhetoric of foreignness builds an identity reliant on an us-them dichotomy, which enhances the moral and spiritual boundaries of the group and reinforces community.[29] The alien-stranger topos thus levies distinctiveness and alienation with respect to gentiles (2:12; 4:3).

By calling Christians aliens and strangers, 1 Peter subverts the biblical picture of outsiders and alienation. The Bible centers God so that human sin is the cause of alienation that is only overcome by Christ's ministry of reconciliation (1 Pet 1:18–21; Gen 3:15; Eph 2:19; 2 Cor 5:18–20). This theologically oriented alienation defines humanity in relationship to God (1 Pet 1:18–19; 2:10; cf. 4:3–4, 17). Philo expressed a similar idea when he called all of creation aliens and strangers against God, the only true citizen (Philo, *Cher.* 121*)*. Given Christians' restored relationship to God in Christ, it would appear that their gentile neighbors are the aliens and strangers.

These believers experience legal and social alienation, but it is their gentile neighbors who are experiencing spiritual alienation. By calling Christians aliens and strangers, the letter considers Christians from the world's perspective because of their relationship to God. The letter employs a then-now literary motif that compares the previous lives of believers, when they lived like the gentiles, to after Christ, when they lived according to God's will (see Table 1). Those comparisons build a portrait of Christians' relationship to God through Christ explicitly but emphasize that it is gentiles who are truly alienated from God.[30] They stumble and fall over Christ (2:7–8), are living sinful and debauched lives (4:3–5) and face a harsher judgment than believers (4:17). Thus, it is gentiles who have diminished relationships with God and his people and need welcome.

---

27 Dunning, "Strangers and Aliens No Longer," 4.
28 Dunning, 3. See Dunning, *Aliens and Sojourners*.
29 Dunning, 87.
30 See Dunning, "Strangers and Aliens No Longer," 1–16.

Verse Reference	Christians' Lives before Christ	Christians' Lives after Christ
1:14	ignorant and conformed to evil desires	suffering grief in all kinds of sorrows holy in all they do
1:18	empty way of life received from their ancestors	
1:22		purified themselves by obeying the truth
1:23		born again of imperishable seed
2:3		they have tasted that the Lord is good
2:4	rejected by humans	chosen by God
2:9		a chosen people, a royal priesthood, a holy nation, God's special possession
2:10a	not a people	people of God
2:10b	had not received mercy	have received mercy
2:16		free people and slaves
2:25	like sheep going astray	returned to the Shepherd and Overseer of your souls
3:15		have hope
4:3	did what gentiles choose to do: debauchery, lust, drunkenness, orgies, carousing, and idolatry	

Missional Implications and Redefining Hospitality Roles

Returning to hospitality as mission, the alien-stranger topos in 1 Peter underscores Christians' unique identity but also asks who is the guest and who is the host. This is a unique situation where individuals, identified as aliens and strangers, are called to extend hospitality to other aliens and strangers (4:9). This calls for embracing a dual nature of being guest and host. How often in our approach to hospitality do we inhabit the role of the host without thought? We open our houses, welcome strangers, minister to others, and then inevitably occupy only the role of host when thinking about hospitality theologically and practically. Escobar stated that the reality of the moment is that evangelical missions have to shift from an "imperial mission mentality" to joining God's plan, which is revealed in Christ and empowered by the Holy Spirit.[31] This means that before determining tools and methods, missions require a different style of presence that responds to the current moment.[32] Foremost this means moving away from positions of superiority toward a Christlike posture and biblically holistic vision. First Peter, through identity, reframes conventional hospitality dynamics by introducing the possibility of another way in mission where Christians are simultaneously host and guest.

When Christians engage in mission work as both host and guest, they integrate the action of mission with identity and internalize God's mission of love and restoration (4:9). Being a host reflects God's generosity and love, inviting others into a space of grace, much like the call to "offer hospitality to one another without grumbling" (4:9). Conversely, being a guest cultivates humility and openness, mirroring our identification as "aliens and strangers" in the world who experienced God's divine hospitality (1 Pet 2:11; Eph 2:11–12). This dual engagement challenges power structures, fostering a mutuality that resonates deeply with the essence of God's kingdom, aligning with the call to "live such good lives among the pagans" (1 Pet 2:12). Through this balanced approach, Christians enact and embody God's mission, transforming it from an external task into an integral part of their identity and existence (2:9).

---

31 Escobar, *New Global Mission*, 25.
32 Escobar, 25.

Eschatological Hospitality

The last discussion focuses on the text of 1 Peter 4:7–11, which links hospitality to eschatology. This shift from exploring the Christian identity as "aliens and strangers" to examining hospitality in an eschatological light reflects how our temporary alienation in the world is met with the promise of ultimate belonging and welcome in God's eternal kingdom. The literary form of verses 7–11 can be recognized as ancient paraenesis from its rhetorical, syntactical, and literary features.[33] This section, particularly verses 7–9, opens with a short statement that the end is near (v. 7a), followed by a brief list of commands that are asyndetic and participial (v. 7b–9).

This section opens with a brief statement that these believers are living in anticipation of the end (v. 7a). Throughout the letter there is a consistent awareness of the immanence of the end that speaks of a living hope (1:4b–5), an eschatological blessing (3:9), future joy (4:13), coming judgment (4:17), and the crown of glory (5:4). Recognizing 4:7's literary form as paraenetic speech clarifies its subtle link to the subsequent commands. Paraenesis involves typical motivations underlying the commands or sanctions in categories such as holiness (1:6), Christology (1:18, 23; 2:13, 21; 3:18; 4:1), and eschatology (4:7a). Seneca wrote that a reason or motive was often added to basic precepts as part of the literary form of paraenesis (Seneca, *Ep.* 94.44). Additionally, the strong inferential conjunction οὖν at the beginning of 4:7b makes a grammatical connection between the beginning of the verse and what immediately follows.[34] Other syntactical and contextual clues affirm that 4:7a is the motivational category for the exhortations and prescriptive speech that follows (vv. 8–11).[35]

Accordingly, the abrupt eschatological statement "the end is near" (Πάντων δὲ τὸ τέλος ἤγγικεν, 4:7a) provides an eschatological motivation for the list of commands that follows in 4:7b–9. First Peter connects missional hospitality to eschatological living and hope through the expectant language of *telos*, meaning the end of a duration or the goal or outcome.[36] Both senses

---

33 Martin, *Metaphor and Composition*, 85–92. See also Keener, *1 Peter*, 313. Some typical characteristics of these texts include lists of commands, prohibitions, admonitions, and warnings, combining imperatival statements with declarations and consequences, and the use of exempla, examples, and comparisons (85–92).

34 Kline, "Ethics for the End Time," 114. Kline remarked that the conjunction is used commonly in the New Testament to introduce paraenesis dependent on doctrine.

35 Martin, *Metaphor and Composition*, 85–92.

36 Kline, "Ethics for the End Time," 114; BDAG, s.v. "τέλος."

are apparent in various translations and capture the literary movement in 1 Peter 4. Twice 1 Peter uses *telos* to speak of outcomes (1:9 of faith; 4:17 of unbelief) and once as "finally" (3:8). Those commands include being soberminded and alert (4:7b) as well as loving each other fervently (4:8) and, as a result of that love, welcoming other believers in hospitality. Although 4:9 specifies hospitality to believers, early Christian writings affirm that the early church practiced hospitality to others outside the church (Rom 12:14–21; Heb 13:2; *1 Clem.* 1.2).[37]

The eschatological motivator of their hospitality is hope for the coming end to present suffering. Following 1 Peter 4:1–4, their suffering takes place in the context of alienation and maligning from the world. They understand that they should persevere in following God's will despite the estrangement from their gentile neighbors (vv. 1–4). Four times in chapter 4, the text uses words from the same Greek root *xenos*, which means host, stranger, guestfriend, and foreigner (vv. 4, 9, 12). This draws a focal point about believers' hospitality (*philoxenos*, v. 9) toward others in the presence of the inhospitality of gentiles who are shocked (*xenizo*) that Christians abstain from sin (v. 4). Yet, the social and cultural inhospitality is temporary (1:5–6, 7a; 4:4) and believers should cultivate attitudes and behaviors in light of that truth (4:8).

Hospitality, given from a place of suffering, embraces the other's suffering and comforts while anticipating the final comfort of God. This requires boldness because they welcome the stigma of other persecuted aliens into their homes and risk worsening their own alienation. This hospitality defies self-protection in offering a welcome to those who are the source of alienation and maligning around them. This hospitality becomes a sanctuary that welcomes even the suffering or hostility of others. From a theological perspective, it calls us back to the shadow of the cross emulating the costly compassion of God toward us in our own hostility (Rom 8:7).

Finally, hospitality reveals a belief in and hope for God's kingdom program. The readers have experienced both joy and suffering (1 Pet 1:13, 17; 4:7–11), and they await the "culmination of something already experienced" and yet unknown.[38] They await the revelation of Christ and the judgment of

---

37 Clement commended the church at Corinth for the magnificence of their habitual hospitality and connected it to their virtue and stable faith.

38 Selwyn, "Eschatology in 1 Peter," 397. This plays off of Selwyn who argued that their eschatology is not awaiting the parousia of Christ but rather the culmination of what they have experienced and know. I suggest that the introduction of the themes of judgment in 1 Peter 4:5–6 is linked to the eschatological statement in 4:7a and represents the unknown.

God (1:7, 18; 4:5–9, 17; 5:1). These are the most common themes of almost every text of the Apocrypha and Pseudepigrapha that features eschatological hospitality and messianic banqueting.[39] First Enoch 62 in the similitudes of Enoch spoke of the judgment of all people and the Lord's righteous followers clothed in garments of glory and eating with the Son of Man. Further, the Old Testament has hints of the idea of eschatological hospitality, but this has primarily been understood in the context of eschatological banqueting (Isa 25:6–9; 55:1–2; Ps 22:26–29).[40] Jesus's hospitality had messianic significance revealed by inclusion and care for the alien and stranger (Matt 8:11–12; 11:19; cf. Isa 25: 6–9).[41] His hospitality looked expectantly forward to the "great multitude that no one could count, from every nation, from all tribes and people and languages" (Rev 7:9). This hospitality offers a glimpse of the fullness of God's kingdom hospitality by subverting earthly power structures (Luke 7:36–50; 14:12–14; 22:24–27). Interestingly, these themes of judgment, eschatology, and hospitality are all present in 1 Peter 4.[42]

Finally, 1 Peter 4:9 exhorts readers to receive other believers without complaint and offers no limits on duration, payback, or status. The reward for welcoming others is not in the material realm but is received at the resurrection of the righteous (Luke 14:12–14).

Conclusion

In exploring diaspora missions through 1 Peter, we challenge traditional hospitality paradigms to foster genuine relationships in migrant communities. This North American perspective considers an identity of alien and stranger can be a legal status but also spiritual and cultural for the church. This identity introduces a powerful dynamic of decentering from the role of host, which invites God as host and permits the discomfort and gift of being a guest. This step is key to becoming truly empathetic in our hospitality and inviting authenticity. We also considered how an eschatology of hope receives those who are suffering in the interim and reflects a hope for the fulfillment of God's kingdom hospitality.

---

39 Priest, "Note on the Messianic Banquet," 222–38; See also Smith, *From Symposium to Eucharist*.
40 Blomberg, *Contagious Holiness*, 20–63; and Wright, *Jesus and the Victory of God*, 322.
41 Lane, *Gospel according to Mark*, 106.
42 Jipp, *Saved by Faith and Hospitality*, 35. Further, Jipp suggested that Jesus's hospitality extended God's hospitality that cared for the people of Israel while inaugurating aspects of eschatological kingdom hospitality (Isa 25:6–9).

These thoughts on hospitality for diaspora mission lean on principles from 1 Peter that applied to early readers and have become increasingly meaningful as churches and ministries respond to a wave of diaspora populations right on the church steps. It is hoped that this offers a new approach to hospitality that is not only reliant on strategies and actions but more intimately on an identity tied to YHWH's care of Israel and Christ's incarnate ministry to humanity.

Bibliography

Aelian. *Historical Miscellany*. Translated by Nigel G. Wilson. Loeb Classical Library 486. Cambridge: Harvard University Press, 1997.

Arterbury, Andrew E. "The Custom of Hospitality in Antiquity and Its Importance for Interpreting Acts 9:43–11:18." PhD diss., Baylor University, 2003.

Arterbury, Andrew E. *Entertaining Angels: Early Christian Hospitality in its Mediterranean Setting*. Edited by Stanley E. Porter. New Testament Monographs 8. Sheffield: Sheffield Phoenix Press, 2005.

Belz, Emily. "Survey: Today's Evangelicals More Likely to Welcome the Stranger." *Christianity Today*, September 27, 2022, https://www.christianitytoday.com/news/2022/september/survey-evangelicals-immigration-reform-dreamers-refugees.html.

Blomberg, Craig L. *Contagious Holiness: Jesus' Meals with Sinners*. New Studies in Biblical Theology. Leicester: Apollos, 2005.

Cicero. *The Verrine Orations 2, Volume I: Against Caecilius. Against Verres, Part 1; Part 2, Books 1–2*. Translated by L. H. G. Greenwood. Loeb Classical Library 221. Cambridge, MA: Harvard University Press, 1928.

Cicero. *De Officiis*. Translated by Walter Miller. Loeb Classical Library 30. Cambridge, MA: Harvard University Press, 1913.

Clement of Alexandria. "1 Clement." In *The Apostolic Fathers, Volume I: I Clement. II Clement. Ignatius. Polycarp. Didache*. Edited and translated by Bart D. Ehrman. Loeb Classical Library 24. Cambridge: Harvard University Press, 2003.

Cook, Erwin. "Homeric Reciprocities." *Journal of Mediterranean Archaeology* 29, no. 1 (2016): 94–104.

Cronshaw, Darren, Hanna Hyun, Peter Laughlin, Titus S. Olorunnisola, and Stephen Parker. "Mission as Hospitality with Refugees and Other Migrants: Exploring Ross Langmead's 'Guests and Hosts' in Australian Churches." *Mission Studies* 40 (2023): 150–76.

Danker, Frederick W., Walter Bauer, William F. Arndt, and F. Wilbur Gingrich. *Greek-English Lexicon of the New Testament and Other Early Christian Literature.* 3rd ed. Chicago: University of Chicago Press, 2000.

Dio Chrysostom. *Discourses 61–80. Fragments. Letters.* Translated by H. Lamar Crosby. Loeb Classical Library 385. Cambridge, MA: Harvard University Press, 1951.

Diodorus Siculus. *Library of History, Volume X: Books 19.66–20.* Translated by Russel M. Greer. Loeb Classical Library 390. Cambridge, MA: Harvard University Press, 1954.

Donlan, Walter. "Reciprocities in Homer." *Classical World* 75, no. 3 (1982): 137–75.

Dunning, Benjamin H. *Aliens and Sojourners: Self as Other in Early Christianity.* Philadelphia: University of Pennsylvania, 2009.

Dunning, Benjamin H. "Strangers and Aliens No Longer: Negotiating Identity and Difference in Ephesians 2." *Harvard Theological Review* 99, no. 1 (2006):1–16.

Elliott, John H. *A Home for the Homeless: A Social-Scientific Criticism of 1 Peter, Its Situation and Strategy.* Minneapolis: Fortress Press, 1990.

Escobar, Samuel. "Migration: Avenue and Challenge to Mission." *Missiology: An International Review* 31, no. 1 (2003): 17–28.

Escobar, Samuel. *The New Global Mission: The Gospel from Everywhere to Everyone.* Christian Doctrine in Global Perspective. Downers Grove, IL: InterVarsity Press, 2003.

Euripides. *Cyclops. Alcestis. Medea.* Edited and translated by David Kovacs. Loeb Classical Library 12. Cambridge: Harvard University Press, 1994.

Flemming, Dean. *Why Mission?* Reframing New Testament Theology. Nashville: Abingdon, 2015.

Green, Joel B. *1 Peter.* Two Horizons New Testament Commentary. Grand Rapids: Eerdmans, 2007.

Jaeggi, Rahel. *Alienation.* Edited by Frederic Neuhouser. Translated by Frederick Neuhouser and Alan E. Smith. New Directions in Critical Theory. New York: Columbia University Press, 2014.

Jipp, Joshua W. *Saved by Faith and Hospitality.* Grand Rapids: Eerdmans, 2017.

Josephus. *Jewish Antiquities, Volume VI: Books 14–15.* Translated by Ralph Marcus, Allen Wikgren. Loeb Classical Library 489. Cambridge, MA: Harvard University Press, 1927.

Keener, Craig S. *1 Peter: A Commentary.* Grand Rapids: Baker Academic, 2021.

Kline, Leslie. "Ethics for the End Time: An Exegesis of 1 Peter 4:7–11." *Restoration Quarterly* 7 (1963): 113–23.

Lane, William L. *The Gospel according to Mark.* New International Commentary on the New Testament 2. Grand Rapids: Eerdmans, 1974.

Langmead, Ross. "Refugees as Guests and Hosts: Towards a Theology of Mission among Refugees and Asylum Seekers." *Exchange* 43, no. 1 (2014): 29–47.

Livy. *History of Rome Volume VI: Books 23–25.* Edited and translated by J. C. Yardley. Loeb Classical Library 355. Cambridge, MA: Harvard University Press, 2020.

Lorencin, Igor. "Hospitality versus Patronage: An Investigation of Social Dynamics in the Third Epistle of John." PhD diss., Andrews University, 2007.

Martin, Troy W. *Metaphor and Composition in 1 Peter.* Society of Biblical Literature Dissertation Series 131. Atlanta: Scholars Press, 1992.

Matthews, John Bell. "Hospitality and the New Testament Church: An Historical and Exegetical Study." PhD diss., Princeton Theological Seminary, 1965.

O'Gorman, Kevin D. "Discovering Commercial Hospitality in Ancient Rome." *Hospitality Review* 9, no. 2 (2007): 44–52.

O'Gorman, Kevin D. "The Essence of Hospitality from the Texts of Classical Antiquity: The Development of a Hermeneutical Helix to Identify the Philosophy of the Phenomenon of Hospitality." PhD diss., University of Strathclyde, 2008.

Phillips, G. Y. "The Use of the Psalms in 1 Peter: An Exegetical and Hermeneutical Study." PhD diss. North-West University, 2013.

Philo. *On the Confusion of Tongues. On the Migration of Abraham. Who is the Heir of Divine Things? On Mating with the Preliminary Studies.* Translated by F. H. Colson and G. H. Whitaker. Loeb Classical Library 261. Cambridge: Harvard University Press, 1932.

Philo. *On the Cherubim, The Sacrifices of Abel and Cain. The Worse Attacks the Better. On the Posterity and Exile of Cain. On the Giants.* Translated by F. H. Colson, G. H. Whitaker. Loeb Classical Library 227. Cambridge, MA: Harvard University Press, 1929.

Philo. *On the Special Laws, Book 4. On the Virtues. On Rewards and Punishments.* Translated by F. H. Colson. Loeb Classical Library 341. Cambridge, MA: Harvard University Press, 1939.

Philo of Alexandria. *The Works of Philo: Complete and Unabridged.* Translated by Charles Duke Yonge. Peabody, MA: Hendrickson, 1995.

Plato. *Laws, Volume II: Books 7–12.* Translated by R. G. Bury. Loeb Classical Library 192. Cambridge, MA: Harvard University Press, 1926.

Plautus. *The Little Carthaginian. Pseudolus. The Rope.* Edited and translated by Wolfgang de Melo. Loeb Classical Library 260. Cambridge, MA: Harvard University Press, 2012.

Plutarch. *Moralia Volume XV: Fragments*. Translated by F. H. Sandbach. Loeb Classical Library 429. Cambridge, MA: Harvard University Press, 1969.

Plutarch. *Lives, Volume IX: Demetrius and Antony. Pyrrhus and Gaius Marius*. Translated by Bernadotte Perrin. Loeb Classical Literature 101. Cambridge, MA: Harvard University Press, 1920.

Pohl, Christine D. *Making Room: Recovering Hospitality as a Christian Tradition*. Grand Rapids: Eerdmans, 1999.

Priest, J. "A Note on the Messianic Banquet." In *The Messiah: Developments in Earliest Judaism and Christianity*, edited by James H. Charlesworth, 222–38. Minneapolis: Ausburg Fortress, 1992.

Sahlins, Marshall. *Stone Age Economics*. Chicago: Aldine-Atherton, 1972.

Seland, Torrey. "Resident Aliens in Mission: Missional Practices in the Emerging Church of 1 Peter." *Bulletin for Biblical Research* 19, no. 4 (2009): 565–89.

Selwyn, E. G. "Eschatology in 1 Peter." In *The Background of the New Testament and its Eschatology*. Edited by W. D. Davies and D. Daube, 394–401. Cambridge: Cambridge University Press, 1956.

Seneca, *Epistles, Volume III: Epistles 93–124*. Translated by Richard M. Gummere. Loeb Classical Literature 77. Cambridge, MA: Harvard University Press, 1925.

Smith, Dennis E. *From Symposium to Eucharist: The Banquet in the Early Christian World*. Minneapolis: Ausburg Fortress, 2005.

Smith, Shively T. J. *Strangers to Family: Diaspora and 1 Peter's Invention of God's Household*. Waco, TX: Baylor University Press, 2016.

Smither, Edward L. *Mission as Hospitality: Imitating the Hospitable God in Mission*. Eugene, OR: Cascade, 2021.

Smither, Edward L. "Missional Hospitality in Hebrews: Welcoming God and Welcoming the Stranger." In *Reading Hebrews Missiologically: The Missionary Motive, Message, and Methods of Hebrews*, edited by Abeneazer G. Urga, Edward L. Smither, and Linda P. Saunders, 71–86. Littleton, CO: William Carey Publishing, 2023.

Steuernagel, Valdir R. "An Exiled Community as a Missionary Community: A Study Based on 1 Peter 2:9." *Evangelical Review of Theology* no. 10.1 (1986): 8–18.

Stewart, Kevin. "Practicing Missional Hospitality in a Suburban Church." *Discernment: Theology and the Practice of Ministry* 3, no. 2 (2017): 23–40.

Tabbernee, William. *Early Christianity in Contexts: An Exploration across Cultures and Continents*. Grand Rapids: Baker Academic, 2014.

Tacitus, Cornelius. *Annals: Books 13–16*. Translated by John Jackson. Loeb Classical Loeb 322. Cambridge, MA: Harvard University Press, 1937.

Wan, Enoch. "Diaspora Missiology and International Student Ministry (ISM)." In *Diaspora Missions to International Students*, edited by Enoch Wan, 10–49. Portland: Western Seminary Press, 2019.

Wright, N. T. *Jesus and the Victory of God.* Christian Origins and the Question of God 2. Minneapolis: Augsburg Fortress, 1996.

Zelnick-Abramovitz, Rachel, and R. Zelnick-Abramowitz. "The Proxenoi of Western Greece." *Zeitschrift für Papyrologie und Epigraphik* 147 (2004): 93–106.

Chapter 11

Suffering in God's Mission

Reflections from 1 Peter

Edward L. Smither

Most commentators agree that Peter's first epistle was written to encourage believers as they endured persecution. Though "chosen" by God for salvation, Peter's readers were also "exiles" dispersed in the region of northern Asia Minor (1 Pet 1:1).[1] Since Peter mentioned suffering in every chapter of the letter (1:6–9; 2:19–25; 3:8–22; 4:1–2, 12–19; 5:1, 10), suffering (*paschō*)—righteous suffering—is a framing motif of his work.[2] Within this broader theme of suffering, in this chapter, I focus on the place of suffering in the mission of God in 1 Peter. That is, how did Peter instruct this first-century church to cross spiritual and cultural boundaries in fruitful witness amid the reality of suffering?

To support this, I begin with a brief survey of Peter's own suffering in mission captured in the Gospels and Acts of the Apostles. Second, I discuss the types of suffering that Peter's readers encounter as the people of God living in a hostile world. Third, I show how Peter's readers are called to imitate Christ and participate in God's mission while suffering. Finally, I conclude with some thoughts on how the global church might read 1 Peter today in their lived reality of suffering in mission.

Peter's Suffering in Mission

When Peter laid down his fishing nets and followed Jesus, he not only put his livelihood in jeopardy but also embraced hardship by living simply, accompanying Jesus on long itinerant preaching journeys, embracing long days of serving the sick and the poor, encountering spiritual warfare, and also inviting the ridicule of those who rejected Christ and his message along the way.[3] Of course, each Synoptic Gospel writer remembered Peter succumbing to fear and failing to suffer with Jesus during a critical point

---

1 Unless otherwise noted, all Scripture references are taken from the New International Version.
2 See Burdick and Skilton, "1 Peter Introduction," 2189; see also Davids, *First Epistle of Peter*, 30–31, 36; Marshall, *1 Peter*, 15; and Williams, *Persecution in 1 Peter*, 4–5.
3 See Smither, *Christian Martyrdom*, 4–6.

of the Passion Week. Despite promising Jesus, "Even if all fall away on account of you, I never will" (Matt 26:35), Peter denied knowing the Lord three times amid the chaotic events of Jesus's arrest and trials (Matt 26:69–75; Mark 14:66–72; Luke 22:56–62; John 18:16–18, 25–27).

Following Christ's resurrection from the dead, his restoration of Peter to the ministry, as well as the outpouring of the Holy Spirit on Pentecost (John 21:15–19; Acts 2:1–47), Peter continued on a faithful path of suffering in mission. While ministering around Solomon's Portico (Acts 3–4), Peter and John healed a lame beggar and then preached the gospel to a captive audience. As a result, they were quickly dragged before the Jewish Sanhedrin, which was "greatly disturbed because the apostles were … proclaiming in Jesus the resurrection of the dead" (Acts 4:2). The Jewish leaders ordered the apostles to stop their activities and then released them. Returning to Solomon's Portico for more healing and preaching (Acts 5:17–41), Peter and the apostles were arrested by the high priest and thrown into prison. During the night, an angel opened the prison doors and instructed them to return to the temple courts and continue their ministry. When brought back before the Sanhedrin and ordered to explain their actions, Peter and the apostles replied, "We must obey God rather than human beings!" (Acts 5:29). Furious with the apostles, the Sanhedrin planned to execute them until an influential Jewish leader, Gamaliel, intervened. Frustrated, the Jewish leaders had them flogged and then released them. Later, King Herod arrested James, the brother of John, and put him to death by the sword. Desiring to win favor with the Jews, Herod tossed Peter in prison ahead of an intended trial. For a second time, Peter was miraculously led out of prison and rejoined a house church that was praying for him (Acts 12:1–24).

Eventually, Peter died a martyr's death. Church tradition claims that around AD 66, Peter was crucified upside down.[4] Peter probably wrote his letters between 62–66 from Rome during Nero's persecution of the church in the city. So when Peter wrote about suffering in his first letter, he was communicating from first-hand experience.

The Suffering of Peter's Audience

Peter addresses his first epistle to "God's elect, exiles scattered throughout the provinces of Pontus, Galatia, Cappadocia, Asia and Bithynia" (1:1). Most biblical scholars agree that these believers were from gentile backgrounds since

---

4 See Marshall, *1 Peter*, 14; also Jobes, *Letters to the Church*, 276.

Peter spoke of when they lived in "ignorance" (1:14), their previous "empty way of life" (1:18), and that they were "not a people" (2:10). He also described their pagan past in which they lived in "debauchery, lust, drunkenness, orgies, carousing and detestable idolatry" (4:3).[5] Though the apostle Paul wrote in Galatians that his mission focus was the gentiles and Peter's was the Jews (Gal 2:7), Peter's relationship with this largely gentile church in Asia Minor shows that these ministry emphases were not so clear cut. Like Paul, Peter's ministry included outreach to both Jews and gentiles.[6]

Though Eusebius of Caesarea asserted that Peter preached in northern Asia Minor, which he inferred from his reading of 1 Peter 1:1, we have no evidence from the New Testament that Peter ever ministered in the region.[7] The most plausible argument is that Peter met these believers in Rome and they later immigrated to Asia Minor.[8] So how did this predominantly gentile community of believers dwelling in Asia Minor encounter suffering for their faith in Christ?

Diaspora Realities

First, Peter's readers suffer because of their diaspora experience. Peter addressed them repeatedly as "exiles" (*parepidēmoi*) and "foreigners" (*paroikoi*). Some Bible translations use the terms "aliens" and "strangers."[9] While it is easy to interpret Peter's words in a strictly spiritual sense (that Christians are citizens of heaven and sojourners in the present world), their lived diaspora reality was both concrete and temporal as well as spiritual.

The "foreigners" (*paroikoi*) of 1 Peter (literally "those who do not belong") were scattered through five provinces in Asia Minor.[10] They were probably not Roman citizens and therefore faced the constant threat of deportation because of their "political, legal, and social status."[11] Though Peter's audience were gentiles, their reality was not unlike the Jewish community expelled from Rome in AD 49 by the emperor Claudius—a community that included Priscilla and Aquila, who immigrated to Corinth where they met and began working with the apostle Paul (Acts 18:2–3).

---

5   See Davids, *First Epistle of Peter*, 8; also Williams, *Persecution in 1 Peter*, 92–95.
6   See Williams, *Persecution in 1 Peter*, 18.
7   Eusebius, *History of the Church* 3.1.
8   See Davids, *First Epistle of Peter*, 8; see also Jobes, *Letters to the Church*, 282.
9   See 1 Peter 1:1, 17; 2:11. In 1:17, Peter employed the verbal form (*paroikia*)—"live out your time as foreigners." See also Dubis, "Messianic Woes in First Peter," 73–91.
10 See Hanciles, *Migration and the Making*, 25.
11 Elliott, *Home for the Homeless*, xxviii; see also Hanciles, *Migration and the Making*, 161.

Striving to make sense of the meaning of foreigners and strangers in the first-century Roman world, Jehu Hanciles proposed four categories:

- Settlers—those who leave their community and become permanent members of another community;
- Sojourners—those passing through an area for a limited time;
- Itinerants—those passing through multiple communities but possessing no permanent residence;
- Invaders—groups such as an armed military that enters an area to take control and displace inhabitants.[12]

Peter's audience could have been a mix of the first three categories.

Karen Jobes argued that Peter's readers were vulnerable people who were often on the move. They experienced "social ostracism" and were "marginal in society."[13] Discussing the hardships of first-century diaspora peoples, Hanciles described the "costs of migration." He spoke of the "trauma of displacement" and the "perils of travel," which included "hunger, adverse weather, disease, armed conflict, piracy and pillage," as well as the "risks of dying."[14]

On top of their vulnerable legal and social status within Roman society, Peter's readers were also gentile followers of Christ, which did not elevate their status or offer them any privileges in the first-century world. Andreas Köstenberger suggested that they were gentile Christians driven from Rome to Asia Minor because of their faith.[15] Peter's readers were not merely believers whose real home was in heaven; they were Christian sojourners dwelling in an unbelieving and hostile pagan society.[16] Though gentiles, Peter likened their faith journey to that of Abraham, the patriarchs, and Israel, who sojourned among the nations even as they longed for "a better country" (Heb 11:16).[17] And like the dispersed Israelites Daniel, Nehemiah, and Esther, Peter's readers were living in a cross-cultural environment where they were the religious minority. As diaspora peoples experiencing hardships, they were always on the mission field.

---

12 See Hanciles, *Migration and the Making*, 26; and Jobes, *Letters to the Church*, 334.
13 Jobes, 282, 284.
14 Hanciles, *Migration and the Making*, 30.
15 See Köstenberger, "Mission in the General Epistles," 201.
16 See Jobes, *Letters to the Church*, 288.
17 See Clowney, *Message of 1 Peter*, 38.

Trials, Accusations, and Insults

In the first of several passages on suffering, Peter noted that his readers "may have had to suffer grief in various trials" (1:6). In language that resembles the opening of James's letter ("consider it pure joy ... when you face trials of many kinds," Jas 1:2), Peter spoke about trials (*peirasmos*) in a general sense.[18] Though trials can be understood in parts of the New Testament as internal temptations toward sin, in Peter these difficulties appear to be external to the believers and caused by the ill will and hatred of others. Davids suggested that these hardships ranged from "economic persecution ... personal rivalries ... [to] physical violence," which were all intended to discourage and dislodge believers in their Christian faith.[19] In the case of slaves and their unbelieving masters (2:18–20), it could be that these servants were suffering violence at the hands of their owners.[20] Because of these trials, Peter's readers "suffered grief"; that is, they became "sad, sorrowful, and distressed."[21]

Though some of Peter's audience probably experienced some form of violence, Christians at this time were not systematically persecuted by the Roman government.[22] Though Nero was oppressing Christians in the city of Rome at the time of Peter's writing, believers in Asia Minor would not experience imperial persecution until half a century later when the Bithynian governor, Pliny, corresponded with Emperor Trajan about dealing with Christians in his province. Because of a "popular dislike of Christians," the church experienced discrimination, harassment, and even violence on a local and community level.[23] These social tensions at the community level are what probably drove Pliny to seek Trajan's advice about keeping order.

The clearest form of suffering Peter's audience experienced was the slander and ridicule they faced from their unbelieving neighbors.[24] Peter described "pagans" who "accuse" (*katalaleō*) Christians of "doing wrong" (2:12). Kistemaker likens these slandering pagans in 1 Peter to those Paul described in Romans as given over by God to a "depraved mind ... filled with every kind of wickedness, evil, greed and depravity" including "envy, murder,

---

18 See Davids, *First Epistle of Peter*, 56–57.
19 Davids, 56–57; see also Williams, *Persecution in 1 Peter*, 132–34.
20 See Kistemaker, *Exposition of the Epistles*, 17.
21 Kistemaker, 46.
22 See Williams, *Persecution in 1 Peter*, 4, 9–10.
23 Davids, *First Epistle of Peter*, 10; see also Kistemaker, *Exposition of the Epistles*, 18; and Marshall, *1 Peter*, 14.
24 See Williams, *Persecution in 1 Peter*, 300–1.

strife, deceit and malice." They are "gossips, slanderers (*katalalos*), God-haters, insolent, arrogant and boastful" (Rom 1:28–30). From this depraved basis, they accused Christians of being criminals. The Roman historian Tacitus added that Christians were "loathed" by the Romans "for their vices."[25]

The Romans accused Christians of engaging in sexual orgies and even incest because they likened their house church agape feasts to their own Roman symposia—banquets followed by drinking parties that often included sexual immorality. The Romans also charged the early Christians with cannibalism because they believed that Christians were consuming actual flesh and blood in the Eucharist. Finally, the Romans accused Christians of atheism because instead of worshiping statues in temples as the Romans did, they worshiped a God they could not see. While worshiping their own God, they were also refusing to pay homage to the Roman deities, including the emperor.[26] In his *First Apology* (ca. 155), Justin Martyr answered each of these accusations, clarifying Christian values and practices in worship.[27]

While some accusations caused psychological stress for early Christians, other charges, such as refusing to venerate the emperor, could have had legal consequences.[28] Pliny's correspondence with Trajan set the stage for a century of legal action against the church. Of course, without any legal basis, Nero made scapegoats of the Christian community in AD 64 by blaming the fire in Rome on them.[29]

In addition to these accusations, Peter acknowledged that Christians suffered by being "insulted because of the name of Christ" (4:14). By using "insulted" (*oneidizō*, which can also mean "reviled" or "upbraided"), Peter seemed to be remembering Jesus's words during the Sermon on the Mount: "Blessed are you when people insult you, persecute you and falsely say all kinds of evil against you because of me" (Matt 5:11; see also Luke 6:22).[30]

Since Jesus was insulted during his saving work on the cross (Matt 27:44; Mark 15:32), it follows that believers would also be insulted for believing in Jesus and proclaiming their faith in him. They were maligned for believing in one God and one "name under heaven given to mankind" for salvation

---

25 Cited in Marshall, *1 Peter*, 82.
26 See Smither, *Christian Martyrdom*, 17–18; Marshall, *1 Peter*, 82; Kistemaker, *Exposition of the Epistles*, 96.
27 See Justin, *First Apology*, 5–6, 65–67.
28 See Clowney, *Message of 1 Peter*, 103; Davids, *First Epistle of Peter*, 97; and Williams, *Persecution in 1 Peter*, 309.
29 See Kistemaker, *Exposition of the Epistles*, 96.
30 See Davids, *First Epistle of Peter*, 167.

(Acts 4:12)—an affront to the polytheistic and syncretistic values of Roman paganism.[31] Early Christians seemed to be especially hated because they no longer participated in the pagan rituals and behaviors that marked their previous way of life. Davids added that these insults implied they were being rejected by family, friends, neighbors, and society as a whole.[32]

Mission through Suffering

Given this sketch of the suffering first-century diaspora church in northern Asia Minor, how did Peter admonish them to participate in God's mission amid their suffering and hardship? Simply put, they were to imitate Christ in his suffering in mission, to live upright and holy lives, to be a vibrant community of believers, and to witness verbally about their hope in Christ.

Imitating Christ in Suffering

As Peter encouraged suffering first-century Christians concerning their "salvation" (1:10)—their "new birth into a living hope" (1:3) and their "inheritance ... kept in heaven" that "can never perish, spoil, or fade" (1:4)—he repeatedly pointed them to the "sufferings of Christ" (1:11). In their suffering, the best thing they could do was to imitate their suffering Savior.[33] He wrote: "Christ suffered for you, leaving you an example, that you should follow in his steps" (2:21). He added that in their sufferings they were also "participat[ing] in the sufferings of Christ" (4:13).

When Peter spoke of Christ's sufferings, he meant Christ's central saving work, which is the heart of the gospel: 1. His death on the cross—Christ shed his "precious blood" (1:19), "'bore our sins in his body' on the cross" (2:23), and was "put to death in the body" (3:18). 2. His burial—he descended to the dead where "he went and made proclamation to the imprisoned spirits" (3:19). 3. His "resurrection ... from the dead" (1:3; 3:21). Through a litany of direct quotes from Isaiah 53 in 1 Peter 2:22–25 ("He committed no sin, and no deceit was found in his mouth ... He himself bore our sins ... by his wounds you have been healed ... you were like sheep going astray"), Peter identified Jesus as Isaiah's suffering servant.[34]

---

31 Kistemaker, *Exposition of the Epistles*, 173–74.
32 See Davids, *First Epistle of Peter*, 167; Marshall, *1 Peter*, 24; Williams, *Persecution in 1 Peter*, 240–44, 323–25; and Dubis, "Messianic Woes in 1 Peter," 115–16, 146–47.
33 See Jobes, *Letters to the Church*, 344–48; and Köstenberger, "Mission in the General Epistles," 205.
34 See Jobes, *Letters to the Church*, 276.

Through his sufferings, Jesus lived out the mission of God. First, he embodied the gospel through his death, burial, and resurrection, which brought redemption for those who believed (1:18). Second, he maintained righteousness and integrity despite being tortured and killed—"he committed no sin" (2:22; Isa 53:9). Third, when he was insulted, he did not respond in kind. Peter wrote, "When they hurled their insults at him, he did not retaliate; when he suffered, he made no threats" (1 Pet 2:23). Fourth, in his sacred humanity, Jesus lived by faith in God. Peter added, "He entrusted himself to him who judges justly" (2:23).

Peter admonished his readers to imitate Christ in his sufferings. At best, this is limited because Jesus's death, burial, and resurrection of Christ were unique and unrepeatable. There is only one Savior. However, they could imitate Christ in his sufferings by embracing suffering as a reality for a Christian in a fallen world and responding to suffering with godly lives and a winsome witness.

Godly Living

In response to the slander and accusations of their pagan neighbors, Peter's readers were to engage in mission through holy living and being people of upstanding character.[35] Peter wrote: "Live such good lives among the pagans that, though they accuse you of doing wrong, they may see your good deeds and glorify God on the day he visits us … For it is God's will that by doing good you should silence the ignorant talk of foolish people (2:12, 15). Peter mentioned two possible outcomes from their witness of "good deeds." Some pagans may embrace the gospel and "glorify God" in worship, while others may simply have their slanderous words silenced because of Christians' virtuous character. I. Howard Marshall rightly noted, "Christian conduct is an important ingredient in evangelism."[36]

To witness through a virtuous life was again to imitate Christ. Peter wrote that those who follow Christ in suffering are "done with sin" (4:1). Because of this they resist indulging in sinful actions from their past: "living in debauchery, lust, drunkenness, orgies, carousing and detestable idolatry" (4:3). They are to "be holy as [God is] holy" (1:6). Though such holy living is attractive to some gentiles and silences others, some will continue to "heap abuse" on Christians for their lifestyles.

---

35 See Köstenberger, "Mission in the General Epistles," 203.
36 Marshall, *1 Peter*, 27.

Peter taught that believers should demonstrate such conduct on every level of society.[37] They should be good citizens, submitting "for the Lord's sake to every human authority," including the "emperor" and "governors" (2:13–14, 17). This is remarkable when we remember that Peter wrote these words during Nero's reign. Peter added that servants should imitate Christ by submitting to their masters (both good and bad ones) to the point of enduring insults and even suffering beatings (2:18–21).

A Communal Witness

While individual Christians were to witness through their godly character in a hostile pagan society, the church was also to be a vibrant communal witness. In contrast to how the Roman pagans viewed the Christians, Peter wrote this about them:

> But you are a chosen people, a royal priesthood, a holy nation, God's special possession, that you may declare the praises of him who called you out of darkness into his wonderful light. Once you were not a people, but now you are the people of God; once you had not received mercy, but now you have received mercy. (2:9–10)

Though the northern Asian Minor believers were from gentile backgrounds ("not a people"), Peter used the language and descriptions for Israel ("a royal priesthood, a holy nation, God's special possession") to describe this new people of God.[38] Just as Israel was to be a light to the nations by keeping God's law and mingling among the neighboring nations in a redemptive way, Peter's audience was also to imitate the ways of Christ before their pagan neighbors.

While Peter addressed the matter of suffering for Christ, he repeatedly spoke of how the members of the church ought to treat one another. Since believers have been "purified ... by obeying the truth," they should "have sincere love for each other, love one another deeply, from the heart" (1:22; 4:8). They should "offer hospitality" and use whatever gifts they possess to serve one another (4:10). They should speak to one another "as one who speaks the very words of God" (4:11) and serve one another "with the strength God provides, so that in all things God may be praised through Jesus Christ" (4:11). Davids referred to these habits of the Christian community as

---

37 See Köstenberger, "Mission in the General Epistles," 204.
38 See Jobes, *Letters to the Church*, 348–49; Ott, Strauss, and Tennent, *Encountering Theology of Mission*, 50–51; and Köstenberger, "Mission in the General Epistles," 202–3.

"communal holiness."[39] He argued that these values preserved the solidarity of the community and made their lives easier as a minority movement within a pagan world. I would also argue that as they suffered, their love and service within the church community also functioned as a collective witness to the pagans who ridiculed them.

Giving An Answer

As believers suffered through ridicule and other hardships, Peter called them to witness verbally about their faith in Christ. He wrote:

> Do not fear their threats; do not be frightened. But in your hearts revere Christ as Lord. Always be prepared to give an answer to everyone who asks you to give the reason for the hope that you have. But do this with gentleness and respect, keeping a clear conscience, so that those who speak maliciously against your good behavior in Christ may be ashamed of their slander. (3:14–16)

Along with their godly and upright conduct, Peter's readers were to open their mouths and give an answer or a defense (*apologia*) for their Christian hope. By *apologia*, Peter imagined a Christian on the witness stand in court providing sworn testimony to what they believe and what they have experienced in Christ.[40] They were not to go on the attack and dismantle pagan beliefs in a polemical manner; instead, they were to defend their faith in Christ.[41]

Ironically, in giving an answer for their faith, this is one area where the Asia Minor believers were not to imitate Christ in his suffering. When Christ suffered on the cross for sins, he did not open his mouth to defend himself or provide an explanation (2:23). Though he had preached the kingdom of God during his earthly ministry, following his arrest and during his trials, he did not offer a defense. This would be the work of his followers through their verbal witness.

Instructing the believers on how to witness, Peter insisted that their tone and manner of speech were important. While proclaiming the gospel, they should do so with "gentleness and respect" or "humility" (3:15).[42] Their gospel speech should align with their godly conduct—their imitation

---

39 Davids, *First Epistle of Peter*, 18–19.
40 See Davids, 131; Clowney, *Message of 1 Peter*, 149; and Williams, *Persecution in 1 Peter*, 314–16.
41 See Kistemaker, *Exposition of the Epistles*, 134.
42 See Clowney, *Message of 1 Peter*, 151.

of Christ—in a hostile environment.[43] Peter reiterated that their righteous and virtuous tones would cause malicious pagans to "be ashamed of their slander" (3:16).

A number of early Christians took seriously their responsibility to give an answer by publishing their faith stories. In Luke's account of Paul's trial before Felix (Acts 24), Paul offered a thorough narrative of his conversion and call to Christ. Later, in his *Dialogue with Trypho* (ca. AD 160), Justin Martyr recounted his journey to faith in Christ to his Jewish counterpart, Trypho. Finally, in the eighth book of his *Confessions* (AD 397), Augustine of Hippo provided an extended account of his faith journey.

As hostilities toward Christians continued into the second century, a group of church fathers, known as apologists, emerged who published literature to provide Christian answers to Roman pagan questions and accusations. This body of literature began with Justin's *First Apology* (ca. 155) in which he adopted the Roman court's template making an appeal (*biblidion*). In the *First Apology*, Justin defended Christians for being good Roman citizens while also explaining some Christian worship practices.[44] Following Peter's admonition to provide an answer with gentleness and respect, Theophilus of Antioch wrote his pagan friend *Autolycus* (ca. 180) with the aim of leading "an intelligent pagan to a cordial acceptance of Christianity."[45]

Perspectives on Suffering

In addition to calling them to mission through holy lives (individually and collectively) and a verbal witness, Peter also imparted a theology of suffering in God's mission. First, he taught them to cultivate a future hope amid their suffering. From the outset of the letter, he praised God for their "living hope" in Christ that cannot "perish, spoil, or fade," an "inheritance ... kept in heaven" (1:3–4). Peter assured them of "the salvation that is ready to be revealed in the last time" and that their faith will "result in praise, glory, and honor when Jesus Christ is revealed" (1:5, 8). Though they suffer, they can also "rejoice" in hope and persevere for "a little while," suffering "grief in all kinds of trials" (1:6–7).[46] Though they presently suffer as they participate in God's mission, the end of mission is praise.[47]

---

43 See Davids, *First Epistle of Peter*, 132; and Kistemaker, *Exposition of the Epistles*, 135–36.
44 See Smither, *Mission in the Early Church*, 113.
45 Dods, "Introductory Note, Theophilus of Antioch," 88.
46 See Dubis, "Messianic Woes in 1 Peter," 286–91.
47 See Köstenberger, "Mission in the General Epistles," 201–2.

Second, Peter reminded them that they were in a spiritual battle. He wrote, "Your enemy the devil prowls around like a roaring lion looking for someone to devour" (5:8). While the Asia Minor believers might be facing resistance from family, neighbors, and even local authorities, Peter affirmed with Paul that their "struggle is not against flesh and blood, but against the rulers, against the authorities, against the powers of this dark world and against the spiritual forces of evil in the heavenly realms" (Eph 6:12). Because of their position in Christ and their future hope, they are able to "resist" the devil, "standing firm in the faith" (5:9; also Eph 6:13–18).

Finally, Peter's readers should be encouraged in their suffering because they are not alone. He continued: "You know that the family of believers throughout the world is undergoing the same kind of sufferings" (5:9). While the church in Asia Minor was to band together in their shared suffering and communal witness, they were also to be encouraged in their solidarity with other believers around the world who understand their pain and suffering.

Conclusion: Reflections for the Suffering Global Church in Mission

Davids called 1 Peter a "highly relevant book wherever the church is suffering."[48] Indeed, Peter's letter is quite relevant to the lived reality of millions of global Christians today—those who suffer for following Christ and those God still calls to participate in his mission. While communities of global Christians ought to reflect on Peter's letter to draw their own applications, I will conclude with a few thoughts.

Discrimination versus Persecution

Though some of Peter's readers experienced persecution and violence, most of their suffering came through ridicule and slander in their local communities. In the present global church, some believers are jailed and even martyred for their faith, but most endure hostility through daily discrimination. In North Africa, some Muslim background believers are denied jobs, educational opportunities, and even the right to marry because of their allegiance to Christ. In China, believers live under tight government surveillance in which their physical and online movements are tracked. In Indian and Ethiopian villages, followers of Christ are the subject of community gossip.

Like Peter's audience, most global Christians today experience discrimination, pressure, and rejection from their communities. In some

---

48 Davids, *First Epistle of Peter*, 3.

ways, this is worse than facing a legal case or imprisonment from an impersonal government. This day-in and day-out discrimination in one's family and community—the center of vital relationships—causes believers to become worn down and discouraged. Some have even abandoned their faith under such pressure.

Suffering global Christians today need Peter's message: to remember the gospel of Christ, to follow Jesus in his sufferings, and to know that their suffering will only last "a little while" compared to their heavenly hope. The church must pray and sing the Psalms, including many prayers about betrayal, slander, and pressure from those in the community. For example, in Psalm 3, as David's own son Absalom sought to take his life, he prayed:

> LORD, how many are my foes!
> > How many rise up against me!
> Many are saying of me,
> > "God will not deliver him."
> But you, LORD, are a shield around me,
> > my glory, the One who lifts my head high.
> I call out to the LORD,
> > and he answers me from his holy mountain.
> I lie down and sleep;
> > I wake again, because the LORD sustains me.
> I will not fear though tens of thousands
> > assail me on every side.
> Arise, LORD!
> > Deliver me, my God!
> Strike all my enemies on the jaw;
> > break the teeth of the wicked.
> From the LORD comes deliverance.
> > May your blessing be on your people.

A Gentle and Humble Answer

God calls his people today to give a verbal witness for their gospel hope. Like Peter's readers, believers today also live in hostile environments. This could be a Muslim, Hindu, or Buddhist context in Asia or a secular post-Christian environment in Western Europe, Canada, or the United States. Peter's admonition to give an answer with "gentleness and respect" remains crucial for global mission today.

These values guided my own gospel conversations when I lived among Muslims in North Africa. Once I was visiting with one of my Muslim friends who was open to hearing the gospel. During my visit, his immediate neighbors, devout Muslims who were quite outspoken about their faith, also stopped in. Very quickly we began to talk about Christ, Islam, the Qur'an, the Bible, and other subjects. Unfortunately, in their defense of Islam, they began to attack Christian beliefs (or what they thought Christians believed), ridicule me, and rudely interrupt me when I tried to speak. Since there was no conversation to be had, I simply stopped talking. After some time, my friend, who is gentle and laid back, raised his voice at his neighbors, declared they were driving him crazy, and he made them leave. After they left, he apologized for their rudeness and then asked me to continue telling him about Christ. I was reminded through this encounter that the manner in which we witness (with gentleness, respect, and humility) is integrally related to the message itself.

I have also learned that a gentle and humble witness can also be a bold witness. While serving in international student ministry in France, I worked alongside a Muslim-background believer from North Africa. As we met Muslim students in the university and began to talk about Christ, some students would allege that Christians worshiped three gods or that Christ was born because God and Mary had sexual relations. My friend would boldly respond: "Who told you that? No Christian has ever believed such horrible things. Do you want to hear from an actual Christian what we believe?" With that permission, my friend would give a spirited and clear explanation of the gospel while laughing, joking, and drinking coffee with these students.

A Communal Witness

Peter admonished his readers to respond to suffering by loving one another as God's people. Most global cultures are communal, and individuals find their identity in the collective whole. The southern African notion of *ubuntu* ("I am because we are") illustrates this well.[49] Often when individuals profess their faith in Christ, they are ostracized from the family and community. They may be forbidden from joining the family for meals, forced to leave their home, or even have a marital engagement called off by the family. To lose such family and social connections in a culture where community is everything is a painful thing for many believers. Though one's blood relatives can never be replaced (and believers in Christ should strive to

---

49 See Ngomane, *Everyday Ubuntu*.

maintain good relationships with their families), the church community can serve as a new spiritual family for ostracized believers. In this sense, Peter's admonitions to be "a people" are quite meaningful to believers today from communal societies.

Because community is so vital, churches in communal societies also have the great opportunity to offer a communal witness. Indeed, as Peter advocated, a believing community's common life together (mutual service, fellowship, kindness, worship) serves as a witness to the non-believing community. And that believing community's witness is further expanded when they reach out to the broader community, caring for the poor, hungry, and sick while also sharing a verbal witness.

Solidarity
Suffering believers today can also find encouragement from Peter's words about solidarity in suffering—"that the family of believers throughout the world is undergoing the same kind of sufferings" (5:9). Each week in corporate worship, Anglican Christians pray "for our brothers and sisters in Christ who are persecuted for their faith."[50] While Western Christians who worship in free contexts pray these prayers for the suffering church, suffering Christians (e.g., Anglicans in Sudan, Nigeria, and India) also intercede for other persecuted believers in their weekly worship gatherings.

At times it is also possible for suffering Christians from different parts of the world to gather and gain a sense of belonging through their shared hardships. I have had the privilege to attend conferences in the Middle East with believers from Sudan, Iran, Iraq, Turkmenistan, Turkey, Morocco, and Tunisia. They have learned from one another how to press on as faithful Christians and how to be a witness to the Muslim majority in their countries.

Accepting Suffering versus Fighting for Religious Freedom
Peter's teachings on imitating Christ in suffering do not mean that global Christians living in contexts of persecution should not work for justice and religious freedom. Adopting Peter's perspective of future hope does not mean defaulting to an escapist posture in the present world. Though we pray that God's kingdom will be done on earth as it is in heaven, and we labor in kingdom mission, we realize that we will not have full justice until Christ returns and makes all things new.

---

50 *Book of Common Prayer*, 128.

In her work for political justice in the Philippines, including peaceful non-violent protest against the regime of Ferdinand Marcos in 1986, evangelical missiologist Melba Padilla Maggay reflected on the tension between Romans 13 (obeying God-established authority) and Revelation 13 (opposing a demonic beast). While many global Christians assume that since Paul wrote Romans during the reign of Nero, Romans 13 should always be obeyed, even when the government is corrupt or tyrannical. Maggay argued that in her context and *kairos* (right moment), a peaceful revolution based on Revelation 13 was a better application of Scripture than the Romans 13 teaching to submit to God-given leaders.[51] Many churches in the world (e.g., China) are presently wrestling with this tension of accepting suffering versus struggling for religious freedom. This requires further reflection.

Bibliography

The Book of Common Prayer. Huntington Beach, CA: Anglican Liturgy Press, 2019.

Burdick, Donald W., and John H. Skilton. "1 Peter Introduction." In *The NIV Study Bible*, edited by Kenneth L. Barker, 2187–90. Grand Rapids: Zondervan, 2020.

Clowney, Edmund. *The Message of 1 Peter: The Way of the Cross*. Bible Speaks Today. Downers Grove, IL: InterVarsity Press, 1988.

Davids, Peter H. *The First Epistle of Peter*. New International Commentary on the New Testament. Grand Rapids: Eerdmans, 1990.

Dods, Marcus. "Introductory Note, Theophilus of Antioch." *The Ante-Nicene Fathers* 2. Accessed August 10, 2023. https://orthodoxchurchfathers.com/fathers/anf02/anf0239.htm.

Dubis, Kevin Mark. "Messianic Woes in First Peter: Suffering and Eschatology in 1 Peter 4:12–19." PhD diss., Union Theological Seminary, 1998.

Elliott, John. *A Home for the Homeless: A Social-Scientific Criticism of 1 Peter, Its Situation and Strategy*. Eugene, OR: Wipf & Stock, 2005.

Eusebius. *The History of the Church from Christ to Constantine*. Edited by Andrew Louth. Translated by G. A. Williamson. London: Penguin, 1989.

Hanciles, Jehu. *Migration and the Making of Global Christianity*. Grand Rapids: Eerdmans, 2021.

Jobes, Karen H. *Letters to the Church: A Survey of Hebrews and the General Epistles*. Grand Rapids: Zondervan, 2011.

Kistemaker, Simon J. *Exposition of the Epistles of Peter and of the Epistle of Jude*. Grand Rapids: Baker Books, 1987.

---

51 Maggay, "Text and Context: Some Missiological Issues."

Köstenberger, Andreas J. "Mission in the General Epistles." In *Mission in the New Testament: An Evangelical Approach*, edited by Willam J. Larkin Jr. and Joel F. Williams, 1892–06. American Society of Missiology 27. Maryknoll, NY: Orbis Books, 1998.

Maggay, Melba Padilla. "Text and Context: Some Missiological Issues in the Search for New Wineskins Post-Pandemic." Plenary address at the annual meeting of the Evangelical Missiological Society (virtual), October 10, 2020.

Marshall, I. Howard. *1 Peter*. IVP New Testament Commentary Series. Downers Grove, IL: InterVarsity Press, 1991.

Ngomane, Mungi. *Everyday Ubuntu: Living Better Together, the African Way*. London: Bantam, 2019.

Ott, Craig, Stephen J. Strauss, and Timothy C. Tennent. *Encountering Theology of Mission: Biblical Foundations, Historical Developments, and Contemporary Issues*. Encountering Mission. Grand Rapids: Baker Academic, 2010.

Smither, Edward L. *Christian Martyrdom: A Brief History with Reflections for Today*. Eugene, OR: Cascade, 2020.

Smither, Edward L. *Mission in the Early Church: Themes and Reflections*. Eugene, OR: Cascade, 2014.

Williams, Travis B. *Persecution in 1 Peter: Differentiating and Contextualizing Early Christian Suffering*. Supplements to Novum Testamentum 145. Leiden: Brill, 2012.

Chapter 12

Ethical Living as Proto-Evangelion

Holiness, Honor, and Hope in 1 Peter

Jessica A. Udall

Introduction

First Peter opens with a reference to the past—we have already been "given new birth into a living hope through the resurrection" (1:3)[1] and a glorious future is also envisioned: an inheritance "is kept in heaven for [us]" (1:4). But in the times in between, how should we live and understand the world? Peter exhorted believers toward an ethic of life characterized by holiness and honor, which God uses to silence critics of the Christian faith and even to inspire questions regarding the great hope that motivates such good lives. As such, this chapter discusses the essential nature of a truly Christian lifestyle as proto-evangelion, removing the barriers—such as preconceived ideas and prejudices—for the sharing of the gospel.

The opening verses of 1 Peter provide a sweeping view of the past, present, and future of those who are followers of the way of Jesus. Peter rooted their present reality in the prophetic past in which "the sufferings of Christ and the subsequent glories" (1:11) as well as "the grace that was to be yours" (1:10) were predicted in order to serve the coming generations.[2] Peter also cast a hope-filled vision for a glorious future: believers have a "living hope" (1:3) because of the resurrection and an "inheritance that is imperishable, undefiled, and unfading, kept in heaven for you, who by God's power are being guarded through faith for a salvation ready to be revealed in the last time" (1:5).

The assurance of God's guarding power would have been good news to the recipients of 1 Peter, who were experiencing intense persecution when the letter was written. While public witnessing would have been extremely difficult during this time, this did not preclude missional living in the author's mind. Instead, 1 Peter is written with a "sensitivity ... for the complexity of

---

[1] Unless otherwise noted, all Scripture verses are from the English Standard Version.
[2] "In 1 Peter the past activity of God among his people is linked organically with his present activity among the new people of God." Green, "Use of the Old Testament," 286.

the social environment."[3] Thus, it can be viewed as "a missionary document," which seeks to consider how gentile converts could live in the world while no longer being of the world,[4] getting into the practical how-to of living a missional Christian life in the midst of an unbelieving world.[5]

Indeed, "the whole letter can and should be read against the background of mission and conversion in early Christianity."[6] As gentile converts, the recipients of 1 Peter must have somehow come to know about Jesus from others who followed him, and they were now called to live their lives as aliens who seek to live in accordance with the laws of the land whenever possible, but whose ultimate authority is the Lord of heaven and earth. As such, Peter invited gentile converts to participate in God's mission as his witnesses through their holy and honorable lifestyles lived with their eyes fixed on Jesus, courageously suffering for his sake and being filled with hope in his second coming.[7]

Old Testament Ethics Reimagined for the New Testament Church

First Peter has much to say about what a Christian lifestyle looks like, with the theme of holiness always in the foreground.[8] In fact, 1 Peter 1:16 is directly taken from Leviticus 19:2: "It is written, 'You shall be holy, for I am holy,'"[9] thus showing the connection between God's character and work in the Old Testament and the New, between the people of God in the Old Testament and the New, and the expectations for holiness among the

---

3 Volf, "Soft Difference," 26.
4 Stenschke, "Mission and Conversion," 250.
5 Volf, "Soft Difference," 16.
6 Stenschke, "Mission and Conversion," 222.
7 Khobnya, "So That They May," 10; and Payne, *Theology of Mission*, 126.
8 For more on the use of the Old Testament in 1 Peter, see Green, "Use of the Old Testament," 276–89. He commented, "There are few books in the NT which make more extensive use of the OT than 1 Peter" (285), which asserts that in the same way "as the call to holiness controls the teaching for those who embarked on the exodus from Egypt, so the same call is applied to those who are the new people of God, separated by the redemption of Christ from immorality" (276).
9 About Leviticus 19:2, Scharlemann commented: "This verse would commend itself to the apostle because of its references to holiness. Yet that is not the only reason for using it as the basis of his exhortation. For we must keep in mind the function of this passage in Israel's religion and life. This verse belongs to what is known as the Holiness Code. In Jewish thinking—and Peter was a Jew by birth and upbringing!—this was the very center of the Old Testament." "Exodus Ethics: Part One," 169.

people of God long ago and today.[10] In using Old Testament passages in his epistle, Peter did not stop at quoting the text verbatim. Instead, he processed the teachings of the Old Testament in his own words and intertwined them with the current situation, making relevant applications of timeless truths.[11] The message of the Old Testament that comes through in 1 Peter was one of both continuity and fulfillment, explained Andrew M. Mbuvi:

> While the injunctions remain the same as in the OT, their function is markedly different in 1 Peter since, unlike the OT, the 'elect' now include Gentiles, and the premise of determining the insider is no longer obedience to the Torah (including the cultic life), but faith and baptism in Jesus Christ (covenant identification) who, significantly, is also the perfect or holy sacrifice (1.18–20; 2.24).[12]

Andreas J. Köstenberger and T. Desmond Alexander elaborated on the contours of the continuity of God's people who are now in Christ—the message of 1 Peter

> is grounded in God's command to the people he called out from slavery in Egypt to be holy and set apart for him. While the external expressions of such distinctiveness (i.e., dietary, ritual and ceremonial laws) have been largely rendered obsolete, the need for God's people to live a distinct Christian lifestyle and to abstain from both physical and spiritual adultery remains. By living holy lives Christians reveal to the surrounding world God's very own nature, just as Israel was called to do.[13]

This call to holiness was received in the context of an alternative community—the church—a "contrastive community"[14] whose members "live an alternative way of life within the political, ethnic, religious, and cultural institutions of the larger society."[15] Robert W. Wall observed that "this [church] community's preoccupation, then, is not with this world per se, whether to accommodate it in response to malicious rumors or to resist it as a countercultural movement; rather, the vocation of a people belonging to God is to be the church, a holy nation, and so to suffer, if need be, simply for doing the will of God (3:13–17)."[16]

---

10 Green, "Use of the Old Testament," 289.
11 Green, 289.
12 Mbuvi, *Temple, Exile and Identity*, 80.
13 Köstenberger and Alexander, *Salvation to the Ends*, 95.
14 Seland, "Resident Aliens," 568.
15 Volf, "Soft Difference," 20.
16 Wall, "Teaching 1 Peter as Scripture," 376.

While these distinct new groups of believers did create some distance from those outside the faith, Torrey Seland asserted that

> life within the Christian communities was not without missional value and implications. Their life was to some extent observable by outsiders, who not only observed that the Christians did no longer "join them in the same excesses of dissipation" (4:4) but might also have observed that the former partygoers now had their source of identity and fellowship in other distinctive settings. The attractiveness of new and hitherto unknown communal settings in which the participants seemed to experience mutual fellowships should not be underestimated.[17]

For the Christian community, said Peter, there is no need to actively retaliate against the world;[18] instead, there is a simple acknowledgment of being on a different path that will naturally lead to differences in lifestyle.[19] Volf explained: "Christian difference from the social environment is … an eschatological one. In the midst of the world in which they live, they are given a new home that comes from God's future. The new birth commences a journey to this home."[20] As a consequence, "What permeates [1 Peter] is not a fixation on distance from the world, but enthusiasm about the eschatological future,"[21] and this "genuine Christian distance has ecclesial shape."[22] Instead of experiencing difference with a negative reaction against "the other," then, believers are empowered to step into a priestly role (2:9) and become conduits of God's goodness who refuse to "repay evil for evil or reviling for reviling, but on the contrary, bless" (3:9).

Walking in this holiness means that believers are living in step with their true identity as image-bearers and imitators of God:[23] "First Peter is convinced that Christian conduct in all aspects of life must be a direct

---

17 Seland, "Resident Aliens in Mission," 575.
18 Shaw observed, "One of the central themes shared by 1 Peter 2:21–25 and 3:8–12 is the emphasis on the non-retaliatory behavior of Jesus in the face of suffering that is likewise expected of those who follow him. In this sense, one might say that the first act of blessing is the (in) action of non-retaliation, that is, a summons to actively absorb evil, thus preventing its perpetuation." Shaw, "Called to Bless," 164.
19 For more on the contrast between being negatively *against* the world versus being positively *for* God's kingdom, see Volf, "Soft Difference," 21, and Khobnva, "So That They May," 12.
20 Volf, "Soft Difference," 18.
21 Volf, 21.
22 Volf, 19.
23 The call to holiness is predicated on the fact that "the premise of holiness is God" himself. Mbuvi, "Christology and *Cultus* in 1 Peter," 149.

consequence of their identity as God's people united by Christ,"[24] and indeed, "Peter grounds moral exhortations in God's action in Christ."[25] "This Christian identity means that they are God's representatives in every respect: in their attitudes and hope (1:13), in their holy conduct (1:14), in love for one another (1:22) and in their abstinence from any evil deeds (2:1)."[26] In addition to this, they are to "stop conforming to the pattern of life established by this world," which is "impermanent"[27] and is "a way of life characterized by a lack of knowledge of God and by misguided desires."[28] Indeed, Scharlemann pointed out that the first verses of 1 Peter lay out the glorious gospel message that believers have received, and then 1:13 begins with the word "therefore," indicating a move from indicative to imperative. Thus, "ethics follow *evangellion* [sic]."[29] But evangelion also follows from ethics, Peter made clear. Indeed, as N. T. Wright commented on ethical teaching in Deuteronomy and similar texts, "There is no biblical mission without biblical ethics."[30]

Living an ethical, holy lifestyle brings the gospel to bear on those who encounter it and leads to one of two responses: mistreatment (rejecting the gospel) or conversion (receiving the gospel). David M. Shaw explained that "the resident-alien-ness of the new Christian community was simultaneously both the reason for their success at winning people to the faith, but also the reason for their persecution!"[31] Thus, holiness and its attendant difference and distance removes neutrality as an option in response to believers. Conversely, observed Köstenberger and Alexander, if the lives of Christians are not distinct from those of non-Christians, "there will be no reason for questions concerning the hope of Christians."[32] Holiness requires differentiation, and "a consistently holy lifestyle ... has certain unique qualities that will render gospel proclamation attractive" to some,[33] but holy believers should also expect to be misunderstood and thus mistreated. Christians follow a Savior

---

24 Khobnya, "So That They May," 10.
25 Keener, *1 Peter*, 91.
26 Khobnya, "So That They May," 10.
27 Scharlemann, "Exodus Ethics," 168.
28 Khobnya, "So That They May," 11.
29 Scharlemann, "Exodus Ethics," 165, emphasis in original.
30 Wright, *Mission of God's People*, 94.
31 Shaw, "Called to Bless," 171.
32 Köstenberger and Alexander, *Salvation to the Ends*, 97.
33 Köstenberger and Alexander, 97.

who was "a stranger to the world because the world into which he came was estranged from God."[34] Indeed, it was Jesus's holiness that made a way back into God's presence for those who trust in him.[35] Along with the mistreatment they would inevitably endure, believers have a sure hope as they follow in their Savior's steps that there will be those who will "see [their] good deeds and glorify God on the day of visitation" (2:12).[36]

Peter did not view a holy lifestyle as an end in itself. Rather, the identity of the church as "a chosen race, a royal priesthood, a holy nation, a people for his own possession" is so "that you may proclaim the excellencies of him who called you out of darkness into his marvelous light" (2:9–10). Indeed, "no part of the New Testament speaks out more eloquently and straightforwardly on [the] theme of holiness of life as a way of Christian witness [than 1 Peter does]."[37] Köstenberger and Alexander commented: "Significantly, this exhortation to holiness, rather than being focused on believers' relationship with God or with one another, is directed towards their responsibility to reflect God's character in the midst of an unbelieving world."[38]

First Peter paints a picture of how believers can live in a holy, God-honoring way within a hostile culture. They are not called to major on protests and petitions and asserting their rights; instead, they are simply to "live in faithfulness to God and to the values of God's kingdom, inviting others to do the same … [and] giv[ing] public witness to a new way of life."[39] Conversely, they are not to fearfully fade into the background of society to avoid interaction with potential persecutors. Instead, they are to be well-known for their holiness and the way they honor others—even those who persecute them without cause. They are to be people whose commitment to what is good and whose reputation for doing good is undeniable.

The Relationship of Holiness and Honor

This commitment to what is good and reputation for doing what is good can be seen both in a believer's holiness—as discussed above—and in their

---

34 Volf, "Soft Difference," 17.
35 Scharlemann, "Exodus Ethics," 169.
36 Keener said of 1 Peter 2:12: "This is not a promise of nonbelievers' conversion (cf. 1 Cor. 7:16), but it is a strategy for it, and an expectation that *at the very least* the effort will be vindicated, and God glorified, on the day of judgment." *1 Peter*, 162, emphasis mine.
37 O'Connor, "Holiness of Life as a Way," 17.
38 Köstenberger and Alexander, *Salvation to the Ends*, 95.
39 Volf, "Soft Difference," 20.

honor. Holiness is recognizing and conducting oneself as a sacred image-bearer of God ("your body is a temple of the Holy Spirit within you," 1 Cor 6:19a), while honor is recognizing and treating others as sacred image-bearers of God ("So God created man in his own image, in the image of God he created him," Gen 1:27a). This honor is to be given both to believers and non-believers since "according to 1 Peter all humans are owed honor as creatures of God. Christians have duties, therefore, not only toward members of the community of believers but also toward outsiders."[40]

Holiness, we see elsewhere in Scripture, is not authentically possible without honor. That is, it is not internally consistent or pleasing to God for a person to recognize their own image-bearer status without also recognizing that of others: "With [our tongues] we bless our Lord and Father, and with it we curse people who are made in the likeness of God. From the same mouth come blessing and cursing. My brothers, these things ought not to be so" (Jas 3:9–10). In other words, real holiness and true honor must exist together or not at all.

Holiness by itself can grate against those who are living only for the pleasures of this world, but honor brings balance. The closer a potential persecutor gets to someone whose life is characterized by both holiness and honor, the more impossible it becomes to make a case against Christ, because to be around someone like this is to feel honored—treated with dignity and respect based on inherent worth and value as someone created in the image of God. Honor is a powerful scrambler of pre-conceived ideas and puts holiness in proper perspective: human lives, bodies, and souls—our own as well as those of others—are sacredly weighty, worthy of being treated with utmost care and reverence. This way of honor stands in stark contrast to the world's "flood of debauchery," which prioritizes short-term passions and self-centered sensuality over the well-being of other humans or the will of God.

Holiness, Honor, and Hope as Proto-Evangelion

In conversations on missional methods, there is frequent talk about word versus deed and their relationship to one another.[41] In these conversations, "deed" is often thought to refer to good deeds done to help those in need, and that is certainly part of what God calls believers to do. However, in

---

40 Richard, "Honorable Conduct among the Gentiles," 412.
41 Seland commented that "words and works belong together as missional aspects of the lives of the Christians in the emergent church of 1 Peter." "Resident Aliens in Mission," 588.

considering the missional methodology of 1 Peter, a broader kind of "deed" becomes apparent—doing good as a general lifestyle, which has the effect of "silenc[ing] the ignorance of foolish people" (2:15) and even causing people to "glorify God" (2:12). As such, ethics and *euangelion* have a dynamic and dialectic relationship—Martin H. Scharlemann is correct that "ethics follow *evangellion* [*sic*],"[42] but it can be equally said that euangelion follows ethics. The two must be found together if they are to be fruitful. Consistently holy and honorable conduct (2:12) is vital proto-evangelion.

When Peter described a person being asked "for a reason for the hope that is in you" (3:15), he made it clear that the person who is asked about the gospel has been suffering for righteousness' sake and presumably is not defending himself with words. In fact, as Christoph Stenschke observed:

> In situations in which Christians are maligned as evildoers (2:12), 1 Peter does not recommend verbal defence but calls for the quiet but effective witness of honourable behaviour: "Conduct yourselves honourable among the Gentiles, so that … they may see your honourable deeds." (2:12). 1 Peter 3:16 offers similar advice: "Keep your conscience clear, so that, when you are maligned, those who abuse you for your good conduct in Christ may be put to shame."[43]

In other words, Peter viewed holy and honorable conduct in the face of persecution as "a catalyst for questions about the faith."[44] How? Why? What hope is powering this perseverance? When these questions are asked, that is the time for Christians to speak.

It should be noted, however, that Christians would not be asked about the hope that was in them if they had been suffering for actually doing wrong, even if that wrong was simply annoying behavior ("let none of you suffer … as a meddler," 4:15). Indeed, the burden is on believers to make sure their behavior is not antagonizing to the gentiles in any way (2:12),

---

42 Scharlemann, "Exodus Ethics," 165, emphasis in original.
43 Stenschke, "Mission and Conversion," 243. Keener helpfully explained the idea of abusers being shamed without guile on the part of believers or the necessity of violence against accusers in this passage: "Earlier in the letter, those who trust in the cornerstone will not be shamed (LXX Isa. 28:16 in 1 Pet. 2:6), but here those who misrepresent God's servants will be shamed. Again, this reversal of shame comes not through retaliation, but through humility and respect that expose the falsehood that Jesus's followers are wrongdoers." *1 Peter*, 262.
44 Shaw, "Called to Bless," 169.

even in relatively mild ways.[45] Keener explained: "One should not act like the world, as if one belongs to it (2:11–12). But neither should one provoke non-gospel offense by failing to submit to its laws or by disrespecting its leaders (cf. 2:13–18; 3:1) ... In modern idiom, believers must choose their battles."[46] Peter's focus on "having a good conscience" is so that "when you are slandered, those who revile your good behavior in Christ may be put to shame" (3:16) because their accusations simply cannot hold up when the holiness, honor, and hope of those they accuse is observed.

First Peter shows the ideal progression of persecutors from slandering believers to glorifying God, giving the sense that increasing proximity leads to a lessening of prejudice. In other words, persecutors have preconceived negative ideas about believers, so they come closer in order to get a better look and to cause harm. As their proximity grows, however, they can see nothing except goodness, holiness, and honor. They find the cheerful hospitality (4:9), mutual service, and support (4:10) of a hope-filled community. There is nothing to attack, only love (4:8).

This ideal picture of believers characterized by holiness and honor, living as part of communities full of love, stands in stark contrast to hypocrisy, that Achilles' heel of the church, where inauthentic believers and communities look commendable from the outside but upon closer inspection are found to be wearing masks that hide unholy behavior, dishonorable conduct, and unloving hearts. Unholiness and dishonorable behavior short-circuits the progress of gospel proclamation because it removes the opportunity to speak of our hope in any authentic way.

Hypocrisy is one of the primary problems that is crippling mission in post-Christian societies today. When hypocrisy is present, potential persecutors sense the counterfeit the closer they get. Indeed, the unbeliever may even be attacked by the Christian in the name of "rights" or "standing up for what I believe," even though believers have been clearly commanded to have "a tender heart" and "a humble mind" and to "not repay evil for evil

---

45 Volf clarified that refraining from antagonizing and having a good conscience does not mean compacting like a chameleon and compromising Christian values in order to please people as an escape from persecution: "As is well-known, a certain kind of meekness is a weapon of the weak. They get their way by avoiding direct confrontations and by seemingly going with the flow." But this supposed meekness is accompanied by "guile," which is deceptive at its root and not in line with a Christian lifestyle. Instead, Volf advocated for "soft difference" that is simultaneously strong in conviction and gentle in manner. "Soft Difference," 24.

46 Keener, *1 Peter*, 162.

or reviling for reviling, but on the contrary, bless, for to this you were called, that you may obtain a blessing" (3:9).

Volf commented that living a life of holiness and honor and hope in suffering "is not simply a missionary method," which would make it more vulnerable to hypocritical co-opting for self-serving ends. "Rather, the soft difference is the missionary side of following in the footsteps of the crucified Messiah. It is not an optional extra, but part and parcel of Christian identity itself."[47] To walk this counterintuitive ethical road of holiness, honor, and hope in the face of persecution is to forego individual rights and instead directly imitate Christ, carrying on his mission of sacrificial, redemptive love:

> For to this you have been called, because Christ also suffered for you, leaving you an example, so that you might follow in his steps. He committed no sin, neither was deceit found in his mouth. When he was reviled, he did not revile in return; when he suffered, he did not threaten, but continued entrusting himself to him who judges justly. He himself bore our sins in his body on the tree, that we might die to sin and live to righteousness. By his wounds you have been healed. (2:21–24)

Whether in the Old Testament or the New, in ancient times or the modern day, believers' words must be backed up by their works, Peter makes clear, if the mission of God is to be carried out fruitfully by his followers: "The proclamation of God's excellencies must be undergirded by 'excellent behavior' … by the new-covenant community in the unbelieving world surrounding it."[48] Ethical living—characterized by holiness, honor, and hope and by an absence of hypocrisy—enables the euangelion to go forth unhindered and in its fullness. "Once [we] were not a people, but now you are God's people; once [we] had not received mercy, but now [we] have received mercy" (2:10), we can say with holy, humble conviction as we declare God's praises while inviting other honored image-bearers to do to the same (2:9).

Bibliography

Green, Gene L. "The Use of the Old Testament for Christian Ethics in 1 Peter." *Tyndale Bulletin* 41, no. 2 (1990): 276–89.

Keener, Craig S. *1 Peter: A Commentary.* Grand Rapids: Baker Academic, 2021.

---

47 Volf, "Soft Difference," 25.
48 Köstenberger and Alexander, *Salvation to the Ends*, 94.

Khobnya, Svetlana. "So That They May Be Won Over without a Word: Reading 1 Peter through a Missional Lens." *European Journal of Theology* 29, no. 1 (2019): 7–16.

Köstenberger, Andreas J. "Mission in the General Epistles." In *Mission in the New Testament: An Evangelical Approach*, edited by William J. Larkin Jr. and Joel F. Williams. American Society of Missiology 27. Maryknoll, NY: Orbis Books, 1998.

Köstenberger, Andreas J., and T. Desmond Alexander. *Salvation to the Ends of the Earth: A Biblical Theology of Mission*. 2nd ed. New Studies in Biblical Theology 53. Downers Grove, IL: InterVarsity Press, 2020.

Mbuvi, Andrew M. "Christology and *Cultus* in 1 Peter: An African (Kenyan) Appraisal." In *Jesus without Borders: Christology in the Majority World*, edited by Gene L. Green, Stephen T. Pardue, and K. K. Yeo, 141–61. Majority World Theology Series. Grand Rapids: Eerdmans, 2015.

Mbuvi, Andrew M. *Temple, Exile and Identity in 1 Peter*. Library of New Testament Studies 345. New York: T&T Clark, 2007.

O'Connor, Dan. "Holiness of Life as a Way of Christian Witness." *International Review of Mission* 80, no. 1 (1991): 17–26.

Payne, J. D. *Theology of Mission: A Concise Biblical Theology*. Bellingham, WA: Lexham, 2021.

Richard, Earl J. "Honorable Conduct among the Gentiles: A Study of the Social Thought of 1 Peter." *Word and World* 24, no. 4 (2004): 412–20.

Scharlemann, Martin H. "Exodus Ethics: Part One—1 Peter 1:13–16." *Concordia Journal* 2, no. 4 (1976): 165–70.

Seland, Torrey. "Resident Aliens in Mission: Missional Practices in the Emerging Church of 1 Peter." *Bulletin for Biblical Research* 19, no. 4 (2009): 565–89.

Shaw, David M. "Called to Bless: Considering an Under-appreciated Aspect of 'Doing Good' in 1 Peter 3:8–17." *Biblical Theology Bulletin* 50, no. 1 (2020): 161–73.

Stenschke, Christoph. "Mission and Conversion in the First Epistle of Peter." *Acta Patristica et Byzantina* 19, no. 1 (2008): 221–63.

Volf, Miroslav. "Soft Difference: Theological Reflections on the Relation between Church and Culture in 1 Peter." *Ex Auditu* 10 (1994): 15–30.

Wall, Robert W. "Teaching 1 Peter as Scripture." *Word and World* 24, no. 4 (2004): 368–77.

Wright, Christopher J. H. *The Mission of God's People: A Biblical Theology of the Church's Mission*. Biblical Theology for Life. Grand Rapids: Zondervan, 2010.

Chapter 13

Evangelism in 1 Peter

The Verbal Proclamation of a People Awaiting the Return of Their King

Will Brooks

In this letter, Peter wrote to a persecuted community of heaven-bound "sojourners" (2:11),[1] who lived in a sinful world while awaiting the appearance of their Savior. Given the fact they were exiles in a world that rejected and persecuted them, we might expect Peter to have encouraged them to simply survive in any way they could. Instead, Peter's missiological and eschatological vision compelled them to engage the world around them. In other words, one of the ways believers set their hope on the return of Christ is by proclaiming to a lost and dying world the message of what God has done in Christ. Especially important for this understanding of the verbal proclamation of the gospel are 1 Peter 2:9b and 3:15, both of which encourage believers to share with those around them. This chapter will first examine those two texts and then consider how the broad themes of 1 Peter contribute to this discussion.

For clarity's sake, let me first state that I follow Christopher Wright's definition of mission: "Fundamentally, our mission (if it is biblically informed and validated) means our committed participation as God's people, at God's invitation and command, in God's own mission within the history of God's world for the redemption of God's creation."[2] That is to say, "Our mission flows from and participates in the mission of God."[3] I also use *missionary task* to speak of the process whereby missionaries cross cultural boundaries, and that task includes entry, evangelism, discipleship, church formation, leadership development, and exit.[4]

That said, in terms of a missiological reading of 1 Peter, instead of forcing an arbitrary framework on the letter, my goal through studying the text is to

---

1 Unless otherwise indicated, all Scripture quotations are from the ESV.
2 Wright, *Mission of God*, 22–23.
3 Wright, 22–23.
4 International Mission Board, *IMB Foundations*, 75–104. The idea of "exit" does not envision abonnement but rather the idea of indigenization and the need to raise up local leaders to whom missionaries can entrust the future of the church. For an excellent article on exit, see Pearce, "Exit: Training and Trusting."

first understand the original author's intention. Only by first understanding the intention in the text and by seeing the various themes that emerge from the text can we then consider missiological implications.[5]

Proclaiming His Greatness (1 Pet 2:9b)

1 Peter 2:9–10 serves as the conclusion for a section of the letter that focuses on the community's identity. They are to be characterized by holiness (1:13–15), fear of the Lord (1:16–21), love for one another (1:22–25), and longing for God's word (2:1–3). They follow in Christ's footsteps for just as he is a living stone (2:4), they too are like living stones (2:5). In his life Jesus was rejected by people but was precious to God because of his covenant faithfulness (2:4). Similarly, believers are rejected by this world and considered exiles (1:2, 17; 2:11), yet because of their relationship with Christ, they will not be put to shame (2:6). If they persevere, they will receive honor when Christ returns (2:7).[6] In the meantime, God is forming them into a spiritual house that offers praise through Christ (2:4).

This description of the community culminates in one of the more well-known verses of 1 Peter where Peter uses Old Testament imagery to describe the new community. Believers are "a chosen race, a royal priesthood, a holy nation, a people for his own possession" (2:9). For our purposes, the key aspect of this verse is in the second half. Here, after this long excursus on the chosen community, Peter explained its purpose: "that you may proclaim the excellencies of him who called you out of darkness into his marvelous light."[7] This holy nation finds its purpose in declaring the greatness of their God.[8]

Thus, by using Exodus 19 in 1 Peter 2:9, Peter is doing good biblical theology—like Israel, these were people who had been chosen (as Israel in Abraham), redeemed (as Israel through the exodus), and brought into covenant (as Israel at Sinai) to display God's glory to the surrounding nations (Deut 4:6–7; 28:9–10). God could have placed Israel virtually anywhere if all

---

5 For more on my hermeneutical approach, see Brooks, *Interpreting Scripture across Cultures*; and Brooks, "Grammatical-Historical Exegesis," 239–67.

6 "黄义信,"希腊文对神学生的必要性 (The Importance of Greek to Theology Students)," 8.

7 The conjunction ὅπως brings out the purpose here. Schreiner and Forbes make the same point: Schreiner, *1 & 2 Peter and Jude*, 122; and Forbes, *1 Peter*, 69.

8 I am aware that some scholars see this statement as pointing to the internal dynamic of the community, that is, declaring God's greatness happens in their worship. Given the dynamic of the letter that Peter is writing to a persecuted community and spends much of the letter helping them understand how to persevere in light of their status as exiles, I find that argument unconvincing. For a brief discussion of this debate, see Forbes, *1 Peter*, 69.

he wanted was a people for himself, but he chose to place them in the midst of other nations—for the sake of those peoples. All that to say, evangelism is not carried out in spite of election but because of it.

The verb in 2:9 is from ἐξαγγέλλω (*exangellō*), and it carries the idea of announcement or proclamation.[9] This specific action envisions communication, meaning that the believing community was expected to use their words—not just their good deeds—to communicate their faith with others. Grudem mentioned the connection with Isaiah 43:21 ("that they might declare my praise") since both texts' promises speak of God's redemptive work in a way that results in proclaiming his glory.[10] Grudem then stated, "This purpose of redemption is too often thwarted by our silence or self-congratulatory pride, but even brief association with a Christian whose speech fulfills this purpose invariably refreshes our spirits."[11]

On this point, Shively T. J. Smith noted the similarity of Peter's readers with the many periods of foreignness in Israel's history.[12] The difference here, as she explained, is that their foreignness is not due to geographical displacement but because of a new way of living. Because they are in Christ, the gospel shapes the way they speak and act, and this new way of living is strange to those around them. As Smith noted, "they are subjected to living as resident strangers in familiar surroundings," but these differences "serve a grand purpose in the life of the believing community and in the period of diaspora … which could draw prospective converts to the faith."[13]

After the verb "proclaim," we see the content of proclamation: the excellencies of God. Craig S. Keener translated the word as "greatness," stating that "it was an aspect of character regarded as praiseworthy."[14] The point here is that this community that sojourns like Christ makes it their aim to proclaim Christ—his works, character, virtues, greatness, and praiseworthiness—to the world around them. The final phrase in the clause further clarifies the excellent one who is worthy of praise, "Him who called you out of darkness into his marvelous light." God's redemptive work is in view here as this dualistic language is often used in Scripture to contrast good

---

9   Louw and Nida, "ἐξαγγέλλω," 411.
10 Grudem, *1 Peter*, 111.
11 Grudem, 112.
12 Smith, *Strangers to Family*, 40–41.
13 Smith, 40–41.
14 Keener, *1 Peter*, 140.

with evil or life with death.[15] God has redeemed them from sin and death and brought them into a right relationship with himself, and his greatness must be declared to the nations.

Giving a Defense (1 Pet 3:15)

A second command related to evangelism is located in a section of the letter that addresses the opposition from the world that believers should expect. Peter's wording, "Have no fear of them, nor be troubled, but in your hearts honor Christ as holy" (3:14–15) harkens back to Jesus's words in Matthew 10:28 and John 14:27. The eschatological reality of Christ's future reign leaves believers unafraid of the potential social or political ramifications of the current situation. On this point, Thomas R. Schreiner noted that the phrase "in your hearts" does not mean that honoring Christ is only done in one's private life, but instead, "The heart is the origin of human behavior," and thus, "The inner and outer life are inseparable because what happens within will inevitably be displayed outwardly, especially when one suffers."[16]

Since the inner and outer life are inextricably connected, it makes sense that one aspect of honoring Christ as Lord means speaking to others about one's faith. Peter explained, "Always being prepared to make a defense to anyone who asks you for a reason for the hope that is within you" (3:15). The first phrase that needs explanation is "make a defense" (ἀπολόγια). This phrase has led to the development of the field of apologetics, which seeks to be "a response to the culture and its *critiques of or questions for* Christianity and is always done in conversation with culture and the people that define it."[17]

While the modern field of apologetics is helpful in terms of Christians providing reasoning or evidence for their faith, as Karen H. Jobes explained, this field is not necessarily what Peter envisioned.[18] For example, Louw and Nida explained the word simply as "to speak on behalf of oneself or of others against accusations assumed to be false."[19] Peter spoke to the need of all Christians to know both the content of the faith and the reasons for their faith. As Norman L. Geisler explained about this verse, "Christians are commanded to know what they believe and why they believe it."[20]

---

15 Keener, 142–44.
16 Schreiner, *1 & 2 Peter*, 197–98.
17 Forrest, Chatraw, and McGrath, *History of Apologetics*, 23; emphasis in original.
18 Jobes, *1 Peter*, 230.
19 Louw and Nida, "ἀπολόγια," 438.
20 Geisler and Turek, *I Don't Have Enough Faith*, 29.

This need helps us understand why Peter introduced the phrase as he does, stating that they should *"be prepared* to make a defense." If believers are to defend themselves against the accusations of others, providing a clear explanation of why they believe what they believe, there must be intentional preparation to do so. "Be prepared" reminds us that discipleship needs to be a key component of the missionary task and a partner to evangelism.

Of course, we need to remember the situation of Peter's original audience. Andrew M. Mbuvi argued helpfully for exile as a controlling metaphor in 1 Peter,[21] and this metaphor points to the issues Peter attempted to address. Unlike the people of Israel in the Old Testament, Peter's audience was not composed of literal exiles, even though they were spread out around the region (1:2). Rather, the metaphor speaks to their position in society as outcasts and misunderstood because of their faith in Christ. Likely, they were frequently questioned about their faith and why they had joined such a strange, new community.

Thus, Peter's admonition to give a defense is best viewed not in terms of a courtroom scene or a modern-day interreligious dialogue where believers provide archaeological or other evidence to support the historical reliability of the faith.[22] Instead, for Peter's original audience, this command is best viewed in terms of everyday evangelistic encounters with family, friends, coworkers, neighbors, and others with whom they interacted. Supporting this view is the internal evidence in the letter related to the trials this community was facing, namely that unbelievers were "surprised" (4:4) that these believers were no longer joining them in sinful exploits and often insulted them (4:14).

Also supporting this view is Peter's explanation that believers must give a defense "for *the hope* that is in you." The concept of hope (ἐλπίδος) is an important one in 1 Peter, given its emphasis on eschatological reward and the need for persevering faith amidst trials. In the Old Testament, the words for "hope" often refer to a longing for the fulfillment of God's saving promises (Ezra 10:2; Job 6:8; 13:15; Pss 33:18, 22; 42:5; 119:81; Isa 51:5; Jer 31:17).[23] In the New Testament it is used in the same way to speak of

---

21 Mbuvi, *Temple, Exile and Identity*, 28.

22 As mentioned above, Jobes, *1 Peter*, 230 makes a similar point. This is contrary to BDAG, which defines the word as a legal term, 117.

23 I am indebted to Kyle Essary for pointing out the different Hebrew words translated as hope. He wrote, "The word for hope is הְוָקְמָ in Ezra 10:2 (see also Jer 14:8; 17:3; 50:7; 1 Chr 29:15). It is הוְקָתּ (a similar but distinct cognate) in Job 6:8 and Jer 31:17. It is לחי in Job 13:15; Ps 33:18, 22; 42:6; 119:81 and Isa 51:5." Personal communication.

the inauguration of these promises. For example, in Acts 26:6–7, Paul said, "I stand here on trial because of my *hope* in the promise made by God to our Fathers, to which our twelve tribes hope to attain, as they earnestly worship night and day." Then in verse 8 he explained what that hope is precisely—that God will raise the dead.

The Old Testament predicted a Messiah who suffers and then is glorified. The surprising twist in the story is the span of time between the promised Messiah's sufferings, declared in the New Testament, and his glorious return, promised in the New Testament. The New Testament does not just look back on the fulfillment of Old Testament hopes, it also looks forward with anticipation to the completion or consummation of those hopes. That is, believers do not hope for something that will be manifested in this life. Rather, their hope is future-oriented; they long for the resurrection that will come at the return of Christ.

Peter used the noun form of hope three times (1:3, 21; 3:15) and the verb form two times (1:13; 3:5), and like other New Testament writers, he used the terms to point believers to the consummation of God's saving promises in Christ. In 1:3 he described the believer's hope as "living." The point is that a believer's hope in what is to come grows stronger and increases over time. As believers walk with the Lord and trust him in the midst of various trials, their certainty of the fulfillment of future promises grows.

In this context where Peter's readers were societal outcasts to such an extent that they were described as exiles, it would have likely seemed strange to unbelievers that this group had such hope within them. It makes sense why they would need to explain the hope within them. Amid insults, rejection, and questions, Peter expected believers to provide reasons for their faith in such a way that it persuaded others to repent and turn to Christ. In fact, this goal is similar to Peter's point in 2:12, "so that when they speak of you as evildoers, they may see your good deeds and glorify God on the day of visitation."[24]

Finally, this verse speaks to the method believers should use to defend the hope within them. Though the word "defend" may connote the sense of

---

[24] In terms of the last part of this phrase, I find Grudem's explanation convincing that what Peter means is that "This glorification is almost certainly the voluntary praise of people who have been converted and not the forced acknowledgment by unbelievers that God has been right." Grudem, *1 Peter*, 117. This is contra Schreiner who stated that "the evidence tilts toward judgment rather than salvation." *1 & 2 Peter and Jude*, 134. For a discussion of the eschatological dimension of this verse, see 唐华德, "彼得前书三章13节至四章11节的终末思想 (The Eschatological Emphasis)," 26–27.

responding to an attack, Peter diminished the negative sense of the word by explaining that believers do so with "gentleness and respect." Their respect for those seeking to harm them grows out of their recognition that all people are created in God's image and are worthy of respect. Keener explained that this admonition echoes 2:18 and 3:2, 4, and "as a minority faith, believers held a subordinate position, and respecting others was valuable not only as a matter of principle but also a prerequisite for survival."[25]

Similarly, believers respond to opposition or questions about their faith with gentleness because they recognize that at one point they too were unbelievers, dead in their sinfulness. In fact, Peter used phrases to speak of their "former ignorance" (1:14), "futile ways inherited from your forefathers" (1:18), and also "For the time that is past suffices for doing what Gentiles do ..." (4:3) to remind his readers of their former sinful ways. Such reminders should have led them away from hating or harboring resentment toward those harming them and instead toward compassion for their oppressors since they themselves were once sinful and in need of Christ.

Thus, Peter's command to give a defense should be understood as a call to the verbal proclamation of the gospel. As believers face opposition to their faith from family, friends, neighbors, coworkers, or others, they use these opportunities to communicate the hope of the gospel within them. That hope believers have within them is an essential part of God's mission completed in the person and work of Christ and is the gospel message that a lost and dying world desperately needs. Rather than this hope leading to arrogance or resentment toward those who are not part of the believing community, believers should communicate this gospel with gentleness and respect, always with a desire that those who initially persecute them will come to faith in Christ.

An Eschatological Community

Now that we have examined two key texts in 1 Peter that command verbal communication of the gospel, we will consider the broad themes that naturally emerge from the letter and how these themes may encourage verbal communication of the gospel. In painting an overall picture of the letter, we have already seen that Mbuvi helpfully argued for exile as the controlling metaphor for the letter.[26] He also added that exile is most meaningful when

---

25 Keener, *1 Peter*, 261.
26 Mbuvi, *Temple, Exile and Identity in 1 Peter*, 28.

combined with the idea of Second Temple "eschatological restoration," which he describes as an "anticipation of eschatological regathering of the diaspora, reestablishing of the temple, forgiving of national sin, eradicating or converting the Gentiles, and implementing measures to maintain purity and holiness."[27] Mbuvi clarified, though, that for Peter's audience, this longing for end times restoration is reinterpreted through the lens of Christ.[28]

Thus, these believers were societal outcasts because of their faith in such a sense that Peter described them with the metaphor of exile. As a result of their commitment to Christ, they faced trials (1:6) that could be described as "fiery" (4:12) and were insulted (4:14), slandered (2:12; 3:16), and misunderstood (4:4). Kelly D. Liebengood explained why this community had difficulty understanding these trials:

> Whereas the Passion Narratives are primarily concerned with explaining why the Christ had to suffer and die and how that fits with what has been revealed in the scriptures, 1 Peter is primarily concerned with explaining why Christian suffering is necessary and to be expected in spite of the fact that, according to early Jesus followers, Jesus is the Lord's messiah… . The question that Peter appears to be addressing throughout the letter then is not *Who is to come?* Or *What are the circumstances surrounding his coming?* But rather, *Why is there still suffering now that the Christ has come?*[29]

This primary question that drives 1 Peter, then, is profoundly eschatological. Peter's explanation and encouragement to them was to persevere by looking forward to their future glory in Christ. He reminded them that, through the resurrection of Jesus, they have been born again into a living hope that will be realized in the future (1:3), an inheritance that will be received in the future (1:4), and a salvation "ready to be revealed in the last time" (1:5). Their faith will result in "praise and glory and honor at the revelation of Jesus Christ" (1:7). They are commanded to set their hope on the return of Christ (1:13). Like Christ (2:4–5), believers are rejected by this world but will receive glory if they persevere until the end for "the honor is for you who believe" (2:7). Even though they suffer for a time, they will "rejoice and be glad when his glory is revealed" (4:13).

Why it is necessary to address the themes of exile, persecution, and

---

27 Mbuvi, 33.
28 Mbuvi, 30.
29 Liebengood, *Eschatology of 1 Peter*, 180, emphasis mine.

eschatology? The reason is because it provides the context for the previous two commands (2:9; 3:15). What did Peter expect of believers during their time of exile? How were they to engage the world as they persevered and awaited future glory? One answer is that Peter expected them to engage in mission by proclaiming the life-changing truth of the gospel to the world around them.[30]

To consider these questions from a different angle, Peter often spoke about the coming judgment (1:17; 2:8; 2:23; 4:5; 4:17–18). In light of the coming judgment, Peter admonished his readers to pursue holiness (1:15–16), to keep their conduct "honorable" (2:12; 3:3), and to do good (2:15; 2:20; 3:16; 4:19). These commands serve a dual purpose of both preparing believers themselves while also providing evidence of their own transformed lives to unbelievers with whom they interact. The evidence of their new lives in Christ supplements their verbal proclamations of the gospel, which are driven by the evangelistic desire that others turn to Christ before the coming judgment.

One example of this perspective comes in 3:1–6, where Peter spoke to wives who have unbelieving husbands. These wives seem to have already shared the gospel with their husbands, and yet the husbands refused to believe (3:1). The wives, though, recognized that a future judgment is coming for all those separated from Christ, and thus with compassionate hearts they desired their husbands to turn to Christ. Even though the husbands had no desire to listen to the word, the wives still hoped that "they may be won" (3:1). Their eschatological perspective provided the motivation for gospel proclamation.[31]

As G. K. Beale explained, "The resurrection marked the beginning of Jesus's messianic reign, and the Spirit at Pentecost signaled the inauguration of his rule through the church."[32] He continued, "The pouring out of the Spirit is a further stage of eschatological fulfillment, which makes the time of the church an eschatological era."[33] From Peter's perspective, this church age is characterized by believers sharing the gospel because, in his words, "The end of all things is at hand" (4:7).

---

30 For a thesis on the importance of witness in 1 Peter, see Yu, "从彼得前书看末世苦难群体的见证 (The testimony of a suffering community)."
31 Jobes, *1 Peter*, 51.
32 Beale, *New Testament Biblical Theology*, 137.
33 Beale, 137.

Missiological Insights

Now that we have considered two key texts and the overall theological themes of the epistle, we can turn our attention to a few missiological implications. First, throughout this study, we have seen the importance of the verbal proclamation of the gospel. This reminder is sorely needed in the contemporary church. As Michael Green stated in his reflections on evangelism in the early church, "Unless there is a transformation of contemporary church life so that once again the task of evangelism is something that is seen as incumbent on every baptized Christian and is backed up by a quality of living that outshines the best that unbelief can muster, we are unlikely to make much headway through techniques of evangelism."[34]

Evangelism, though, does not need to be only personal and individual. In 1 Peter, there is a corporate dynamic built into the commands to evangelism in such a sense that it is expected that the church will evangelize together. For example, in 2:9 the verb ἐξαγγείλητε is second person plural, as is the pronoun that is the object of the participle ὑμᾶς καλέσαντος ("who called you")—meaning that there is a corporate dimension to their calling and purpose to declare God's greatness. Lucy Witten explained the application of this principle for missions:

> The task of evangelism is rightly accomplished with both personal and corporate evangelism. Evangelism must connect to the local church. Missionaries need to evangelize in partnership with new and established churches in their context. Helping the local church to flourish as an evangelistic community enlarges the reach of the missionary.[35]

One way this happens in mission contexts where no church exists is when missionaries share the gospel with entire families or communities. Since many contexts, like many in the Majority World, have collectivistic value systems, it makes sense for people to hear the gospel in community. One example of this is the video "Ee-taow" in which the Mouk people in Papua New Guinea gathered together over a period of time to hear the biblical story and evaluate it together.[36] Of course, this does not dismiss the need for people to make an individual decision to follow Christ. It simply recognizes the collectivistic dynamic in many cultural contexts that influences the way people choose to hear and respond to important information.

---

34 Green, *Evangelism in the Early Church*, 381.
35 Witten, "Evangelism: Sharing the Gospel."
36 "Ee-Taow," *Ethnos* 360, May 13, 2014.

Likewise, Peter's emphasis on evangelism with gentleness and respect means that, when missionaries are sent cross-culturally, they should take the time to learn the worldview in the places they are serving. They must learn the thoughts, beliefs, and values of those people and then learn to communicate in culturally appropriate ways. Doing so is an act of respect and shows that they value all people as created in the image of God. One example is that in Asian contexts, missionaries should recognize indirect communication patterns and not be overly direct or pushy in calling for a response. Moreover, missionaries need to recognize that this type of communication, combined with an honor-shame dynamic, means that people will respond positively if pushed—not because they are interested in the gospel but because they do not want to shame the evangelist. Though the recipient seeks to avoid damaging the relationship, it will not be a positive outcome toward the gospel or Christianity.

Second, studying 1 Peter is a reminder of the need for missionaries to prepare for evangelistic encounters. As we have seen, Peter emphasized that in the midst of questions or attacks from unbelievers, believers need to have the ability to defend the faith and provide reasons for the hope within them. Doing so means preparing for those questions or concerns *in advance*. As Benjamin K. Forrest and others have said, these responses are done "in conversation with the culture."[37] Such a statement is challenging for missionaries since the questions raised will be different in different cultural contexts, and as the gospel spreads to new peoples and places, those peoples and places will likely produce new questions.

Twenty years ago, I was living cross-culturally in an urban area, and I shared the gospel with a young professional. His only response to the gospel was, "If I believe in Jesus will it make me successful? And will Jesus help me find a beautiful girlfriend?" I had never encountered someone with such a thought process and did not know how to respond. Years later, I was in a different context where the people were largely animistic. The gospel conversations there and unbelievers' questions were quite different since they were concerned (and often fearful of) the spirit world. Some responded, "If I believe in Jesus, no one will care for my ancestors."

These different responses serve as a reminder of the need for rigorous training for missionaries who are sent cross-culturally. They will face questions that they have never considered before, and thus, need to be

---

37 Forrest, Chatraw, and McGrath, *History of Apologetics*, 23.

equipped with a biblical and theological foundation so that they can respond to unique concerns not discussed in seminary. To that point, theological education (especially as it relates to training for missionaries) does not exist to answer every question. Rather it exists to equip students with the skills to do theology in context, and this is especially critical for cross-cultural missionaries who will be wrestling with cultural issues and concerns they have never considered.

Considering the missionary task, as missionaries share the gospel and lead others to faith, this point about defending the faith is a reminder of the need for discipleship. Missionaries must disciple local believers—especially those in contexts formerly untouched by the gospel—to defend the faith. Doing so means missionaries need to have a deep understanding of the local culture and its worldview such that they recognize the key elements that contradict the gospel and may serve as stumbling blocks. Again, the goal of missionary discipleship is not just to provide these new believers with all the answers, but it is to put them on the path to Christian maturity (Col 1:28), which means they can go to Scripture and apply its unchanging truth to the ever-changing questions of people in their context.

Third, it is worth stating that theology matters. In 2:9 Peter framed the evangelistic task in terms of proclaiming God's excellencies. Such an understanding of evangelism means that missionaries need to have a healthy doctrine of God and strong theological foundations.[38] For example, considering the need for missionaries not only to share the gospel but also to train believers to share the gospel, we can see that this training

> will include theological discussions of what Scripture says about God's nature and character. It will also involve setting the biblical-theological foundation for *why* believers evangelize, not just the practical training of *how* to evangelize. Moreover, it will also involve the *what* of evangelism, ensuring that believers are sharing the true gospel. The priority of a firm understanding of the gospel message is what motivated Paul to begin many of his letters with teaching on the gospel.[39]

Finally, reflecting on the teaching of 1 Peter and the reality that Christ will return, the church must recognize that, until he returns, they should share the gospel. Part of their status as exiles is strategic in that God has placed all believers around those who need to hear the gospel. Such a point

---

[38] For a longer argument on this point, see Tan and Brooks, "Theological Education," 177–203.
[39] Tan and Brooks, 179.

is consistent with Peter's emphasis on election for service (Exod 19; 1 Pet 2:9). A time of judgment is coming, and as we have already seen, Peter encouraged his readers to live and speak in ways that persuade people to turn to Christ so that on the day Christ returns they may join the believing community in glorifying him.

From a negative perspective, Peter's emphasis on the certainty of Christ's return does not lead to a monkish approach that abandons the world and waits for his return. Nor does it encourage the kind of attitude I heard some years ago from a missionary at a church who said, "We should all share the gospel because I want Jesus to come back sooner." Sharing the gospel with urgency will not speed up Jesus's return. Instead, in Peter's mind anticipating Jesus's return leads the church to live and labor for the right kind of things—things with eternal impact.

Peter's eschatological perspective compels his readers to share the gospel with the world around them. Believers have been ransomed by the blood of Christ (1:18–19) and have tasted the goodness of God (2:3), and as they set their hope on his return (1:13), they proclaim his excellencies to a lost and dying world. This is the beauty of the gospel: that the one who has called them "out of darkness and into his glorious light" (2:9) now sends them back toward darkness filled with compassionate, loving hearts to proclaim the greatness of God to those still separated from him.

Bibliography

Beale, G. K. *A New Testament Biblical Theology: The Unfolding of the Old Testament in the New*. Grand Rapids: Baker Academic, 2011.

Brooks, Will. "Grammatical-Historical Exegesis and World Mission." In *World Mission: Theology, Strategy, & Current Issues*, edited by Scott N. Callaham and Will Brooks, 239–67. Bellingham, WA: Lexham, 2019.

Brooks, Will. *Interpreting Scripture across Cultures: An Introduction to Cross-Cultural Hermeneutics*. Eugene, OR: Wipf & Stock, 2022.

Danker, Frederick W., Walter Bauer, William Arndt, and F. Wilbur Gingrich. *Greek-English Lexicon of the New Testament and Other Early Christian Literature*. 3rd ed. Chicago: University of Chicago Press, 2000.

"Ee-Taow." Ethnos 360. May 13, 2014. https://www.ethnos.nz/videos/2020/ee-taow-the-mouk-story.

Forbes, Greg. *1 Peter*. Exegetical Guide to the Greek New Testament. Nashville: B&H Academic, 2014.

Forrest, Benjamin K., Joshua D. Chatraw, and Alister E. McGrath, eds. *The History of Apologetics: A Biographical and Methodological Introduction*. Grand Rapids: Zondervan Academic, 2020.

Geisler, Norman L. and Frank Turek. *I Don't Have Enough Faith to Be an Atheist*. Wheaton, IL: Crossway, 2004.

Green, Michael. *Evangelism in the Early Church*. Rev. ed. Grand Rapids: Eerdmans, 2003.

Grudem, Wayne. *1 Peter*. Tyndale New Testament Commentaries 17. Grand Rapids: Eerdmans, 1988.

International Mission Board. *IMB Foundations*. Richmond: IMB, 2018.

Jobes, Karen H. *1 Peter*. Baker Exegetical Commentary on the New Testament. Grand Rapids: Baker Academic, 2005.

Keener, Craig S. *1 Peter: A Commentary*. Grand Rapids: Baker Academic, 2021.

Liebengood, Kelly D. *The Eschatology of 1 Peter: Considering the Influence of Zechariah 9–14*. Society for New Testament Studies Monograph Series 157. Cambridge: Cambridge University Press, 2013.

Louw, Johannes P., and Eugene A. Nida. "ἐξαγγέλλω." In *Greek–English Lexicon of the New Testament based on Semantic Domains*. 2nd ed. New York: United Bible Society, 1989.

Mbuvi, Andrew M. *Temple, Exile and Identity in 1 Peter*. Library of New Testament Studies 345. New York: T&T Clark, 2007.

Pearce, Preston. "Exit: Training and Trusting." *Great Commission Baptist Journal of Missions* 1, no. 1 (2022). https://doi.org/10.31046/gcbjm.v1i1.3054.

Schreiner, Thomas R. *1 & 2 Peter and Jude*. Christian Standard Commentary 37. Nashville: B&H Academic, 2020.

Smith, Shively T. J. *Strangers to Family: Diaspora and 1 Peter's Invention of God's Household*. Waco, TX: Baylor University Press, 2016.

Tan, Sunny, and Will Brooks. "Theological Education as Integral Component to World Mission Strategy." In *World Mission: Theology, Strategy, & Current Issues*, edited by Scott N. Callaham and Will Brooks, 177–203. Bellingham, WA: Lexham, 2019.

Witten, Lucy. "Evangelism: Sharing the Gospel in Community." *Great Commission Baptist Journal of Missions* vol. 1, no. 1 (2022). https://serials.atla.com/gcbjm/article/view/3055.

Wright, Christopher J. H. *The Mission of God: Unlocking the Bible's Grand Narrative*. Downers Grove, IL: IVP Academic, 2006.

Yu, Mu. "从彼得前书看末世苦难群体的见证 [The Testimony of a Suffering Community with an Eschatological Perspective from 1 Peter)." 神说论文 ThM thesis, Malaysia Baptist Theological Seminary, 2023.

黄义信. "希腊文对神学生的必要性 [The Importance of Greek to Theology Students]." 神学文集 *MBTS Theological Journal* 7 (2021): 4–10. https://www.mbts.org.my/theological-journal-vol-7.

唐华德. "彼得前书三章13节至四章11节的终末思想 [The Eschatological Emphasis of 1 Peter 3:13 through 4:11]." 神学文集 *MBTS Theological Journal* 7 (2021): 21–35. https://www.mbts.org.my/theological-journal-vol-7.

Chapter 14

Missional Implications of Christ's Proclamation to the Spirits

Sigurd Grindheim

In 1 Peter 3:18–22, Peter painted a picture of Christ's death and resurrection. This picture involves his proclamation to the disobedient spirits. Perhaps because this worldview is so alien to modern, Western readers, the missional implications of this passage have largely gone unnoticed.

This chapter will attempt to remedy this shortcoming. I will argue that the account undergirds Peter's various calls to evangelism. The spirits that were disobedient at the time of Noah are the spirits that were leading the nations astray. Announcing Christ's victory over these spirits, Peter subtly encouraged the audience to believe that their evangelistic efforts would meet with success. There is reason to hope that their oppressors may be converted and come to faith in Christ.

Largely following the consensus of modern scholarship, this chapter will first offer a brief exegesis of this passage, still referred to as "perhaps the most difficult in the NT."[1] Then follows a sketch of the spiritual warfare theme. Finally, I will draw the missiological implications and offer a modern application of spiritual warfare.

1 Peter 3:18-22

First Peter was written to encourage believers in a perplexing situation. They had turned away from a life characterized by shameful desires and had adopted the honorable life of God's people (1:14; 2:12; 4:4). However, their new lifestyle actually caused them to suffer shame and dishonor in society (2:12; 3:16; 4:13–14, 16).[2]

In these circumstances, Peter called on the audience to persist in doing good to all, even to those who abuse them (3:9–12). If they do, they should expect to be treated well in return (3:13). Even if they are not, however, Peter insisted that it is better to suffer for doing good, should it be God's will, than for doing evil (3:17).

---
1 Jobes, *1 Peter*, 236.
2 Campbell, *Honor, Shame, and the Rhetoric*, 29.

To substantiate this claim, Peter invoked the example of Christ himself. The passage in 3:18–22 may be translated as follows:[3]

> For even Christ suffered for sins once, a righteous one for unrighteous ones, in order to bring us into the presence of God. While he was put to death with respect to flesh, he was made alive with respect to spirit, in this state he went and made a proclamation to the spirits in prison, those who once disobeyed when God's patience waited in the days of Noah, when the ark was fashioned. Into this ark a few, that is, eight souls, were saved through water. The antitype, baptism, now also saves you—not a putting off of the dirt of the flesh, but the pledge of a good conscience before God—through the resurrection of Jesus Christ, who is at the right hand of God, having gone into heaven, as angels and authorities and powers have been made subject to him.

The introductory conjunctions "for even" (ὅτι καί) serve to emphasize the surprising fact: Not even the most honorable Lord Jesus Christ was exempt from the fate of suffering while doing good. Even though he was righteous, he also underwent suffering. His affliction served a great purpose; he suffered for the sake of the unrighteous. Peter did not enter into a more detailed explanation of the nature of Christ's suffering, except to state its glorious purpose: his suffering made it possible for Peter and his audience to have a relationship with God and to be in his presence.[4]

While this portrait of Christ refers to the uniqueness of his suffering, its purpose lies elsewhere: to undergird Peter's exhortation that his audience accept unjust suffering.[5] The recipients therefore may be led to consider the parallels between Christ's suffering and their own afflictions.

In the preceding section, Peter encouraged wives to submit to their husbands. As motivation, he indicated that unbelieving husbands may be won over without words by their wives' lifestyle (3:1). Having just received this encouragement, the audience may have heard in the prior description of Christ's suffering a hint that their own unjust suffering would serve a similar purpose. When they suffer in this way, they may prepare for their abusers to acknowledge Christ as well.

---

[3] Unless otherwise noted, all translations from the New Testament are my own.

[4] The verb προσάγω is used with the meaning "to bring into someone's presence" (BDAG, s.v. "προσάγω"), as in Genesis 48:9 LXX, where it refers to Ephraim and Manasseh being brought before Jacob to be blessed by him, in Exodus 19:4 LXX, where God's deliverance of his people from Egypt is said to have brought (προσηγαγόμην) them to himself, and in Numbers 16:5 LXX, where those deemed holy are allowed to approach (προσηγάγετο) the Lord.

[5] Note the use of the term ἅπαξ ("once"), which highlights the singularity of Christ's sacrifice.

In any case, Peter proceeded to describe Christ's death with the contrasting images "put to death with respect to flesh" and "made alive with respect to spirit."[6] The terms "flesh" and "spirit" probably refer to Christ's physical body in its state of weakness and his spiritual resurrection body, respectively.[7] While his "fleshly" body died, he was made alive with a spiritual body.[8]

Being made alive with respect to spirit, Christ "went and made a proclamation to the spirits in prison." The identity of these spirits and the nature of Christ's proclamation have been the object of intense discussion in the history of interpretation. According to a view that appears to go back to Clement of Alexandria, Christ went to the realm of the dead and proclaimed the gospel.[9] Rejecting the idea of a post-mortem conversion, Augustine argued that the reference was to the pre-existent Christ, who had preached through Noah at the time of the flood (*Letters* 164.15–17).[10]

---

6   The two datives σαρκί and πνεύματι (here translated as "with respect to the flesh" and "with respect to the spirit," respectively) are usually understood as datives of respect. It is difficult to decide whether to take "the spirit" as a reference to the Holy Spirit (as in the translations that capitalize the term) or in a more general sense, in contrast to "flesh" (as above). For the understanding of the datives as instrumental, see Achtemeier, *1 Peter*, 250. The difficulty with this interpretation is that "flesh" (σαρκί) cannot refer to Jesus's own flesh but instead must be understood as "unbelieving humanity," denoting the agent that put Jesus to death.

7   Similarly, Dalton, *Christ's Proclamation to the Spirits*, 127; Michaels, *1 Peter*, 204; Elliott, *1 Peter*, 645; Jobes, *1 Peter*, 239; and Reese, *1 Peter*, 211–12. Reading the expression in light of Kenyan Akamba cosmology, Mbuvi maintained that "even after going through death, Jesus was still alive in the spirit world, where he made proclamation" ("Christology and *Cultus* in 1 Peter," 156). He explained that death is "a transition into a different state of being" (Mbuvi, 157). However, the text says that Christ was "made alive" (ζῳοποιηθείς), not that he was alive, an important distinction for which Mbuvi's interpretation is not able to account.

8   For the contrast between "flesh" and "spirit" being used in this way, cf. 1 Pet 4:6; 1 Cor 5:5; Col 2:5; 1 Tim 3:16; John 3:6, and for a more detailed account of the distinction between a "natural body" (σῶμα ψυχικόν) and a "spiritual body" (σῶμα πνευματικόν), cf. 1 Cor 15:42–50.

9   Origen, *Principiis* 2.5.3; cf. *Against Celsus* 2.43; and Clement of Alexandria, *Stromata* 6.6.44–46. See also Goppelt, *Der Erste Petrusbrief*, 246–54; Klumbies, "Die Verkündigung unter Geistern," 207–28; and Feldmeier, *First Letter of Peter*, 203–6.

10 In modern times, this interpretation has been forcefully defended by Grudem (*1 Peter*, 157–61, 203–39; cf. Feinberg, "1 Peter 3:18–20," 303–36; Skilton, "A Glance at Some," 6–9). Grudem maintained that the term "spirit" (πενῦμα) refers to humans. To support this interpretation, he made an important argument regarding the background in Genesis 6:4, which refers to the "sons of God" who had intercourse with "daughters of humans." In Jewish tradition, these "sons of God" are often understood to be fallen angels, but Grudem pointed to equally well-established traditions according to which these "sons of God" are taken to be humans. These arguments are unconvincing. Even though the

However, following the convincing study of William Dalton, a near consensus has emerged that the preaching was not directed to humans, but to angels and demons.[11] Jewish writings from the Second Temple period attest that the period before the flood was a time of intense activity by fallen angels or evil spirits, leading humans astray and inspiring the great moral decay that took place in the antediluvian generation. When God judged the world and sent the flood, these spirits were also subject to judgment and imprisonment.[12] These ideas help explain Peter's reference to "the spirits in prison, those who once disobeyed when God's patience waited in the days of Noah." Apparently alluding to Jewish traditions regarding the fallen angels, 1 Peter affirms that Christ made his proclamation to these spiritual beings.[13]

If evil spirits were the audience of this proclamation, it rules out the possibility that the proclamation was evangelistic because Christ died for humans, not for demons. His proclamation must then be understood as the declaration of his victory and of the ultimate defeat of the disobedient spirits. This interpretation is confirmed by the clause that concludes this paragraph, declaring that "angels and authorities and powers have been made subject to him."

The reference to Noah gave Peter an occasion to mention the ark, which also allowed him to relate Noah's situation to that of the audience. He makes the connection by portraying the flood as a prefiguration of baptism. The "water," which in the story of Noah functions as the means of God's judgment of the ungodly, is now seen as the means by which he saves

---

term "spirit" (πνεῦμα) may be used for humans, the predominant meaning of the term in the New Testament, when used absolutely, is for spiritual beings such as angels and demons (Matt 8:16; Mark 9:20; Luke 9:39; 10:20; 13:11; Acts 16:18; 23:9; Eph 2:2; 1 John 4:1). Regarding the Jewish interpretation of Genesis 6:4, the earliest sources attest to the understanding that the "sons of God" were angels. The evidence cited by Grudem for interpreting the "sons of God" as humans is from later Rabbinic sources.

11 Dalton, *Christ's Proclamation*; similarly, Selwyn, *First Epistle of St. Peter*, 198–201. Among recent commentators, cf. Elliott, *1 Peter*, 656; Jobes, *1 Peter*, 243–47; Keener, *1 Peter*, 272–75; and Reese, *1 Peter*, 214–17.

12 *1 Enoch* 6.1–11.2; *2 Enoch* 18.4–6; *Jubilees* 5.1–11. For further references, see Elliott, *1 Peter*, 653.

13 These traditions also appear to be reflected in 2 Peter 2:4–5; Jude 6. The background is the note in Genesis 6:4 that the "sons of God went to the daughters of humans and had children by them." These "sons of God" were understood as fallen angels who were having intercourse with human women, an idea that appears to contradict what Jesus said in Mark 12:25 par. Regarding such ideas, Frank Thielman wisely observed, "There is no reason to think that Peter embraced every element of Enoch's interpretation of Genesis 6:1–9:17, but he apparently found in the basic structure of this myth an apt description of Christ's defeat of all invisible, malevolent powers." *Theology of the New Testament*, 583n39.

the faithful. In this subtle way, Peter reinforced the theme that salvation comes through judgment. As Peter previously affirmed, Christ brought salvation by undergoing judgment (3:18; cf. 2:24).

Baptism is more than a ritual act, ensuring outward cleansing (Heb 9:13). It presupposes an inward cleansing of the conscience (9:14) so that the baptized may make their commitment to God with a good conscience. The source of baptism's power is the resurrection of Christ. His resurrection forms the cornerstone of Peter's argument. The one who was made alive with respect to spirit is the one who ensures that baptism may bring salvation to the audience. Christ's resurrection represents his decisive victory, which is affirmed by his ascension to the right hand of God and his position of total sovereignty because all powers have now been subjected to him. The emphasis in 1 Peter squarely falls on realized eschatology, even if Peter previously referenced a future inheritance (1 Pet 1:4–5, 7, 9, 13).

Spiritual Warfare

Peter's focus on the defeat of the spirits seems misplaced because there is no indication in the letter that the audience is being tormented by demons. Rather, their suffering is inflicted by the members of their society. They are victims of social prejudice and are subject to slander and possibly legal persecution.[14]

Nevertheless, Peter showed no interest in telling his audience to oppose the Roman Empire. Instead, he had in his sights an even more formidable enemy, the devil. His concluding exhortations, in which he recapitulated the main themes of his letter, gave a stern warning: "Your accuser the devil is prowling around like a roaring lion seeking someone to devour. Resist him, being firm in the faith, as you know that the same sufferings are undergone by your family of believers in this world" (1 Pet 5:8b–9).[15]

This exhortation is closely related to the troubled situation of the church, which may be seen from how the devil is named. His name (διάβολος) means "slanderer," and he is also identified as "your accuser (ἀντίδικος)." These two terms correspond closely to the predicament of the audience. Their opponents slander them and bring accusations against them (2:12, 15; 3:16; 4:14–16). It is as if Peter is saying that the mastermind behind their suffering is the devil himself.[16]

---

14 Holloway, *Coping with Prejudice*, 66–73.
15 Horrell, Arnold, and Williams, "Visuality, Vivid Description," 713–16.
16 Asumang, "Resist Him," 26; and Reese, *1 Peter*, 297.

The image of the devil as a roaring lion recalls a theme from the Old Testament, in which this predatory animal was used as a metaphor for the enemies of God's people (e.g., Ps 22:21; Jer 50:17). To the audience living as subjects of the Roman Empire, however, the most obvious association would likely have been the lions that were used in the Roman theater. A spectacular method of execution was to have convicts thrown into the theater for lions to devour them.[17] By using this image, Peter associated the empire with the devil and reinforced his implicit message, that the empire is a tool of Satan.

At the same time, Peter communicated that resistance against the empire was a matter of spiritual warfare. The real battle to be fought is a battle against the devil. To resist him, it is necessary to stand firm in the faith.

That the audience is engaged in a spiritual battle is repeatedly implied in 1 Peter. With military terminology, the letter begins with an assurance that the audience is guarded (φρουρουμένους) by God's power (1 Pet 1:5; cf. Eph 6:11, 13). Against this background, the exhortation to gird up their loins (1 Pet 1:13) may be read against the background of military preparedness (cf. Exod 12:11; Eph 6:14). Peter encouraged the audience to "abstain from the fleshly desires which wage war (στρατεύονται) against the soul" (1 Pet 2:11) as well as to be free from fear (3:14). The call not to fear is likely an allusion to Isaiah 8:12–13, which in its original context is a promise that God will protect Judah in the war against Samaria and Syria. Finally, Peter encouraged the audience to "arm yourselves (ὁπλίσασθε) with the same thought, that the one who has suffered in the flesh has put an end to sin" (1 Pet 4:1).[18]

This understanding of the audience's situation, that they are engaged in a spiritual war, explains Peter's interest in Christ's victory over the spirits. A closer look at the Jewish traditions to which he apparently alluded may further illuminate his line of thought. In these traditions, the disobedient spirits are known as watchers, or fallen angels. According to *1 Enoch* (ca. 200–160 BC), these angels had intercourse with women on earth and had children with them. They also taught humans how to excel in evil works, including magical practices, the art of warfare, "all (forms of) oppression," and occult practices, summarily described as "eternal secrets which are performed in heaven" (*1 Enoch* 9.6).[19] Indeed, "the whole world has been corrupted by Azazel's teaching" (10.8).

---

17 Paschke, "Roman *ad bestias* Execution," 489–500; and Horrell, Arnold, and Williams, "Visuality," 705–12.
18 Asumang, "Resist Him," 30–37.
19 Cf. *1 Enoch* 7.1; 8.1–3; 10.7; 64.1–2; 65.6–7; 69.4–15; *Jubilees* 7.27; 8.3; 10.2.

According to the book of *Jubilees* (ca. 160 BC), all of the nations and peoples except Israel were ruled by spirits. The Lord himself had ordained it that way so that these spirits "might lead them astray from following him" (15.31).

Compared to the detailed narratives in *1 Enoch* and the book of *Jubilees*, 1 Peter's account is strikingly sparse. There is no reference to the idea that the evil upon the earth traces its origin to the fallen angels having intercourse with women. Neither is this idea directly evidenced anywhere else in the New Testament.

Peter was content to mention the spirits that are known to have been active in the days of Noah, apparently assuming that such a reference would generate the appropriate associations among his audience. When they heard about evil spirits, they would likely have thought of the powers that inspire humans to do evil.

Aside from these narrative elements characteristic of the Jewish traditions, this view of human evil is well-attested in the New Testament as well. The Synoptic Gospels include numerous accounts of humans that are occupied by unclean spirits or demons and whose speech and behavior are controlled by these evil spirits.[20]

The epistolary literature reflects a more universal understanding of demonic beings and their influence in the world. According to Ephesians 2:2, there was a time when the audience "conducted themselves according to the era of this world, according to the ruler of the domain of the air, the spirit that is now at work in the children of disobedience." The unbelievers were ultimately controlled by a power outside themselves. This power was the devil, the ruler of the evil spirits.[21]

The outlook that is reflected in Ephesians may be described as dualistic. Every person's conduct is either determined by the Holy Spirit (Eph 1:13; 3:16) or by the devil and his minions (2:2).[22]

The letter proceeds to describe Christ's salvific work as triumphant divine warfare. However, the enemy is now defined as enmity itself, as Christ's military victory consists in his "tearing down the wall of partition, namely enmity" (Eph 2:14), thereby "killing the enmity" (2:16) that exists between Jews and gentiles.[23]

---

20 Mark 1:21–28 par., 32–34 par., 39; 3:11–12 par.; 5:1–20 par.; 6:13; 7:24–30 par.; 9:14–29 par., 38 par.; Matt 4:24; 9:32–34; 12:22–23 par.; Luke 6:18; 7:21; 8:2; 13:10–17.
21 Similarly, Gombis, "Ephesians 2 as a Narrative," 410.
22 Similarly, Best, *Critical and Exegetical Commentary*, 205–6.
23 Gombis, "Ephesians 2," 414.

A similar view of the devil is also reflected in the book of Revelation, in which he is portrayed as the king of the evil army (9:11). As elsewhere in the New Testament (2 Cor 11:14), he is known as the one who is constantly occupied with deception and leading people astray. With graphic, apocalyptic imagery, two illuminating passages portray his downfall.

The first is the allegory of the woman and the dragon (Rev 12:1–17), which refers to a battle between the archangel Michael and the dragon, also known as "that ancient serpent," the devil, and Satan. The battle ends with the dragon being cast out of heaven and hurled down to earth. When he has lost his place in heaven, he also loses his authority to accuse the people of God (v. 10). Regarding his activities, we also learn that he "leads the whole world astray" (v. 9).

An even more consequential defeat is described in Revelation 20:1–3, a passage that mentions the capture and imprisonment of the dragon (v. 2). An angel from heaven, which may represent Jesus himself, seizes him and locks him in the Abyss "in order that he might no longer lead the nations astray until the thousand years were completed" (v. 3).[24]

The concept of a millennium in Revelation 20:1–6 has given rise to many different interpretations. One of the most difficult questions concerns whether the binding of Satan should be understood as a future, eschatological event or a description of the victory that Christ has already won. In other words, are divided on whether the seer portrays a future millennium or a symbolic account of what Christ has already accomplished through his death and resurrection.[25]

In the latter interpretation, the binding of Satan would explain why the time following Christ's ministry is also the time of Christian mission. The nations are no longer invariably and unfailingly blinded by Satan, but

---

24 For a christological interpretation of this angel, note the parallel with Revelation 10:1, where an angel also descends from heaven (cf. 18:1). This angel "was wrapped in a cloud," recalling the image of Jesus in 1:7 (cf. 14:14), "with a rainbow (characteristic of the divine throne [cf. 4:3]) over his head, and his face was like the sun," like that of Jesus (1:16), "and his feet like pillars of fire," not unlike Jesus's feet that were "like bronze glowing in a furnace" (1:15; cf. 2:18). The angel in 20:1 has "the key to the Abyss." Elsewhere in Revelation, Jesus is the one holding "the keys of death and Hades" (1:18) and "the key of David" (3:7). The power to cast into the Abyss is also attributed to Jesus in Luke 8:31. See further Gundry, "Angelomorphic Christology," 663–72; contra Hannah, *Michael and Christ*, 151–55; Hoffmann, *Destroyer and the Lamb*, 68–76.

25 For a strong argument that this passage should not be read as describing events in chronological order (leading to understanding the millennium as future) but as a recapitulation (representing yet another description of Christ's decisive eschatological victory through his crucifixion and resurrection), see Beale, *Book of Revelation*, 972–83; contra Osborne, *Revelation*, 702–3.

they are open to persuasion through the proclamation of the gospel. The time when the devil could control the nations like marionettes is now past because he has been locked up in the Abyss.

In this interpretation, the vision in Revelation 20:1–3 has much in common with Christ's proclamation to the spirits in 1 Peter 3:18–22. As Christ triumphs over the prince of demons (Rev 20:1–3), so his ultimate victory is manifested (1 Pet 3:18–22) when he is made alive after having been put to death. In Revelation, his victory makes possible the conversion of the nations, and the demons' defeat in 1 Peter makes a similar point: Christ's vindication means that the demons are made subject to him, preventing them from leading people astray and making possible the conversion of the gentiles who now oppress the believers.

The Missional Contribution of 1 Peter

While the account of Christ's proclamation to the spirits assures the audience of their ultimate vindication, it contains a hint of a glorious purpose, which in a broader sense may be described as missional. A qualification is necessary, however. In my opinion, mission is best defined as the crossing of ethnic and linguistic boundaries in order to proclaim the gospel in word and deed. Of mission in this sense, 1 Peter has precious little to say.[26] Torrey Seland therefore fruitfully suggested studying the letter in light of the concept of a missional church. He understood "missional" to mean that the church participates in God's work of proclaiming his kingdom in this world.[27]

As 1 Peter was written in order to strengthen the audience's Christian identity in the midst of hostile surroundings, there is a strong evangelistic undercurrent that runs through the letter. Even though they are met with opposition and oppression, believers are encouraged to see their oppressors as possible converts to the Christian faith.

First of all, they are reminded of their own background, mired in a sinful lifestyle (1:14, 18; 2:1; 4:3) when they "were not a people" (2:10). Through God's great mercy, however, they have been born again (1:3) and are now God's chosen people (2:9–10). If God could perform such a miracle in their lives, then he might be expected to do similar things for their enemies as well.[28]

---

26 While he noted the importance of testimony in 1 Peter, Hahn correctly observed that the oppression suffered by the audience means that "all missionary activity is denied to them." *Mission in the New Testament*, 141. Therefore, "we can speak of an understanding of the mission only in a modified way" (142).

27 Seland, "Resident Aliens in Mission," 567–68.

28 Schnabel, *Paul and the Early Church*, 1521–22.

Peter repeatedly hinted at such expectations. He exhorted the audience to conduct themselves in such a manner that while the gentiles "slander you as evildoers, they may glorify God on the day of visitation because they are noticing your good works" (2:12). More specifically, he addressed the wives of unbelieving husbands and urged them to submit and demonstrate a "pure and reverent lifestyle," holding out hope that unbelieving husbands "may be won without words by the lifestyle of their wives" (3:1–2).

The audience's testimony is not exclusively non-verbal, however.[29] They are also exhorted to "always be ready to give a defense to everyone who holds you to account for the hope that is in you" (3:15).[30] In this way, they fulfill their purpose, to "proclaim the great works of the one who called you out of darkness and into his marvelous light" (2:9).[31]

Faced with seemingly insurmountable obstacles to the success of such evangelistic activities, Christ's proclamation to the spirits subtly helps the audience to look at the situation from a different perspective. The powers that are deceiving the nations and leading the people astray have been made subject to the supremacy of Christ. One may, therefore, put one's hope in him and expectantly wait for the conversion even of one's enemies.

In this way, 1 Peter points to a kind of cultural engagement that preserves the distinctiveness of the church.[32] Recent post-colonial studies of the letter have

---

29 See especially Seland, "Resident Aliens," 579–88; cf. Boyley, "1 Peter: A Mission Document?," 72–86; and Stenschke, "Reading First Peter," 120–22.

30 There is some discussion about whether the setting for this "defense" (ἀπολογίαν) is specifically the court of law, referring to the possibility that the believers may be held to account for their failure to participate in the emperor cult and other religious activities that were considered mandatory. In light of the general language that is used ("everyone who asks you") and the wider context pointing to hostility in everyday situations, it seems unwarranted to restrict this exhortation to such a specific setting. Elliott, *1 Peter*, 627; and Seland, "Resident Aliens," 588.

31 Balch narrowed the term unnecessarily when he insisted that the verb ἐξαγγέλλω ("declare") only refers to praise given to God, not to the public. *Let Wives Be Submissive*, 132–35. It also has a wider usage that is appropriate here. Seland, "Resident Aliens," 583–85.

32 The debate between David Balch and John Elliott has set the agenda for much of subsequent scholarship on 1 Peter. Whereas Balch read 1 Peter as a call for Christians to assimilate to the society in which they lived (*Let Wives*, 81–109, esp. 109; "Hellenization/ Acculturation in 1 Peter," in Talbert, *Perspectives on First Peter*, 79–101), Elliott capitalized on the letter's portrait of the audience as strangers and aliens, reading it as a specimen of a sectarian outlook and noting its exhortations to distinctiveness and internal cohesion (*Home for the Homeless*, 73–84, 101–50; "1 Peter, Its Situation and Strategy, 61–78). Avoiding this bifurcation, Seland correctly argued that the letter is better understood as a re-acculturation from the audience's previous gentile culture to their new, Christian community. *Strangers in the Light*, 168–87.

found in it a quiet form of resistance to the oppressive empire.[33] Indeed, the letter envisions a form of resistance that is expected to be crowned with victory.

However, this resistance is neither an overt effort to overturn the existing political structures nor a subversive attempt to undermine them. As Miroslav Volf argued, 1 Peter points to what he calls a soft difference, the way between isolation and accommodation.[34] He observed that the letter calls for gentleness (3:4, 15), a well-known method for the powerless to accomplish their goals. By combining gentleness with deception, their subversive behavior may pass undetected. But deception is precisely what 1 Peter prohibits (2:1–2, 22). Instead, the letter urges openness and transparency (cf. 1:22; 2:16), qualities that presuppose fearlessness (3:6, 14). According to Volf, therefore, soft resistance is not weak but strong. Its weapons are good works, performed with a pure heart and a good conscience (1:22; 3:16). Its outcome is the transformation, not the suppression, of the enemy (2:12).

In modern times, the use of such weapons has been described beautifully by Martin Luther King Jr. In a speech given on the occasion of Ghana's birth as a nation in 1957, he explained the goal for which he was working:

> The aftermath of nonviolence is the creation of the beloved community. The aftermath of nonviolence is redemption. The aftermath of nonviolence is reconciliation. The aftermath of violence are emptiness and bitterness. This is the thing I'm concerned about. Let us fight passionately and unrelentingly for the goals of justice and peace. But let's be sure that our hands are clean in this struggle. Let us never fight with falsehood and violence and hate and malice, but always fight with love, so that, when the day comes that the walls of segregation have completely crumbled in Montgomery, that we will be able to live with people as their brothers and sisters. Oh, my friends, our aim must be not to defeat Mr. Engelhardt, not to defeat Mr. Sellers and Mr. Gayle and Mr. Parks. Our aim must be to defeat the evil that's in them. But our aim must be to win the friendship of Mr. Gayle and Mr. Sellers and Mr. Engelhardt. We must come to the point of seeing that our ultimate aim is to live with all men as brothers and sisters under God, and not be their enemies or anything that goes with that type of relationship. And this is one thing that Ghana teaches us: that you can break aloose from evil through nonviolence, through a lack of bitterness.[35]

---

33 Bauman-Martin, "Speaking Jewish: Postcolonial Aliens," 144–77; Horrell, "Between Conformity and Resistance," 117–43; Asumang, "Resist Him"; Smith, *Strangers to Family*; and Hall, "Christian Mission in the Contemporary World," 119–45.

34 Volf, "Soft Difference," 24–25; similarly, Asumang, "Resist Him," 37–38.

35 King, *Call to Conscience*, 32–33.

King understood that the battle he was fighting was spiritual. It was not "a struggle against flesh and blood, but against the rulers, against the authorities, against the world-rulers of this darkness, against the evil spiritual powers in the heavenly domains" (Eph 6:12). Or, as he put it,

> through violence you may murder a murderer, but you can't murder murder. Through violence you may murder a liar, but you can't establish truth. Through violence you may murder a hater, but you can't murder hate through violence. Darkness cannot put out darkness; only light can do that.[36]

With love, good works, and purity of heart as weapons, our spiritual enemies will be defeated. Light will drive out darkness.

Conclusion

According to 1 Peter, the decisive spiritual battle has been won by Jesus Christ through his crucifixion and resurrection. He defeated the spirits "who once disobeyed when God's patience waited in the days of Noah" (3:20) so that "angels and authorities and powers have been made subject to him" (3:22). Therefore, he offers his followers the promise of victory and the prospect that their oppressors will be converted. His struggle is the blueprint for believers' own spiritual battle. He is the ultimate example of someone fighting with the weapons of light.

> He who did not sin, nor was there found deceit in his mouth, he who was abused, but did not return the abuse, was suffering, but made no threats, leaving it to the one who judges righteously; he who bore our sins himself in his body on the cross, so that we, having died to sins, might live to righteousness—by whose wounds you have been healed. (1 Pet 2:22–24)

By following in his footsteps, believers may fulfill their missional purpose. Assured by Jesus's complete victory over the spirits, they may do so with the expectation that their enemies may be won for the gospel.

Bibliography

Achtemeier, Paul J. *1 Peter: A Commentary on First Peter*. Hermeneia. Minneapolis: Fortress Press, 1996.

Asumang, Annang. "'Resist Him' (1 Pet 5:9): Holiness and Non-Retaliatory Responses to Unjust Suffering as 'Holy War' in 1 Peter." *Conspectus* 11 (2011): 7–46.

---

36 King, 191.

Balch, David L. "Hellenization/Acculturation in 1 Peter." In *Perspectives on First Peter*, edited by Charles H. Talbert, 79–101. NABPR Special Studies Series 9. Macon, GA: Mercer University Press, 1986.

Balch, David L. *Let Wives Be Submissive: The Domestic Code in I Peter*. Society of Biblical Literature Monograph Series 26. Atlanta: Scholars Press, 1981.

Bauman-Martin, Betsy. "Speaking Jewish: Postcolonial Aliens and Strangers in First Peter." In *Reading First Peter with New Eyes: Methodological Reassessments of the Letter of First Peter*, edited by Robert L. Webb and Betsy Bauman-Martin, 144–77. Library of New Testament Studies 364. London: T&T Clark, 2007.

Beale, G. K. *The Book of Revelation: A Commentary on the Greek Text*. New International Greek Testament Commentary. Grand Rapids: Eerdmans, 1999.

Best, Ernest. *A Critical and Exegetical Commentary on Ephesians*. International Critical Commentary. Edinburgh: T&T Clark, 1998.

Boyley, Mark. "1 Peter: A Mission Document?" *Reformed Theological Review* 63, no. 2 (2004): 72–86.

Campbell, Barth L. *Honor, Shame, and the Rhetoric of 1 Peter*. Society of Biblical Literature Dissertation Series 160. Atlanta: Scholars Press, 1998.

Dalton, William J. *Christ's Proclamation to the Spirits: A Study of 1 Peter 3:18–4:6*. Analecta Biblica 23. Rome: Pontifical Biblical Institute, 1965.

Elliott, John H. *1 Peter: A New Translation with Introduction and Commentary*. Anchor Bible 37B. New York: Doubleday, 2000.

Elliott, John H. "1 Peter, Its Situation and Strategy: A Discussion with David Balch." In *Perspectives on First Peter*, edited by Charles H. Talbert, 61–78. NABPR Special Studies Series 9. Macon: Mercer University Press, 1986.

Elliott, John H. *A Home for the Homeless: A Sociological Exegesis of 1 Peter, Its Situation and Strategy*. Philadelphia: Fortress, 1981.

Feinberg, John S. "1 Peter 3:18–20, Ancient Mythology, and the Intermediate State." *Westminster Theological Journal* 48, no. 2 (1986): 303–36.

Feldmeier, Reinhard. *The First Letter of Peter: A Commentary on the Greek Text*. Translated by Peter H. Davids. Waco, TX: Baylor University Press, 2008.

Gombis, Timothy G. "Ephesians 2 as a Narrative of Divine Warfare." *Journal for the Study of the New Testament* 26, no. 4 (2004): 403–18.

Goppelt, Leonhard. *Der Erste Petrusbrief*. Edited by Ferdinand Hahn. Kritisch-exegetischer Kommentar über das Neue Testament 12.1. Göttingen: Vandenhoeck & Ruprecht, 1978.

Grudem, Wayne. *1 Peter*. Tyndale New Testament Commentaries 17. Grand Rapids: Eerdmans, 1988.

Gundry, Robert H. "Angelomorphic Christology in the Book of Revelation." In *Society of Biblical Literature 1994 Seminar Papers*, ed. E. H. Lovering, 662–78. Society of Biblical Literature Seminar Papers 33. Atlanta: Scholars Press, 1994.

Hahn, Ferdinand. *Mission in the New Testament*. Translated by Frank Clarke. Studies in Biblical Theology 47. Naperville, IL: Allenson, 1965.

Hall, Josiah D. "Christian Mission in the Contemporary World: A Dialogue between 1 Peter and Postcolonial Studies." *Horizons in Biblical Theology* 43, no. 2 (2021): 119–45.

Hannah, Darrell D. *Michael and Christ: Michael Traditions and Angel Christology in Early Christianity*. Wissenschafttliche Untersuchungen zum Neuen Testament 2/109. Tübingen: Mohr Siebeck, 1999.

Hoffmann, Matthias Reinhard. *The Destroyer and the Lamb: The Relationship between Angelomorphic and Lamb Christology in the Book of Revelation*. Wissenschafttliche Untersuchungen zum Neuen Testament 2/203. Tübingen: Mohr Siebeck, 2005.

Holloway, Paul A. *Coping with Prejudice: 1 Peter in Social-Psychological Perspective*. Wissenschafttliche Untersuchungen zum Neuen Testament 244. Tübingen: Mohr Siebeck, 2009.

Horrell, David G. "Between Conformity and Resistance: Beyond the Balch-Elliott Debate towards a Postcolonial Reading of First Peter." In *Reading First Peter with New Eyes: Methodological Reassessments of the Letter of First Peter*, edited by Robert L. Webb and Betsy Bauman-Martin, 111–43. Library of New Testament Studies 364. London: T&T Clark, 2007.

Horrell, David G., Bradley Arnold, and Travis B. Williams. "Visuality, Vivid Description, and the Message of 1 Peter: The Significance of the Roaring Lion (1 Peter 5:8)." *Journal of Biblical Literature* 132, no. 3 (2013): 697–716.

Jobes, Karen H. *1 Peter*. Baker Exegetical Commentary on the New Testament. Grand Rapids: Baker, 2005.

Keener, Craig S. *1 Peter: A Commentary*. Grand Rapids: Baker Academic, 2021.

King, Martin Luther, Jr. *A Call to Conscience: The Landmark Speeches of Dr. Martin Luther King, Jr.* Edited by Clayborne Carson and Kris Shepard. New York: IPM/Warner Books, 2001.

Klumbies, Paul-Gerhard. "Die Verkündigung unter Geistern und Toten nach 1 Petr 3,19 f. und 4,6." *Zeitschrift für die neutestamentliche Wissenschaft* 92 (2001): 207–28.

Mbuvi, Andrew M. "Christology and *Cultus* in 1 Peter: An African (Kenyan) Appraisal." In *Jesus without Borders: Christology in the Majority World*, edited by Gene L. Green, Stephen T. Pardue, and K. K. Yeo, 141–61. Majority World Theology Series. Grand Rapids: Eerdmans, 2014.

Michaels, J. Ramsey. *1 Peter*. Word Biblical Commentary 49. Waco, TX: Word, 1988.

Osborne, Grant R. *Revelation*. Baker Exegetical Commentary on the New Testament. Grand Rapids: Baker Academic, 2002.

Paschke, Boris A. "The Roman *ad bestias* Execution as a Possible Historical Background for 1 Peter 5.8." *Journal for the Study of the New Testament* 28, no. 4 (2006): 489–500.

Reese, Ruth Anne. *1 Peter*. New Cambridge Bible Commentary. Cambridge: Cambridge University Press, 2022.

Schnabel, Eckhard J. *Paul and the Early Church*. Vol. 2 of *Early Christian Mission*. Downers Grove, IL: InterVarsity Press, 2004.

Seland, Torrey. "Resident Aliens in Mission: Missional Practices in the Emerging Church of 1 Peter." *Bulletin for Biblical Research* 19, no. 4 (2009): 565–89.

Seland, Torrey. *Strangers in the Light: Philonic Perspectives on Christian Identity in 1 Peter*. Biblical Interpretation Series 76. Leiden: Brill, 2005.

Selwyn, Edward G. *The First Epistle of St. Peter*. Grand Rapids: Baker, 1947.

Skilton, John H. "A Glance at Some Old Problems in First Peter." *Westminster Theological Journal* 58, no. 1 (1996): 1–9.

Smith, Shively T. J. *Strangers to Family: Diaspora and 1 Peter's Invention of God's Household*. Waco, TX: Baylor University Press, 2016.

Stenschke, Christoph W. "Reading First Peter in the Context of Early Christian Mission." *Tyndale Bulletin* 60, no. 1 (2009): 107–26.

Thielman, Frank. *Theology of the New Testament: A Canonical and Synthetic Approach*. Grand Rapids: Zondervan, 2005.

Volf, Miroslav. "Soft Difference: Theological Reflections on the Relation between Church and Culture in 1 Peter." *Ex Auditu* 10 (1994): 15–30.

Chapter 15

The Pilgrimage Motif in 1 Peter and Its Implications for Evangelism

Sofia Papaspyrou

This chapter explores the evangelistic implications of pilgrimage through a case study and emphasizes its potential as a testimony of faith and a means of spreading the gospel. Ultimately focusing on 1 Peter 2:11, this chapter contemplates the Christian call to be strangers in the world, maintaining a unique identity while engaging with the culture and embracing a missionary outlook.

Sojourners and Exiles in 1 Peter

Throughout Christian tradition, few passages have been as frequently employed to establish a connection between the Christian way of life and the identity of a stranger, sojourner, or pilgrim as 1 Peter 2:11. This verse introduces a pivotal passage in the letter and acts as a descriptive title for it. The apostle Peter addressed his audience, summarizing their identity as beloved, sojourners and exiles living among gentiles who were accused of wrongdoing (2:12), and he urged them to abstain from the passions of the flesh that wage war against their souls.[1]

> Beloved, I urge you as sojourners and exiles to abstain from the passions of the flesh, which wage war against your soul.[2] Ἀγαπητοί, παρακαλῶ ὡς παροίκους καὶ παρεπιδήμους ἀπέχεσθαι τῶν σαρκικῶν ἐπιθυμιῶν αἵτινες στρατεύονται κατὰ τῆς ψυχῆς.[3] (1 Pet 2:11)

The verse starts with the vocative ἀγαπητοί (beloved). The address is particularly apt in this context, given that love has been highlighted as the defining attribute of the community, as mentioned earlier in 1:22. Furthermore, this verbal adjective not only signifies the interconnection among Christians but also emphasizes their beloved status. Thus, this attribute encapsulates the earlier discussion, particularly regarding God's election (2:9) and his mercy and compassion as the bedrock of the new

---

[1] Green, *1 Peter*, 66–68.
[2] Unless otherwise noted, all Scripture quotations in this chapter come from the ESV.
[3] References to the Greek New Testament are based on Aland et al., eds., *Novum Testamentum Graece*.

community. The address is reiterated in 4:12, reinforcing the designation of "chosen ones" (ἐκλεκτοί) in the introduction (1:1) with a specific emphasis on God's love as the foundation of their election.[4]

Peter addressed the community as being παροίκους καὶ παρεπιδήμους, terms that he had previously used in the epistle (1:1, 17). Though the two terms, παρεπιδήμοις in 1:1 and τῆς παροικίας ὑμῶν χρόνον in 1:17, have nearly the same meaning, they carry distinct nuances. In 1:1, the term is specifically connected to the historical circumstances of the addressed communities. On the other hand, the phrase in 1:17 has a broader connotation, implying enduring conditions that govern the life of a holy community.[5]

The term πάροικος (*paroikos*) originally denoted a neighbor, but over time, it evolved to signify a resident alien. This status implied that the individual, although not a full citizen and thus lacking both the responsibilities and privileges of citizens, still possessed a recognized standing and was not entirely devoid of legal protection. In the New Testament, it was predominantly used to convey the notion of an alien, except one instance outside of 1 Peter, where it is applied to Christians (Eph 2:19). As for παρεπίδημος (*parepidēmos*), it does not pertain to a specific class of individuals but rather someone who has temporarily settled in a particular place, a sojourner. Consequently, they lack the recognized status even of a πάροικος. Παρεπίδημος appears only one other time in the New Testament outside of its usage in 1 Peter (Heb 11:13).[6]

In the Septuagint, πάροικος καὶ παρεπίδημος occur in conjunction only in Genesis 23:4 and in Psalms 39:12 (38:13 LXX). In the Genesis account, Abraham referred to himself as both a "stranger" and "sojourner" when negotiating with the Hittites to secure a burial site for his late wife Sarah in the land where he had settled. As a foreigner, he lacked inherited rights and faced difficulties in finding a place to bury his deceased spouse. Similarly, the recipients of 1 Peter were addressed as individuals belonging to the lowest social stratum because the terms "foreigners" and "sojourners" denoted their limited ownership rights over land and property. Additionally, this same terminology conveys the characteristic of "exile" both in a literal and metaphorical sense (1 Pet 1:17).[7]

---

4 Feldmeier, *First Letter of Peter*, 146–47.
5 Selwyn, *First Epistle of St. Peter*, 169.
6 Achtemeier, *1 Peter*, 173–74.
7 Mbuvi, *Temple, Exile, and Identity*, 39.

Abson P. Joseph claimed that the use of these terms illustrates how the author's understanding of his audience is dependent on the Old Testament's description of the people of God.[8] Central to Israel's essence as a nation was the recollection of their foreign and pilgrim status.[9] This recollection emphasizes God's unwavering loyalty to them and serves as a constant reminder of the imperative to live in accordance with God's commands and to show compassion to the foreigners among them.[10]

On the other hand, John H. Elliott brought attention to the Hellenistic and Roman context of the letter, carefully considering the political, legal, and social implications associated with the terms used.[11] He interpreted the terms literally, arguing that the word πάροικοι does not designate the recipients as "exiles" or "pilgrims." Instead, it is comparable to the official term "resident alien" used in legal national codes, signifying a particular group of people with restricted political, legal, and social rights due to their foreign origin and allegiances.[12]

Furthermore, Karen H. Jobes introduced a different perspective on the literal interpretation of the recipients' identity as πάροικοι καὶ παρεπίδημοι. Observing the absence of evidence regarding the evangelization of northern Asia Minor, Jobes proposed that Peter addressed Christians who had embraced Christianity in other regions, maintained some connection with Peter prior to his correspondence, and were dispersed as foreigners and resident aliens throughout Asia Minor.[13]

Conversely, Moses Chin debated that terms are not confined to a legal or secular-social sense only. He presented copious evidence indicating their frequent usage in a cosmological and spiritual context. Acknowledging the social status of the recipients in 1 Peter is essential, but it is equally vital to recognize the greater significance of their cosmic and spiritual journey on earth, as suggested by a longstanding theological and literary tradition.[14]

Comparably, Janette H. Ok proposed that Peter addressed his audience as strangers, not literal strangers before conversion but cultural strangers because of their conversion. When taken metaphorically, these terms reveal the social alienation experienced by the recipients due to their divine

---

8   Joseph, *Narratological Reading of 1 Peter*, 74.
9   Shaw, *Pilgrim People of God*.
10 Joseph, *Narratological Reading of 1 Peter*, 74.
11 Elliott, *Home for the Homeless*, 33.
12 Elliott, *Conflict, Community, and Honor*, 20–21.
13 Jobes, *1 Peter*, 23–41.
14 Chin, "A Heavenly Home," 111.

selection. Ok argued that Peter urged them to see themselves as foreigners to the prevailing pagan values of the surrounding world they once embraced. He wanted them to find belonging among fellow believers by constructing a new ethnic identity and reidentifying as the "people of God" (2:9–10).[15]

In addition, Miroslav Volf explained how this new identity is a result of a new birth (1:3). As he said, Christian identity is not that of an outsider who either seeks to become an insider or strenuously maintains the status of outsider. Christians are insiders who have diverted from their culture by being born again.[16]

Despite their status as strangers, the πάροικοι καὶ παρεπίδημοι are not expected to confine themselves within isolated spheres. On the contrary, they are encouraged to exhibit their virtuous conduct openly. The character of the people of God, their inherent qualities that manifest in their deeds, is a matter of public interest and contributes to the magnification of God's glory.[17] According to Vassilis Stogiannos, this dual purpose serves two main objectives: first, it enables them to uphold their unwavering identity, which is impervious to the world's influence; second, it allows them to function as missionaries, actively engaging with the world.[18] As Romualdas Babarskas stated, when we consider Christian witness, it typically refers to verbally sharing our account of coming to Christ or how God has impacted our lives. While speaking is undoubtedly part of our witness, we are equally called to testify through our actions and lifestyle, which entails resisting conformity to worldly ways.[19] Likewise, M. Eugene Boring mentioned that the new life to which Christians are called is not just a life of personal piety but of an active mission.[20]

Moreover, Andrew M. Mbuvi explored further the idea that the letter serves a dual purpose, being both apologetic and missionary in nature. He contended that these two facets are essential to address the core issues faced during exile, namely, the preservation of faith and identity while striving to endure and survive in a foreign world. The way to do this is their καλή ἀναστροφή ("good conduct") among the nations (2:12). The Jews living in dispersion saw their moral life intertwined with their identity, and adherence to the Jewish moral code defined their Jewishness. The letter of 1 Peter

---

15 Ok, *Constructing Ethnic Identity*, 56–57.
16 Volf, "Soft Difference," 18–19.
17 Wells, *God's Holy People*, 229.
18 Στογιάννος, *Πρώτη Επιστολή Πέτρου*, 244.
19 Babarskas, "1 Peter," 1586.
20 Boring, *1 Peter*, 114.

follows a similar pattern, emphasizing moral conduct alongside identity. However, on this occasion, Peter applied this principle to a gentile-inclusive community. The call for responsibility and holiness is rooted in believers' identification with God, with conduct serving to preserve their identity as exiles. Assimilation into surrounding cultures poses a constant threat, demanding focused vigilance to maintain their distinct Christian identity.[21] So, as Elliott commented, being a stranger in society is not a status to avoid but to cherish. Embracing this identity with confidence and joy allows the believing community to preserve its distinct holy nature and unwavering allegiance to God.[22]

In conclusion, irrespective of the ethnic or social identity of the Petrine community, the theological significance of this verse prompts us to contemplate our manner of living within diverse environments. Nevertheless, a prevalent issue is our frequent failure to acknowledge the "gentile world" surrounding us and the extent to which we conform to its norms, even if we do not explicitly admit it. Therefore, engaging in a mission or pilgrimage can provide an opportunity for us to achieve physical detachment from the customary social frameworks, enabling us to gain a clearer perspective on our own status and culture. As asserted by Ellen Badone, "defamiliarization heightens cultural awareness." In one's native society, culture is often overlooked, much like the air we breathe. Only by completely distancing oneself from familiar customs and fully engaging with those of different cultures can we realize that both are products of social construction, distinct from the natural world.[23] One can attain physical detachment from the usual structures of social interaction by embarking on a mission or a pilgrimage.

Tourists, Pilgrims, and Missionaries

Pilgrimage has a firm foundation in the Bible and has been a vital element of Christian tradition throughout history. Nonetheless, in the context of the twenty-first century, I raise the question of whether the concept of pilgrims remains applicable, or if modern practices are more akin to tourism.

The line between the pilgrim and the tourist used to be clear. To use the words of the poet Horace, tourists are those "who rush across the sea, changing the sky but not their soul."[24] In a way, a pilgrim is the exact

---

21 Mbuvi, *Temple, Exile, and Identity*, 39–43.
22 Elliott, *Conflict, Community, and Honor*, 41.
23 Badone, "Crossing Boundaries: Exploring," 184.
24 "Caelum non animum mutant qui trans mare currunt." Horace, *Epistula* 1.9.27.

opposite. However, the line separating the two recently became a bit blurrier. The widespread accessibility of travel has sparked a contemporary resurgence in pilgrimage, which in turn caused the development of an infrastructure and economy oriented around meeting pilgrims' needs, both spiritual and physical. In time, other activities were added to their itineraries and schedules, such as museum visits, culturally immersive experiences, and more.[25] Gradually the pilgrim was transformed into a religious tourist. Boris Vukonić was the first to talk about the *Homo Turisticus Religiosus* (The Religious Tourist Man), and he separated the religious tourists from simple tourists based on their motivation for traveling and their specific expectations and demands for the journey.[26]

Both the tourist and the pilgrim are aware of the transient nature of their presence in a given location. They both share the common aspect of being strangers and foreigners, being sojourners. However, their approaches to life diverge fundamentally. First Peter 2:11 serves as a poignant reminder that regardless of where we live in the world, we are pilgrims—purposefully journeying toward a specific destination. Unlike tourists, our journey is not aimless or devoid of purpose. Moreover, our identity as pilgrims imparts a sense of vulnerability and reliance on external assistance. Exiles, by their very nature, possess a distinct and relatively powerless status.[27] Tourists do not really need anybody; pilgrims need all the help they can get. Ultimately, the distinction between being a tourist or a pilgrim is primarily contingent on the prevailing attitude rather than merely the observable actions. As Jim Forest noted: "Walking a pilgrimage route, wearing a pilgrim's badge, and sleeping in pilgrim hostels are not what make a pilgrim… . Pilgrimage is a conscious act of seeking a more vital awareness of God's living presence."[28]

In essence, a true pilgrim ought to conduct themselves in a manner more akin to a missionary rather than a tourist. Although rarely explored in existing literature, there is an integral connection between pilgrimage and mission. Martin Robinson contended that pilgrimage and mission share not only a common origin but also an inseparable connection. These facets of the journey of faith are mutually reliant in order to sustain hope and vitality, and they are equally important in the life of the church. He said: "It might be possible to think of these encounters as different aspects of the breath

---

25 Olsen, Trono, and Fidgeon, "Pilgrimage Trails and Routes, 1–2.
26 Vukonić, *Tourism and Religion*.
27 Paas, *Pilgrims and Priests*, 168.
28 Forest, *Road to Emmaus: Pilgrimage*, 13.

or Spirit of God. Just as in breathing we must both inhale and exhale, so in encountering God there is a time to breathe in and a time to breathe out. Both dimensions of breathing are important."[29] Furthermore, Robinson elaborated on the interplay between pilgrimage and mission. First, before being sent out to mission, believers are called out by God. This calling sets them on a journey of faith as perpetual wanderers. The journey commences with an invitation to engage in the *missio Dei*, making it an inherent pilgrimage. While specific pilgrimages offer a space for reflection on the broader call, the "pilgrim principle" becomes paramount from the mission's perspective, guiding the church's focus toward its future hope.

Second, both pilgrimage and mission seek genuine encounters with God. Notably, genuine pilgrimage is inherently imbued with a missionary objective, recognizing that encountering God is more than an endpoint and rather is an integral act of mission. Lastly, a deeper element unites both pilgrims and missionaries throughout their journey. The initial divine calling remains an ongoing encouragement along the way, a continuous beckoning that endures.[30]

However, if we are *citizens of heaven* walking in spirit toward the *city of God*, as Augustine said, then why do we need physical pilgrimages? According to Mircea Eliade, in recent times, by desacralizing space in the West, we have lost our sense of orientation and purpose in our world. In spite of that, the reality and importance of sacred places in our lives are so undeniably great that admittedly even for non-religious people there are "holy places" in their private universes. As Eliade argued, a profane space still includes values that to some extent recall the non-homogeneity peculiar to the religious experience of space.[31] Evidently, the human inclination toward sacred spaces is grounded in the need for tangible, physical experiences alongside the intangible and spiritual. As creatures of habit, our learning process is enriched through ritual and experiential encounters. As a result, engaging in a physical pilgrimage, where each step of the journey is traversed thoughtfully, allows for contemplation of the lessons gleaned along the way and fosters meaningful connections with fellow pilgrims. Such experiences contribute significantly to our comprehension of our transient sojourner status. In addition, it can provide valuable insights into cultivating the appropriate mindset when traveling for mission.

---

29 Robinson, "Pilgrimage and Mission," 175.
30 Robinson, 174–78.
31 Eliade, *The Sacred and The Profane*, 24.

In Greece, foreign missionaries have been coming for quite some time, even before the country's official establishment in 1830.[32] Additionally, after the European migrant crisis in 2015, the number of missionaries rapidly increased. Greece, due to its geographical location, serves as a major entry point for refugees arriving by sea, and over the past decade, it has accepted millions of them.[33] Consequently, alongside the presence of many long-term missionaries, a new wave of short-term volunteers arrived in the country.[34] Presently, Greece hosts a considerable number of missionaries, primarily concentrated in major cities and specific islands. Among them are those who approach their mission with a pilgrim's mindset, making significant sacrifices for the sake of spreading the gospel. These dedicated individuals build meaningful connections with the locals, share their joys and sorrows with a humble spirit, and persist and struggle in a country that poses constant challenges. They are driven by their devotion to Christ and his church. However, it is important to acknowledge that some missionaries adopt a tourist mentality. They fail to invest in learning the language and form superficial relationships, knowing they will soon depart. Frequently, these individuals prioritize their personal development and the benefits they can derive from interacting with the local community.

Paradoxically, these missionaries exhibit a reluctance to engage in genuine learning opportunities, as they perceive the local culture as inferior to their own, adopting an approach reminiscent of colonialism. Similar to the North Americans with whom Robert Ellis Haynes conversed, many individuals feel that Greeks need to learn a thing or two about how to run their country.[35] Essentially, their primary objective is to engage in a subjective and imaginative form of personal pilgrimage, or, regrettably, they might even be here just for the pictures. Yet, as Robinson asserted: "Personal devotion, however intense and sincere, which is not related to a desire to see a changed world, betrays historic Christian spirituality and does indeed take on something of the character of spiritual tourism."[36] Derek Tidball said: "When tourists go home, they leave their litter behind for someone else to clean up. When pilgrims pass through, they transform the world for the better."[37]

---

32 For further details see Saloutos, "American Missionaries in Greece," 152–74; and Παπαγεωργίου, *Αμερικανοί Ιεραπόστολοι Στην Ελλάδα*.
33 Lodovici et al., "Integration of Refugees in Greece," 19–21.
34 Thornton, "Strangers in a Foreign Land."
35 Haynes, *Consuming Mission: Towards a Theology*, xii.
36 Robinson, "Pilgrimage and Mission," 182.
37 Tidball, "Pilgrim and the Tourist: Zygmunt Bauman," 196.

Case Study

The impetus behind the contemplation on tourism, pilgrimage, and mission stemmed from a research undertaking, wherein I was afforded the privilege to embark on a pilgrimage following in the footsteps of Paul while studying the experience of all participants involved in the journey. It is becoming increasingly common for pilgrims to rush through their visits, using a variety of quick means of transportation. Unfortunately, this superficial approach results in an incomplete and fragmented narrative, failing to effectively convey the intended message or overarching story of the route. So, the traveler became a tourist, the experience became a photo opportunity, the visit became a check on a bucket list. Yet, in recent times, a discernible shift has occurred within the tourism industry, with an increasing number of individuals actively seeking more authentic and immersive experiences.[38] However, it is hard to talk about authenticity when we have alienated ourselves completely from the landscape and time. Of course, we cannot travel back in the past. But we can experience time, or more accurately the passing of time, in a similar way that people in Roman times did. Frédéric Gros contended that the prevailing belief that speed equates to time-saving is illusory. Instead, he proposed a paradigm shift, advocating for a deliberate slowdown in daily activities, which would result in longer and more fulfilling days. A practical approach to achieving this objective is through the simple act of walking. As he wrote:

> The illusion of speed is the belief that it saves time… . But haste and speed accelerate time, which passes more quickly, and two hours of hurry shorten a day. Every minute is torn apart by being segmented, stuffed to bursting. Days of slow walking are very long: they make you live longer, because you have allowed every hour, every minute, every second to breathe, to deepen, instead of filling them up by straining the joints.[39]

"Come over to Macedonia," an experimental hiking expedition conducted in 2021 which drew its name from Acts 16:9, focused on the concept of slow tourism and the authenticity of the touring experience, acting as a counterproposal to the prevailing trend of the mass consumption of tourist

---

38 Yeoman, Brass, and McMahon-Beattie, "Current Issue in Tourism," 1128; Garau-Vadell, Orfila-Sintes, and Batle, "Quest for Authenticity," 210; Tiberghien, Bremner, and Milne, "Authenticity and Disorientation," 1–2; and Moore et al., "Authenticity in Tourism Theory," 1–5.
39 Gros, *Philosophy of Walking*, 37.

destinations. Rather, those taking part endeavored to establish connections with the local communities they encountered during the journey.

During the pilgrimage, we walked from the city of Kavala[40] to Thessaloniki,[41] covering a total of 215 kilometers in eight days. The route Kavala–Thessaloniki, with the main intermediate stops at Philippi, Amphipolis, and Apollonia, is part of the "Footsteps of Paul" route in northern Greece and was ideal for the present research.[42] The route lacks systematic organization, signposted trails, guidebooks with maps tailored for pilgrims, and often lacks essential facilities along the way. Polyxeni Moira, referring to cultural-religious routes and their tourism valorization, underlined the challenges the development of the route has as a consequence of the multitude of public and private entities engaged in monument management, compounded by the absence of a central management agency.[43] Among others, she mentioned the serious lack of appropriate infrastructure, which is something all the volunteers of the project pointed out as well. At this point it is worth mentioning that, outside of specific areas, camping in the open is not allowed in Greece.[44] Hence, without accommodations within walking distance, we faced two options: cancel the journey or depend on the hospitality of the locals.

To our surprise, this problem turned out to be an opportunity. Although organizing such an endeavor proved to be particularly tricky and challenging, our dependence on the local communities offered us an entirely different perspective. We started this journey thinking about how we could help the locals and what could we teach them; ultimately though, they ended up helping us and teaching us some valuable lessons. The volunteers' feedback highlighted that one of the most significant aspects of their experience was the connections formed not only between the team and the locals but, above all, among the team members themselves. Shalini Singh pointed out how pilgrimage can be an agent of social cohesion, as the traditions and rituals

---

40 Kavala is the contemporary name of ancient Neapolis.
41 Thessaloniki is also known as Thessalonica.
42 The route was chosen based on historical significance, practicality, and accessibility, allowing the team to follow Via Egnatia. The project's duration was carefully balanced to provide a meaningful pilgrimage experience while accommodating individuals with work commitments. Kavala and Thessaloniki were selected as accessible starting and ending points.
43 Moira, "Cultural-Religious Routes," 168.
44 For further details, refer to *Government Gazette* Issue no. 392 (1976) [ΦΕΚ Α' 199/1976], Issue no. 4055 (2012) [ΦΕΚ Α' 51/ 12.3.2012].

of a pilgrimage can reinforce social relations among participants.⁴⁵ This was evident in the findings of the current experiment. As mentioned above, all participants recognized the significance of the interpersonal bonds forged within the group, considering them a pivotal aspect of their journey. Two volunteers mentioned in their daily journals: "Without my fellow travelers the journey would be extremely difficult, perhaps even impossible," and "Something that will sound like a cliche, but it was proven today, is that traveling is not only about a place but also about people."

Additionally, another volunteer connected something that they saw in a site with the concept of hospitality that we were experiencing during the trip. More specifically, on our second day we visited the Holy Baptistery of Saint Lydia of Philippi, where the volunteer noticed a fresco depicting the "Philoxenia of Abraham."⁴⁶ Although they already knew the story of Abraham's hospitality, seeing it while we were walking as strangers in the land struck a different chord. It is interesting that in Greek the word for hospitality is *philoxenia*, literally love of the stranger, the outsider, the *xenos*. The fresco of the baptistery and the generous love we received, even as *xenoi*, sparked a marvelous conversation that evening. We delved into discussions about Paul's experiences in Philippi, expressions of gratitude, and ways to become more hospitable in our daily lives. In this instance, the pilgrimage not only served as a catalyst for contemplation and conversation but also presented us with a unique chance to integrate what we observed at the site with our immediate experiences. This valuable combination would not have been possible during a more conventional visit.

Apart from that, it is essential to highlight that the project was not organized as an evangelistic event. While it was explicitly communicated that the route follows the path of apostle Paul and all participants were aware of this Christian connection, the primary objective was not to discuss God or convince anyone of anything. The sole purpose was conducting research. Of course, throughout our journey, we often talked about Paul, his life and work, his beliefs, his teaching, and consequently about God within the team or with others, but it never felt coerced. It flowed naturally and organically during our conversations. No one attempted to "evangelize" anyone; instead, we simply lived our lives, walked together, and engaged in honest discussions. That is precisely the beauty of a pilgrimage.

---

45 Singh, "Tourism in the Sacred Indian Himalayas," 377–78.
46 The "Philoxenia (hospitality) of Abraham" refers to the story in Genesis 18:1–18, when the Lord appeared to Abraham by the Oak of Mamre in the form of three men.

In summary, I'm not advocating that everyone must walk the route to fully appreciate it. However, I firmly believe that we can gain valuable insights from adopting a pilgrim's mindset and engaging in a slower form of tourism. By doing so, we have the opportunity to forge meaningful connections with our environment, including both people and places along the way. My experience with the pilgrimage described in this chapter yielded considerable academic value. The immersive opportunity to briefly assume the role of a pilgrim provided first-hand insight into the essence of such a journey. Additionally, the observation of fellow pilgrims' dynamics and experiences proved to be a rare and enlightening perspective. This comprehensive engagement encompassed establishing meaningful connections with various sites and local communities and facilitating daily focus group discussions to extract profound insights into participants' perceptions and viewpoints concerning both the project and the route itself. From this erudite experience, a multitude of valuable lessons surfaced, the most notable of which is the empirical differentiation between tourist and pilgrim mindsets and behaviors and their consequential ramifications on evangelistic endeavors.

Conclusion

In conclusion, the theological significance of 1 Peter 2:11 urges us to examine our way of life in diverse environments, regardless of our ethnic or social background. A common issue is our failure to recognize the influence of the surrounding "gentile world" and unintentional conformity to its norms. Engaging in a mission or pilgrimage offers an opportunity for physical detachment from familiar social frameworks, enabling us to gain clarity about our own identity and culture. By fully immersing ourselves in unfamiliar customs, we heighten cultural awareness and recognize the constructed nature of cultures. Engaging in a physical pilgrimage encourages contemplation, fosters connections with fellow travelers, and enriches our understanding of our transient sojourner status. Such experiences also provide valuable insights for traveling with the right mindset during missions. Embracing a pilgrim's mindset, even without physically walking the route, can foster meaningful connections with people and places along the journey. The "Come over to Macedonia" project offered profound academic value, revealing the essence of pilgrimage and the differentiation between tourist and pilgrim behaviors. These insights hold relevance for evangelistic efforts and underscore the importance of embracing a pilgrim's approach to life's journey.

In 1 Peter 2:11, Christians are referred to as "sojourners and exiles" in the world, emphasizing their distinct identity as God's chosen people living amidst a secular society. This spiritual alienation suggests that we, as Christians, are not of the world, but rather, we are emissaries of a higher, heavenly kingdom. In the context of evangelism, this verse serves as a foundational reminder of the Christians' role as ambassadors of Christ. Nevertheless, it is imperative to acknowledge that this awareness should instill not a sense of pride or disdain but, rather, one of humility and gratitude. Approaching people with a tourist-like mentality typically stems from a sense of arrogance and signifies a lack of genuine concern for their well-being. Such an approach reduces people to mere instruments for achieving a goal, even when that objective is evangelization. Conversely, adopting a pilgrim's mindset signifies a humble disposition, one that genuinely cares for others without exploiting them. While the content of the message may remain constant, the attitude with which it is delivered holds significant weight. Indeed, the virtuous conduct advocated in 1 Peter 2:12, apart from self-betterment, primarily serves the purpose of the public manifestation of God's love so that people will see the good deeds of Christians and glorify God. All in all, it is of paramount importance to bear 1 Peter 2:11–12 in mind throughout all evangelistic initiatives because it establishes a vital foundation for the appropriate mindset in this sacred work.

Bibliography

Achtemeier, Paul J. *1 Peter: A Commentary on First Peter*. Hermeneia. Minneapolis: Fortress Press, 1996.

Aland, Barbara, Kurt Aland, Eberhard Nestle, Erwin Nestle, Johannes Karavidopoulos, Carlo Maria Martini, Bruce M. Metzger, Holger Strutwolf, and Institut für Neutestamentliche Textforschung, eds. *Novum Testamentum Graece*. 28th rev. ed. Stuttgart: Deutsche Bibelgesellschaft, 2012.

Babarskas, Romualdas. "1 Peter." In *Central and Eastern European Bible Commentary*, edited by Corneliu Constantineanu and Peter Penner, 1581–95. Carlisle, UK: Langham Global Library, 2022.

Badone, Ellen. "Crossing Boundaries: Exploring the Borderlands of Ethnography, Tourism, and Pilgrimage." In *Intersecting Journeys: The Anthropology of Pilgrimage and Tourism*, edited by Ellen Badone and Sharon R. Roseman, 180–90. Urbana: University of Illinois Press, 2004.

Boring, M. Eugene. *1 Peter*. Abingdon New Testament Commentaries. Nashville: Abingdon, 1999.

Chin, Moses. "A Heavenly Home for the Homeless: Aliens and Strangers in 1 Peter." *Tyndale Bulletin* 42, no. 1 (1991): 96–112. https://doi.org/10.53751/001c.30498.

Eliade, Mircea. *The Sacred and the Profane: The Nature of Religion*. New York: Harcourt, Brace & Company, 1959.

Elliott, John H. *Conflict, Community, and Honor: 1 Peter in Social-Scientific Perspective*. Eugene, OR: Cascade, 2007.

Elliott, John H. *A Home for the Homeless: A Sociological Exegesis of 1 Peter, Its Situation and Strategy*. Eugene, OR: Wipf & Stock, 2005.

Feldmeier, Reinhard. *The First Letter of Peter: A Commentary on the Greek Text*. Translated by Peter H. Davids. Waco, TX: Baylor University Press, 2008.

Forest, Jim. *The Road to Emmaus: Pilgrimage as a Way of Life*. Maryknoll, NY: Orbis Books, 2007.

Garau-Vadell, Joan B., Francina Orfila-Sintes, and Julio Batle. "The Quest for Authenticity and Peer-to-Peer Tourism Experiences." *Journal of Hospitality and Tourism Management* 47 (2021): 210–16. https://doi.org/10.1016/j.jhtm.2021.03.011.

Green, Joel B. *1 Peter*. Two Horizons New Testament Commentary. Grand Rapids: Eerdmans, 2007.

Gros, Frédéric. *A Philosophy of Walking*. Translated by John Howe. London: Verso, 2014.

Haynes, Robert Ellis. *Consuming Mission: Towards a Theology of Short-Term Mission and Pilgrimage*. Eugene, OR: Pickwick, 2018.

Jobes, Karen H. *1 Peter*. Baker Exegetical Commentary on the New Testament. Grand Rapids: Baker Academic, 2005.

Joseph, Abson Prédestin. *A Narratological Reading of 1 Peter*. Library of New Testament Studies 440. New York: T&T Clark, 2012.

Lodovici, Manuela Samek, Serena Marianna Drufuca, Nicola Orlando, Chiara Crepaldi, Flavia Pesce, Spyros Koulocheris, and Szilvia Borbély. "Integration of Refugees in Greece, Hungary and Italy: Comparative Analysis." Brussels: European Union, 2017.

Mbuvi, Andrew M. *Temple, Exile, and Identity in 1 Peter*. Library of New Testament Studies 345. New York: T&T Clark, 2007.

Moira, Polyxeni. "Cultural-Religious Routes and Their Tourism Valorization: 'In the Footsteps of the Apostle Paul' in Greece." In *The Bible and Global Tourism*, edited by James S. Bielo and Lieke Wijnia, 147–75. The Bible in Contemporary Culture Series. New York: T&T Clark, 2021.

Moore, Kevin, Annæ Buchmann, Maria Månsson, and David Fisher. "Authenticity in Tourism Theory and Experience. Practically Indispensable and Theoretically Mischievous?" *Annals of Tourism Research* 89 (2021): 103208. https://doi.org/10.1016/j.annals.2021.103208.

Ok, Janette H. *Constructing Ethnic Identity in 1 Peter: Who You Are No Longer*. Library of New Testament Studies 645. New York: T&T Clark, 2021.

Olsen, Daniel H., Anna Trono, and Paul R. Fidgeon. "Pilgrimage Trails and Routes: The Journey from the Past to the Present." In *Religious Pilgrimage Routes and Trails: Sustainable Development and Management*, edited by Daniel H. Olsen and Anna Trono, 1–13. CABI Religious Tourism and Pilgrimage Series. Boston: CABI, 2018.

Paas, Stefan. *Pilgrims and Priests: Christian Mission in a Post-Christian Society*. London: SCM, 2019.

Παπαγεωργίου, Σόφη Ν. *Αμερικανοί Ιεραπόστολοι στην Ελλάδα 1820–1850*. Αθήνα: Δωδώνη, 2001.

Robinson, Martin. "Pilgrimage and Mission." In *Explorations in a Christian Theology of Pilgrimage*, edited by Craig G. Bartholomew and Fred Hughes, 170–83. Burlington, VT: Ashgate, 2004.

Saloutos, Theodore. "American Missionaries in Greece: 1820–1869." *Church History* 24, no. 2 (1955): 152–74. https://doi.org/10.2307/3161652.

Selwyn, Edward G. *The First Epistle of St. Peter: The Greek Text with Introduction, Notes, and Essays*. 2nd ed. Thornapple Commentaries. Grand Rapids: Baker Book, 1987.

Shaw, Joseph M. *The Pilgrim People of God: Recovering a Biblical Motif*. Minneapolis: Augsburg, 1990.

Singh, Shalini. "Tourism in the Sacred Indian Himalayas: An Incipient Theology of Tourism?" *Asia Pacific Journal of Tourism Research* 11, no. 4 (2006): 375–89. https://doi.org/10.1080/10941660600931226.

Στογιάννος, Βασίλης Π. *Πρώτη Επιστολή Πέτρου*. Ερμηνεία Καινής Διαθήκης 15. Θεσσαλονίκη: Π. Πουρναρά, 1980.

Thornton, Jill. "Strangers in a Foreign Land: A Study of the Christian Missionary Response to Refugees in Greece and Italy." Master's thesis, Radboud University, 2018.

Tiberghien, Guillaume, Hamish Bremner, and Simon Milne. "Authenticity and Disorientation in the Tourism Experience." *Journal of Outdoor Recreation and Tourism* 30 (2020): 100283. https://doi.org/10.1016/j.jort.2020.100283.

Tidball, Derek. "The Pilgrim and the Tourist: Zygmunt Bauman and Postmodern Identity." In *Explorations in a Christian Theology of Pilgrimage*, edited by Craig G. Bartholomew and Fred Hughes, 184–200. Burlington, VT: Ashgate, 2004.

Volf, Miroslav. "Soft Difference: Theological Reflections on the Relation between Church and Culture in 1 Peter." *Ex Auditu* 10 (1994): 15–30.

Vukonić, Boris. *Tourism and Religion*. Tourism Social Science Series. New York: Pergamon Press, 1996.

Wells, Jo Bailey. *God's Holy People: A Theme in Biblical Theology*. Journal for the Study of the Old Testament Supplement Series 305. Sheffield: Sheffield Academic, 2000.

Yeoman, Ian, Danna Brass, and Una McMahon-Beattie. "Current Issue in Tourism: The Authentic Tourist." *Tourism Management* 28, no. 4 (2007): 1128–38. https://doi.org/10.1016/j.tourman.2006.09.012.

About the Contributors

Yimenu Adimass Belay (PhD candidate, Vrije Universiteit, Amsterdam and Ethiopian Graduate School of Theology) is academic dean at Meserete Kristos Seminary and a lecturer in New Testament studies. His research areas are New Testament studies and the Ethiopic (Geʻez) Tradition. Recently he published two articles related to his research: "Paul's View of the Law in Romans and the Ethiopian Orthodox Tewahedo Church's (EOTC) Use of the Law as *həgga ləbbunā*, 'həgga Orit' and 'həgga wangle.'" *Stellenbosch Theological Journal* 6, no. 4 (2020): 59–82; and "Scripture and Context in Conversation: The Ethiopian *Andəmta* Interpretative Tradition." *Conspectus* 34, no. 1 (2022): 41–49.

Joshua Bowman (PhD, Southeastern Baptist Theological Seminary) is assistant professor of missions and theology at Cedarville University. He and his wife, Amy, along with their four children, served in Zambia and South Asia with the International Mission Board for seventeen years as a church planter, church-strengthening strategist, and team leader. He is the author of *Cross-Cultural Missional Partnership* (Pickwick, 2023).

Will Brooks (PhD, Southern Baptist Theological Seminary) lives in Southeast Asia with his wife and three children. He is the acting provost and director of DMiss and MAIS programs at a seminary in Asia. He is the author of *Love Lost for the Cause of Christ* (2018), *Interpreting Scripture across Cultures* (2022), and a co-editor of *World Mission* (2019). He is an avid runner and has completed multiple ultra-marathons and endurance obstacle course events.

Jacob Chengwei Feng (PhD, Fuller Theological Seminary) is fellow and co-coordinator of Oxford Interfaith Forum. He earned a PhD at Fuller Theological Seminary in Pasadena, CA, majoring in theological studies. He earned his BE from Tsinghua University (Beijing), MA from Rutgers University, and MAT from Fuller Theological Seminary. His area of expertise includes North America, China, and Southeast Asia. His research interests include systematic theology, Theological Interpretation of Scripture, Chinese theology, theology-science-religion trialogue, *Jingjiao* ("Nestorian" Christianity), and the Church of the East.

Rudolf K. Gaisie (PhD, Akrofi-Christaller Institute) is a senior research fellow at the Akrofi-Christaller Institute of Theology, Mission and Culture, Akropong-Akuapem, Ghana. He serves as director of the Institute's Centre for the Study of Early African Christianity (CESEAC) and as director of Information Communication Technology. He is a fellow at the Center for Early African Christianity (CEAC), New Haven, CT, USA. His teaching and research interests are in the areas of early Greco-Roman and North African Christianity, contemporary African Christology and missiology, mother-tongue biblical studies, African Christian leadership, and technology in theological education. His doctoral thesis is published as *Jesus Christ as Logos Incarnate and Resurrected Nana (Ancestor): An African Perspective on Conversion and Christology* (Pickwick, 2020).

Sigurd Grindheim (PhD, Trinity Evangelical Divinity School) is professor of Christianity, religion, worldview, and Ethics at Western Norway University of Applied Sciences, and he has also taught at the Mekane Yesus Seminary, Trinity Evangelical Divinity School, and other institutions in Ethiopia, the United States, and Norway. His publications include *The Letter to the Hebrews*, *The Crux of Election*, and *God's Equal*, as well as many other books and articles on topics related to the New Testament, biblical theology, and missiology. He and his wife, Kidist Bahru Gemeda, have one son, Per.

Markus T. Klausli (PhD, Dallas Theological Seminary) is an ordained presbyter in the Anglican Church of North America and has served as professor of New Testament and Greek at Columbia International University since 2013. Before coming to CIU he was both lecturer and dean of CIU's European School of Culture and Theology in Korntal, Germany (AWM), where he continues to teach as an adjunct faculty member. An active member of the Evangelical Theological Society, his research interests are primarily in the General Epistles and New Testament theology. He is married to Julia and together they have four daughters on the cusp of adulthood.

Grant LeMarquand (ThD, Wycliffe College/University of Toronto) is emeritus professor of biblical studies, Trinity School for Ministry, and retired Anglican bishop for the Horn of Africa (Ethiopia, Eritrea, Djibouti, Somalia). He has written and edited numerous articles and books in biblical studies, missiology, and Anglicanism including *Why Haven't You Left? Letters from the Sudan* (Church Publications) and *A Comparative Study of the Story of the Bleeding Woman (Mk 5:25–34; Mt 9:20–22; Lk 8:43–48) in North Atlantic and African Contexts* (Peter Lang, 2004). He and his wife, Wendy, a retired medical doctor, are Canadians. They have two grown children and one grandchild.

About the Contributors

Sarah Lunsford (PhD, Columbia International University) lives with her four children in the metro-Atlanta area and is an instructor of global studies for Liberty University Online. She previously served as an international church planter in East Asia and has ministered short term in several countries across five continents. Sarah is the author of *Missiological Triage: A Framework for Integrating Theology and Social Sciences in Missiological Methods.*

Gift Mtukwa (PhD, University of Manchester) is a lecturer and chair of the department in the School of Religion and Christian Ministry at Africa Nazarene University in Nairobi, Kenya. He was born and raised in Harare, Zimbabwe, and currently lives in Nairobi, Kenya. He is an ordained minister with the Church of the Nazarene and he teaches New Testament and Greek. He earned a bachelor's degree in theology, a Master of Arts in religion from Africa Nazarene University, and a Master of Arts in theology and a PhD from the University of Manchester in England, UK. Dr. Mtukwa is the author of *Work and Community in the Thessalonian Correspondence* (Langham Monographs, 2021).

Sofia Papaspyrou (PhD candidate, The National and Kapodistrian University of Athens) is an archaeologist-museologist with extensive experience in the museum sector, having worked in various museums and museological projects throughout Greece. Additionally, she served as a co-curator and museum educator at the National Historical Museum of Greece, contributing to research, exhibition design, and digitization initiatives. Over the past decade, she has been leading tours centered around the "Footsteps of Paul" cultural route, focusing on Greek and Roman archaeology, contemporary tourism, and pilgrimage aspects. Her ongoing university research explores the impressions and experiences of the traveler following in the footsteps of the apostle Paul from archaeological, museological, sociological, and touristic perspectives.

Boubakar Sanou (DMin, PhD, Andrews University) serves as an associate professor of mission and intercultural leadership and chair of the Department of World Mission at Seventh-day Adventist Theological Seminary, Andrews University, Michigan.

Edward L. Smither (PhD, University of Wales; PhD, University of Pretoria) serves as professor of intercultural studies and history of global Christianity and dean of the School of Missions and Intercultural Ministry at Columbia International University. Previously, he served for fourteen years in intercultural ministry in North Africa, France, and the United States. His recent books include *Christian Mission: A Concise Global History* and *Mission in the Way of Daniel*.

Tricia Stephens (PhD candidate, Asbury Theological Seminary) is a current doctoral student in New Testament studies at Asbury Theological Seminary. She earned her BASc from the University of Toronto, MEng from Texas A&M, MSc from IFP in France, and her ThM from Dallas Theological Seminary. Tricia has traveled to and worked in over sixty countries as a student of life and in her former career as a senior engineer. After spending a fruitful year studying the Bible in Israel, she started a new journey of full-time biblical studies. She is an evangelist with a particular fondness for the Middle East because of the rich tradition of hospitality, which is her primary research area. Her other research interests include alienation, household rituals, Christology, and eating.

Jessica A. Udall (PhD, Columbia International University) is professor of Intercultural Studies at Evangelical Theological College in Addis Ababa, Ethiopia, and adjunct professor of Intercultural Studies at Columbia International University. She is a member of Equip International and SIL International/SIL in Ethiopia. She has worked in cross-cultural ministry in Ethiopia and among immigrants in the United States since 2007. She is the author of *Loving the Stranger: Welcoming Immigrants in the Name of Jesus*.

Abeneazer G. Urga (PhD, Columbia International University) is the department head for the MA in Biblical Studies and lectures in biblical studies at Evangelical Theological College in Addis Ababa, Ethiopia, and is an adjunct professor at Columbia International University and Ethiopian Graduate School of Theology. He is a member of Equip International and SIL in Ethiopia/International. He has authored several books and articles. His recent book is *Intercession of Jesus in Hebrews* (Mohr Siebeck, 2023).

Scripture Index

Genesis

1:3-5   26
1:11   117
1:27a   187
1:28   117
2:7   130
2:17   117, 130
3:15   8, 151
4:8   130
5:1, 4, 10   117
5:5   130
6:1-4   88
6:2   88
9:1-2, 7   117
12   22
12:1   43
12:1-3   84, 117
12:3   11, 14, 117
15:15   131
23:4   42, 226
49:10   8
49:29   131
50:24-26   131

Exodus

12:5-7   101
12:11   126, 214
12:23   130
13:29   130
14:31   121
19   53, 194, 205
19:5-6   117
19:6   23, 53, 89
19:9   121
24:1-8   102
28:2   22
40:9   22

Leviticus

5:5-11   102
6:18, 23   102
14:19   102
16:3-5   102
19:2   22, 106, 182
22:3   22

Numbers

14:11   121
16:30-33   131
20:12   121
32:19   118

Deuteronomy

1:32   121
2:12   118
4:6-7   194
9:23   121
12:9   118
18:15-18   8
25:19   118
26:1   118
28:9-10   194
30   81
30:15   131
30:17-18   81

Joshua

11:23   118

2 Samuel

7:12-16   14
7:18   14
7:22-26   14

1 Kings

13:24   130

2 Kings

4:29   126
4:31-37   131
9:1   126
13:21   131
19:35   130

Ezra

9:2   22
10:2   197

Job

6:8   197
13:15   197
14:12   131

Psalms

3   175
6:4-5   131
6:5   131
9:14   124
16:8-11   8
22   13
22:1   13
22:18   13
22:21   214
22:26-29   156
22:27-28   13
30:3   131
33:13-16   106

33:18, 22 197	40:1-2 82	**Jeremiah**
34 109	40:1-5 81	
34:12-16 106	40:6-8 10	1:17 126
39:12 226	42 11	31:17 197
41 117	43:1-7 81	50:17 214
42:5 197	43:7 26	**Ezekiel**
57 14	43:20 24	
57:11 14	43:20-21 53	32:26-27 131
65-67 82	43:20-22 23	36 17
67 14	43:21 24-26, 90, 195	36:12 81
71:15 124	43:25 82	36:27 82
73:28 124	49:6 53	37 81, 86
79:13 124	51:5 197	37:9-10 82
86 14	52 11	39:29 82
97-100 82	52:4 11	40-48 82
105:11 118	52:7 11	47:14, 22-23 81
107:22 124	52:10 11	**Daniel**
117 14	52:13 119	
119:81 197	52:13-14 11	9 7
Proverbs	52:13-53:12 71	9:2 7
	53 10, 102, 104, 169	9:6 7
11:31 101	53:4 104	9:11 8
Isaiah	53:5 102	9:14-15, 24-25 82
	53:6 102	9:24-25 8
2:1-5 82	53:7 104	12 86
2:2-3 11	53:9 101, 104, 170	12:1-2 81
2:3-4 24	53:11 13	12:1-3 82
8:12-13 214	54 117	12:2 131
8:13 125	55:1-2 156	12:6, 8 8
11 82	57:13b 81	12:8 8
11:1-5 89	58:11 81	12:9 8
19:16-22 11	60:1-14 82	12:12-13 8
19:16-25 82	60:21 81	**Hosea**
19:21-22 11	65:9 81	
25:6-8 82	65:17-25 82	2:23 103
25:6-9 156		**Joel**
25:8 131		
		2:28 82

Matthew

1:1-17 12
1:20 73
3:16-17 12
4:1 73
5:5-7 59
5:11 168
5:16 91
6:9-10 9
6:14-15 9
7:24-27 60
7:25 41
8:11-12 156
10:7 74
10:19-20 74
10:28 196
11:1 59
11:4 74
11:19 156
13 9
16:24-26 56
19:29 118
25:34 118
26:35 164
26:69-75 164
27:35 13
27:44 168
27:46 13
28:16-20 84
28:19 43, 132
28:19-20 61, 145

Mark

8:34-37 56
10:17 118
12:26-27 136
14:66-72 164
15:32 168
16:10, 15 74
16:17-18 132

Luke

1:35 73
1:46-55 12
1:67-79 12
4:1 73
4:14 65
6:22 168
7:22 74
7:36-50 156
9:23-25 56
10:25 118
12:11-12 74
14:12-14 156
14:25-33 56
14:25-34 59
15 59
16:13 60
18:1-14 59
18:18 118
19:11-26 59
22:56-62 164
24:25-27 9
24:26 117

John

3:16 84
5:39-40, 45-47 9
8:32 60
8:56, 58 12
8:59 12
13:35 125
14:26 74
14:27 196
15:1-10 60
15:1-17 59
18:16-18, 25-27 164
21:15-19 164

Acts

1:6 12
1:8 43, 65, 68, 132
1:1-12 68
2:1-43 67
2:1-47 164
2:4 132
2:14-40 67
2:14-47 8
2:24 132
2:24, 32 129
2:25-31 130
2:25-35 132
2:30-31 8
2:31 8
2:33 132
2:36 8, 132
3:4 164
4:2 164
4:12 169
5:17-41 164
5:29 164
6:7 8
7:1-53 8
7:5 118
7:6, 20 120
7:54-60 9
12:1-24 164
16:9 234
17:2-4 13

18:2-3   165
24   173
26:6-7   198
26:8   198
26:18   27

Romans

1:28-30   168
8:1-4, 26-27   73
8:2-4   66
8:7   155
8:11   73
8:19, 22   124
12:13   148
12:14-21   155
13   178
15:16   69
16:25-27   11

1 Corinthians

1:2   70
6:9-10   118
6:19a   187
7:16a   93
12:4-7   73
13   40
15:40-43   117

2 Corinthians

1:5-6   123
3:8   74
4:6   27
4:17   74
5:18-20   151
11:14   216

Galatians

2:7   165
3:7   42
3:18   119
4:6   66
4:30   119
5:16   66
5:21   119

Ephesians

1:3   117
1:10   84
1:11, 14   119
1:13   215
2:2   215
2:11-12   153
2:12   119
2:14   215
2:16   215
2:19   120, 151, 226
2:21   40
3:4-6   11
3:16   215
5:5   119
5:21-6:9   92
6:11, 13   214
6:12   174, 220
6:13-18   174
6:14   126, 214

Philippians

1:5, 27   42
3:21   117

Colossians

1:12   119

1:12-13   27
1:15-23   84
1:24   123
1:28   204
3:4   74
3:18-4:1   92
3:24   119

1 Thessalonians

1:6   73
4:13   119

2 Thessalonians

2:13   70

1 Timothy

3:2   148
5:9-10   148

Titus

1:8   148

Hebrews

2:14-18   75
4:15   122
9:13   213
9:14   213
11   14
11:9-10   121
11:9, 13   42
11:13   120, 226
11:13-16   119
11:16   166
11:35-40   14
13:2   148, 155
13:15-16   90

Scripture Index

James
1:2   167
3:9–10   187

1 Peter
1   14, 18–20, 183
1:1   4, 17, 21, 79, 103, 120, 148–49, 163–65, 226
1:11–12   91
1:1–12   6, 85
1:2   5, 52, 66, 68–70, 75, 102–3, 197
1:2–3   5
1:2, 11–12   65, 76, 77, 83
1:2, 14–22   66
1:2, 17   194
1:3   22, 83, 89, 100, 102, 117, 119, 132, 169, 181, 198, 200, 217, 228
1:3–4   173
1:3–5   105
1:3–12   5, 6, 86, 87
1:3, 13, 21   82
1:3, 21   102, 198
1:4   5, 105, 118–19, 132, 169, 181, 200
1:4–5, 7, 9, 13   213
1:4–5, 7–12, 18–19, 22–23   52
1:4b–5   154
1:5   5, 105, 118, 132, 181, 200, 214
1:5–6, 7a   155
1:5, 7, 13, 20   83
1:5, 8   173
1:5, 9   5, 10

1:5, 9, 10   83, 90
1:6   4–6, 52, 103, 105, 154, 167, 170, 200
1:6–7   13, 173
1:6–8   107
1:6–9   163
1:6–10   132
1:7   101, 104–5, 134, 200
1:7–8   5, 117
1:7–9   105
1:7, 11   82
1:7, 13   105
1:7, 17   110
1:7, 18   156
1:8, 22–23   125
1:9   5, 101, 105, 155
1:9–10   6
1:10   7, 9, 169, 181
1:10–11   10–11, 101
1:10–12   4–5
1:10–12   3–5, 10–11, 13
1:11   12–13, 101, 169, 181
1:11–12   66, 70–72, 75
1:12   4, 10, 14, 86, 102, 108, 140
1:12, 25b   102
1:13   5, 55, 87, 101, 105–6, 119, 126, 133, 185, 198, 200, 205, 214
1:13–2:10   6
1:13–15   194
1:13–16   54
1:13, 17   155
1:14   21, 100, 103, 106, 118, 152, 165, 185, 199, 209

1:14–16   21
1:14, 18   217
1:15   21, 30
1:15–16   106, 201
1:15–16, 22   66
1:15, 18   54
1:16–21   194
1:17   83, 103, 108, 118, 120, 201, 226
1:18   100, 106, 152, 165, 170, 199
1:18–19   101, 109, 133, 151, 205
1:18–21   133, 151
1:18, 23   154
1:18, 24   102
1:19   102, 169
1:19–20   100
1:20   83, 105
1:21   21, 102, 117, 119, 132–33
1:21–23   119
1:22   55, 102, 106, 152, 171, 185, 219, 225
1:22–25   69, 194
1:23   100, 102, 118, 152
1:24–25   10
2:24   183
2:1   55, 106, 125, 133, 185, 217
2:1–2, 22   219
2:1–3   194
2:1–12   89
2:2   83, 106, 133
2:3   91, 152, 205
2:4   91, 133, 152, 194
2:4–5   200

1 Peter

2:4–5, 7 104
2:4, 6 103
2:4–7 103, 107
2:4–10 83
2:5 39, 41–42, 54, 66, 123–24, 133, 194
2:5, 9 23, 54, 61, 66
2:5, 9–10 52
2:5–11 35–36, 45, 47
2:6 90, 103, 194
2:7 102, 194, 200
2:7–8 151
2:8 100, 201
2:9 23–24, 27, 30, 54, 69, 103, 106, 123–24, 152, 184, 190, 194–95, 201–2, 204–5, 218, 225
2:9–10 23, 53–54, 68–69, 75, 83, 171, 186, 194, 217, 228
2:9–11 29
2:9, 13–17 106
2:9b 193
2:10 101, 103, 151, 165, 190, 217
2:10a 152
2:10b 152
2:11 42, 53, 103, 106–7, 120, 148–50, 153, 193–94, 214, 225, 230, 236–37
2:11–3:12 6
2:11–12 28, 54–55, 189, 237
2:12 19, 26, 54, 56, 83, 90–92, 94, 103–4, 116–17, 125, 150–51, 153, 167, 186, 188, 198, 200–1, 209, 218–19, 225, 228, 237
2:12–15 54
2:12, 15 93, 170, 213
2:12, 18 52
2:12, 20 106
2:13 116
2:13–3:7 23, 27, 29
2:13–14, 17 171
2:13–16 99
2:13–17 55, 92
2:13–18 189
2:13, 21 154
2:14 107, 116
2:14–15 107
2:15 92, 103, 108, 188, 201
2:15, 20 54
2:15, 26 106
2:16 102, 152, 219
2:17 55, 106
2:18 55, 92, 103, 107, 199
2:18–3:6 108, 122
2:18–20 110, 167
2:18–21 171
2:18–25 92
2:19 92, 104
2:19–21 107
2:19–25 163
2:20 92, 107, 116, 201
2:20a 92
2:20b 92
2:20b–21 104
2:21 4, 19, 22, 93, 102, 104, 107, 123, 169
2:21–23 55, 133
2:21–24 122, 190
2:21–25 10, 56, 71
2:22 93, 104, 170
2:22–24 220
2:22–25 104, 133, 169
2:23 83, 92–93, 101, 104, 118, 169, 170, 172, 201
2:24 101–2, 104, 134, 213
2:24a 101
2:24b 102–3
2:24c 102
2:24–27 156
2:25 100, 102, 152
3:1 26, 31, 79, 93, 99, 107, 123, 189, 201, 210
3:1–2 106, 218
3:1–2, 15 150
3:1–2, 16 54
3:1–6 55, 92, 103, 201
3:2 54
3:2, 4 199
3:2, 16 54
3:3 201
3:4 93
3:4, 15 219
3:5 93
3:5, 15 82
3:6 104, 116
3:6, 13, 17 54
3:6, 14 219
3:6, 17 106
3:7 92, 109, 110

Scripture Index

3:8 55, 155
3:8-22 163
3:9 22, 51, 105, 109, 123, 154, 184, 190
3:9-12 209
3:10 109
3:10-11 125
3:10-12 106, 109-10
3:11a 106
3:12 109
3:13 106-7, 209
3:13-4, 19 56
3: 13-5, 11 6
3:13-16 28
3:13-17 93, 109, 183
3:14 52, 214
3:14-17 133
3:14-15 196
3:14-16 108, 172
3:14, 17 105
3:15 23, 29-30, 56, 66, 69, 75, 79, 87, 115, 122-23, 152, 172, 188, 193, 196, 198, 201, 218
3:15-16 99, 106
3:16 54, 108, 150, 173, 188-89, 200-1, 209, 213, 219
3:17 87, 108, 118, 122, 209
3:18 4, 13, 73, 89, 93, 100, 102, 122, 133, 154, 169, 213
3:18-19 65, 70, 73, 75-77, 136
3:18-22 87, 129, 133-34, 136-37, 209, 210, 217

3:19 89, 134-35
3:19a 73
3:20 100, 118, 220
3:20-21 89
3:21 83, 102, 132, 135, 169
3:21-22 102, 104
3:22 72, 89, 119, 122, 134-35, 138, 220
4 156
4:1 100, 102-3, 107, 154, 170, 214
4:1-2, 6 103
4:1-2, 12-19 163
4:1-2, 13-19 122
4:1-4 155
4:2 105-6
4:3 100, 148-52, 165, 170, 199, 217
4:3-4 51, 150
4:3-4, 17 151
4:3-5 151
4:4 54, 102-3, 150, 155, 184, 197, 200, 209
4:4-5 104
4:4, 9, 12 155
4:4, 12-14 52
4:4, 14-15 51
4:5 101, 118, 135, 201
4:5-6 99, 129, 136
4:5, 6, 17 83
4:5-9, 17 156
4:5, 17-18 118
4:6 99, 102, 104, 137
4:6, 14 83
4:7 83, 105-6, 201
4:7-11 154-55

4:7a 154
4:7b 155
4:7b-9 154
4:8 125, 155, 171, 189
4:8, 14a 106
4:9 55, 106, 125, 147-48, 153, 155-56, 189
4:10 61, 189
4:10-11 103, 125
4:11 171
4:11, 16 117
4:12 4, 91, 103, 200, 226
4:12-13 108
4:12-16 10
4:13 4, 82-83, 92, 104-5, 107-8, 110, 119, 154, 169, 200
4:13-14, 16 209
4:14 65-66, 70, 74-77, 92, 103, 105, 108, 168, 197, 200
4:14-16 213
4:15 91-92, 188
4:15-16 110
4:16 92, 103, 107
4:16, 19 4
4:17 83, 100, 110, 151, 154-55
4:17-18 101-2, 109, 201
4:18 100-1
4:19 54, 104, 118, 201
5:1 83, 107, 119, 156
5:1-4 68, 102
5:1, 4, 10 82
5:1, 8-10 4

5:1, 10   105, 163
5:2–3   106
5:4   105, 154
5:4, 5   110
5:5–6   106–7
5:8   102–3, 174
5:8–9   104
5:8b–9   213
5:9   174, 177
5:9–10   4
5:10   104, 119, 123, 140
5:11   44
5:12   52, 105–6
5:14   125

2 Peter

1:16–18   119
3:9   22
3:13   19
3:18   60, 139

Revelation

1:6   42
7:9   156
9:11   216
12:1–17   216
13   178
20:1–3   216–17
20:1–6   216
21:1–22, 25   119

visit us at missionbooks.org

Reading Hebrews Missiologically
The Missionary Motive, Message, and Methods of Hebrews
Abeneazer G. Urga, Edward L. Smither, and Linda P. Saunders, Editors

The discussion on the theology of mission in the New Testament usually focuses on Jesus and Paul, with minimal attention given to the General Epistles. However, *Reading Hebrews Missiologically* tries to fill that gap by focusing on the theology of mission in the book of Hebrews and fleshing out the unique contribution it has to the discussion of a New Testament theology of mission. The twelve contributors—from various theological, geographical, and missiological contexts—explore the missionary motive, the missionary message, and the missionary method of the Epistle to the Hebrews. All Scripture can be read missiologically, and the letter to the Hebrews, with its emphasis on the supremacy of Christ, is no exception. We pray that this book will inspire fresh approaches to practical mission in the world today.

Mission in the Way of Daniel
Empowering Believers to Live into God's Plan
Edward L. Smither

While many books and Bible studies explore the work ethic and character of Daniel, Ed Smither takes those discussions to a new level, illustrating why each of Daniel's qualities and skills is a necessary component of mission today.

Mission in the Way of Daniel probes mission theology and practice in the Old Testament, exploring the well-known story of Daniel through the lenses of mission history and mission practice. Providing relevant application for contemporary issues like diaspora, power encounters, and divine favor in mission, the themes in *Mission in the Way of Daniel* advance the ongoing conversation about how to do mission.

visit us at missionbooks.org

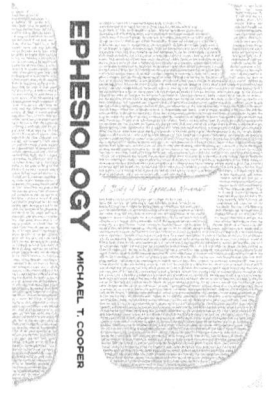

Ephesiology
A Study of the Ephesian Movement
Michael T. Cooper

Ephesiology is not another methodology or attempt to re-contextualize evangelicalism. Rather, it is a journey from the launch of the church in Ephesus as it became a movement grounded in God's mission and led by those who multiplied generations of disciples. Michael T. Cooper focuses on Paul and John as missiological theologians who successfully connected Jesus's teaching with the cultural context and narrative of the people in Ephesus. Their ability to relate the God of all creation to a people who sought him in vain resulted in "the Way" transforming the religious, intellectual, economic, and social fabrics of the Ephesian society.

This book offers a comprehensive view of the redemptive movement of the Holy Spirit in this city and compels us to ask the question: how can we effectively connect Christ to our culture? Through this study of a movement, discover how the Holy Spirit still changes lives, cities, and the world.

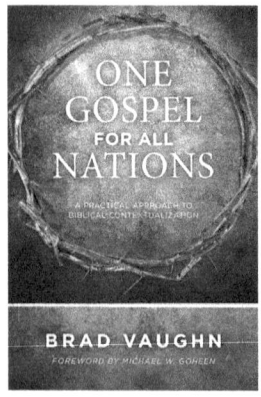

One Gospel for All Nations
A Practical Approach to Biblical Contextualization
Brad Vaughn

The Bible tells us what to believe—the gospel. But did you know it also shows *how* to contextualize the gospel?

In *One Gospel for All Nations*, Brad Vaughn (formerly Jackson Wu) does more than talk about principles. He gets practical. When the biblical writers explain the gospel, they consistently use a pattern that is both firm and flexible. Vaughn builds on this insight to demonstrate a model of contextualization that starts with interpretation and can be applied in any culture. In the process, he explains practically why we must not choose between the Bible and culture. Vaughn highlights various implications for both missionaries and theologians. Contextualization should be practical, not pragmatic; theological, not theoretical.

www.ingramcontent.com/pod-product-compliance
Lightning Source LLC
Chambersburg PA
CBHW052135070526
44585CB00017B/1830